Strengthening Peace in Post–Civil War States

Strengthening Peace in Post–Civil War States

Transforming Spoilers into Stakeholders

Edited by
MATTHEW HODDIE AND
CAROLINE A. HARTZELL

The University of Chicago Press
Chicago and London

Matthew Hoddie is assistant professor of political science at Towson University. **Caroline A. Hartzell** is professor of political science at Gettysburg College. Together they are coauthors of *Crafting Peace: Power-Sharing Institutions and the Negotiated Settlement of Civil Wars*.

The University of Chicago Press, Chicago 60637
The University of Chicago Press, Ltd., London
 Published 2010
Printed in the United States of America

19 18 17 16 15 14 13 12 11 10   1 2 3 4 5
ISBN-13: 978-0-226-35124-7 (cloth)
ISBN-13: 978-0-226-35125-4 (paper)
ISBN-10: 0-226-35124-6 (cloth)
ISBN-10: 0-226-35125-4 (paper)

Library of Congress Cataloging-in-Publication Data

Strengthening peace in post civil war states : transforming spoilers into stakeholders / edited by Matthew Hoddie and Caroline A. Hartzell.
p. cm.
Includes index.
ISBN-13: 978-0-226-35124-7 (cloth : alk. paper)
ISBN-13: 978-0-226-35125-4 (pbk. : alk. paper)
ISBN-10: 0-226-35124-6 (cloth : alk. paper)
ISBN-10: 0-226-35125-4 (pbk. : alk. paper) 1. Peace-building. 2. Civil war. I. Hoddie, Matthew, 1969– II. Hartzell, Caroline A.
JZ5548.S874 2010
303.6'6—dc22

2010007698

♾ The paper used in this publication meets the minimum requirements of the American National Standard for Information Sciences—Permanence of Paper for Printed Library Materials, ANSI Z39.48-1992.

For Donald Rothchild—
teacher, scholar, mentor, and friend

CONTENTS

PREFACE

This book's origins lie in the effort by a group of scholars to critically assess current models of peace maintenance in the aftermath of civil wars and to suggest alternative means by which the international community might help divided societies construct an enduring peace. Meeting to discuss these issues over a period of three years, our group was struck by the lack of attention many strategies for building and keeping peace pay to fostering a sense among the citizens of postwar societies that they have a personal stake in maintaining stability. We came to believe that attention to this matter was critical if we were to understand why, following some civil wars, individuals and groups have committed themselves to the hard work of rebuilding and managing conflict peacefully, whereas in other instances actors have opted to defect from postwar arrangements and reinitiate hostilities. Guided by this concern, we formulated three central sets of questions we sought to answer via this project. First, what are the interests of actors within postwar environments that must be addressed for them to believe that they have a personal stake in supporting the peace? Second, what role can the international community play in helping to serve those interests and create stakeholders in a stable peace? And finally, what policy implications follow from third-party actors' efforts to create stakeholders in stability?

The approach we take to answering these questions was shaped to a significant degree by one of the contributors to this volume, Donald Rothchild, who has authored pathbreaking works on conflict management in divided societies. Don's scholarship on and engagement with these issues has challenged all of us who work in this field to think about how incentives can—and at times cannot—be used to foster stakeholders in an enduring peace. Drawing on Don's research on third-party conflict management and institutionally generated incentives, we asked the scholars contributing to the two parts of this book to focus on the effects third-party involvement in the restructuring of postconflict institutions (part 1) and soft (nonmilitary) intervention (part 2) have had in convincing actors that it is in their interest to help maintain the peace. As these authors demonstrate, the international community has made use of these strategies with considerable success in some instances and much less success in others. We hope that our analysis of the reasons for this mixed record will help to inform the growing debate on the issue of how third parties can best help to generate support for a fragile peace following civil war.

This project has enjoyed the support of a good many people and organizations, to whom we are profoundly grateful. Sponsorship from the Program in the Cross-National Study of Politics at Texas A&M University made it possible to bring together a group of scholars at a conference in College Station in May 2006 to begin a discussion of strategies used to stabilize peace in postconflict states. A grant from the International Studies Association's Workshop Grant Program provided an opportunity for a follow-up meeting in March 2007. A final meeting at the University of California at Davis in October 2007 was made possible by generous funding from the Dean of the College of Letters & Science at UC Davis, the Rothchild Memorial Fund, and the University of California's Institute on Global Conflict and Cooperation. We thank David Lake and Phil Roeder for their suggestions and assistance in the process of applying for the latter grant. Our thanks to Robert Huckfeldt, chair of the Political Science Department at UC Davis, and other members of the department for their support of the conference. We are also grateful to Cynthia Simmons, Sande Dyer, and Helen Olow for their help in navigating the shoals of conference organization and grant management. Joseph Rudolph provided insightful comments and suggestions for final revisions to the book manuscript. Finally, we owe a debt of gratitude to David Pervin of the University of Chicago Press for guiding this project to a successful conclusion.

Our work as editors on this book proved to be a bittersweet experience. The pleasure we experienced in bringing together and working with top scholars in the field, including our former professor and mentor, Donald Rothchild, was dimmed by Don's death during the course of the project. Don's intellect, passion, and generosity of spirit were and are sorely missed by all of us who had the good fortune to know and work with him. We dedicate this book to Donald Rothchild—scholar, friend, teacher, and mentor—a gentle soul with a fierce dedication to learning and teaching about peace.

ONE

Introduction

MATTHEW HODDIE AND CAROLINE A. HARTZELL

One unanticipated consequence of the invasion of Iraq by US-led forces in March 2003 was the initiation of a civil war among the country's different communities. In the wake of Saddam Hussein's fall from power, Sunnis and Shiites opposed one another in a violent struggle for control of the state.[1] By the third anniversary of the invasion, at least thirty thousand people had died in the fighting (Sambanis 2006).

What is most striking about the Iraqi civil war is that it was initiated at a time when there was an overwhelming presence of foreign troops within the country. Hundreds of thousands of soldiers, deployed to maintain order in the postinvasion state, were unable to bring about cooperation among the country's rivals. Extremist militias, including most notably the Shiite Mahdi Army, continued to undermine efforts at conciliation through acts of violence. Critics of the invasion fear that the bloodshed may become more intense once intervening states scale back their troop commitments.

If considered in the context of recent history, events in Iraq may not seem so surprising. Iraq joins many other states in which the presence of foreign soldiers also failed to bring a definitive end to civil violence. UN troops were unable to halt Rwanda's 1994 genocide in which an estimated 891,000 citizens, primarily members of the Tutsi minority, were murdered.[2] In a similar vein, Indian peacekeeping troops withdrew from Sri Lanka in 1990 after a presence on the island of more than two years, acknowledging that an operation intended to end the war between the Sinhalese majority and the Tamil minority had proved ineffective. Taken together, these examples suggest that military intervention alone is often insufficient for securing an enduring peace in the aftermath of civil war.

The argument we advance in this book is that the successful resolution of civil wars requires more than the efforts of peacekeepers to end the fighting. Success also depends on fostering a sense within the postwar population that peace will serve the individual interests of citizens. Aligning the self-interest of individuals with the society-wide goal of ending war enhances the potential that citizens will seek to maintain and defend an emerging stability rather than acting as challengers to the incipient peace. We conceptualize this as a process of creating stakeholders in stability.

If successful civil war resolution depends upon actors having a personal stake in peace, how might third parties encourage such an understanding within a postwar population? In this volume, contributors explore two complementary approaches: restructuring institutions and soft intervention. Contributors focus on the impact these approaches have on fostering a commitment to peace on the part of political elites, civil society, and economic actors. With an emphasis on the domestic aspect of the peace process in countries emerging from civil war, restructuring institutions involves replacing failed governing structures with new state institutions intended to enhance the security of citizens.

Soft intervention is focused on the international dimension of the peace process, and it takes the form of actions by third parties that are intended to foster peace through means falling short of the use of military force. As we describe in detail below, the strategies of restructuring institutions and soft intervention share in common an emphasis on establishing incentives for individuals and groups to support a fragile peace and disincentives for defecting from an agreement. By linking rewards and punishments to the peace process, these mechanisms seek to ensure that self-interested behavior is supportive of efforts to bring an end to conflict.

In the following sections we discuss, first, one of the central challenges confronting post–civil war states: individuals and groups who act as opponents of an emerging peace with the intention of reinitiating hostilities. Next we consider the value of peacekeepers as a means of dealing with these enemies to stability. While the introduction of peacekeepers is the most frequently advocated solution to the challenges confronting countries emerging from war, we find that peacekeepers have a mixed record of success in creating effective incentives for local actors to support the incipient peace. The subsequent two sections explore the tactics of restructuring institutions and soft intervention that form the focus of this volume. We consider how these strategies serve to discourage those opposed to the peace and create new stakeholders in stability.

Challenges to the Post–Civil War Peace Process

At first impression it might seem as if every segment of society emerging from an environment of domestic warfare should have an interest in backing a peace process that promises security and an end to bloodshed. Yet the record demonstrates that maintaining support for an end to conflict can be extremely difficult. For the years between 1945 and 1999, sixty-three countries fought and ended 108 civil wars. Thirty-four of these states experienced more than one civil war, with renewed conflict taking place among at least two of the same warring factions in twenty-three of the countries (Hartzell 2009).

The recurrence of civil wars points to the fact that there are often powerful opponents of peace seeking to derail the settlement process if given an opportunity. Often described as spoilers, actors who seek a reinitiation of hostilities may appear among different segments of post–civil war society. Below we describe some of the most common origins of such adversaries of the peace.[3]

The most immediate challenge to efforts at creating a sustainable peace is likely to come from groups who opposed or boycotted the negotiations resulting in an end to hostilities. In the context of civil war, rebels do not usually speak in unison. Instead, factional divisions make it challenging or impossible to conclude an agreement satisfactory to all interested parties. Those who are left out of the negotiations, or who are critical of the planned compromise, may thus view the settlement as offering even greater motivation for continued armed resistance.

An effort to end civil war in the Philippines illustrates this point. Following three years of negotiations, an agreement was reached between the Philippine government and the Moro National Liberation Front (MNLF) in 1996. The settlement provided the MNLF with governing autonomy on their home island of Mindanao; it also required that a referendum be held three years later to determine whether the population supported a continuation of the autonomy arrangement. Once the peace deal was made public, two competing rebel organizations announced their opposition. Both the Moro Islamic Liberation Front and Abu Sayaff accused the MNLF of betraying the cause of securing independence for Mindanao and vowed to continue their armed struggle. It is estimated that membership in these organizations grew rapidly in the wake of the settlement as MNLF soldiers, unhappy with the terms of the settlement, defected and joined their ranks (Hartzell and Hoddie 2007, 125–138).

A similar dynamic appears to be heightening the challenge of establishing a negotiated settlement to resolve the current conflict in the Sudan. At talks held in Libya during October 2007, only seven of the estimated twenty-eight rebel factions involved in fighting the government in the Darfur region were present.[4] The fact that some of the largest of the rebel organizations opted not to attend these negotiations further dimmed the negotiations' prospects for success (Gettleman 2007).

Challengers to peace may also emerge among the very same people who were the original signatories to an agreement to end conflict. Two scenarios serve to illustrate this possibility. First, group leaders may fundamentally distrust that their rivals will actually fulfill the commitments specified in the peace process—such as the requirement to disarm and demobilize soldiers. Because of concern that acting to fulfill obligations unilaterally will create vulnerabilities inviting attacks, peace deals may fall apart as mutual suspicions inhibit cooperation (Walter 2002).

A second scenario suggesting the potential for defections among signatories to an agreement centers on concerns about loss of prestige or wealth. By definition, negotiating an end to conflict requires compromise with adversaries; these concessions force all involved to scale back their ambitions and acquiesce to sharing power with rivals. In the case of rebel organizations, it will also likely require leaders to disband the armed forces that offer access to power and wealth during wartime. A reluctance to cede power may thus encourage a leader to act as a spoiler and return to war (Lyons 2005).

This type of defection from an agreement is reflected in the history of Angola's civil wars. Jonas Savimbi, leader of the rebel group UNITA until his death in 2002, reneged on two separate peace agreements once he recognized that his power would be substantially diminished in the postwar state. In the case of the 1991 Bicesse Accords, Savimbi reinitiated the war soon after he failed to receive a majority of the vote in the country's presidential election in 1992. His desire to hold on to his army was also an important factor leading to the collapse of the 1994 Lusaka Protocol. It was not until after Savimbi's death that the present peace among rivals in Angola was secured (Hartzell and Hoddie 2007, 110–125).

Lastly, the organizations that constitute civil society also have the potential to derail incipient peace processes. Civil society is defined as those organizations with a voice in political debates, aside from groups contending directly for public office. Included are groups as distinct from one another as unions, women's organizations, and neighborhood associations. Since there is an extensive literature describing a vibrant civil society as critical to the survival of democracy, it might appear counterintuitive to suggest that such organizations may oppose the development of a sustainable peace (Putnam 1993, 2000). Yet, given that civil society is a product of the environment in which it develops, it often reflects and reinforces the wartime polarization of groups.[5]

The absence of civil-society organizations shared by the constituencies of wartime rivals is predictable and extensively documented.[6] In the context of this division, civil-society organizations may well oppose a peace process they consider threatening to the interests of their community. This was the case during efforts to foster peace in Northern Ireland; civil-society organizations, predisposed toward favoring either Catholic or Protestant interests, acted as barriers to peace rather than its supporters (see Foley, chapter 8, this volume).

In sum, a central challenge confronting states emerging from civil war is ensuring that societal actors support the developing peace. Given the incentives and norms established during wartime, however, such support cannot be assumed to exist. Instead, there is a need to identify strategies that discourage the emergence of those opposed to a settlement and create incentives for individuals and groups to recognize that the maintenance of peace is in their own self-interest.

Peacekeeping in Post–Civil War States: Promise and Limitations

Much of the literature on the role of third parties in civil war resolution has focused on the role of peacekeepers in containing elements that are antagonistic to the peace.[7] To an extent, this emphasis on peacekeepers is disproportionate to the role they have played in facilitating stability in post–civil war states. In her study of intervention following civil war, Virginia Page Fortna calculates that international peacekeepers were deployed in only 36 percent of the civil wars ending between 1947 and 1999 (Fortna 2004).[8]

In those instances in which peacekeepers are actually deployed, the number of soldiers associated with such missions often proves insufficient to the task of providing security. The failure of Angola's 1991 Bicesse Accords can be explained, at least in part, by the fact that the United Nations approved deployment of only 350 military observers to the country in the aftermath of the settlement. The present UN mission to the Darfur region of Sudan suffers from a similarly limited presence. As of the end of July 2008, there were approximately ten thousand uniformed personnel on site to monitor a region the size of France.[9]

The central expectation associated with peacekeeping research is that introducing third-party troops in the immediate aftermath of civil war tends to establish an environment conducive to conciliation among former enemies. Peacekeepers foster such an environment by addressing concerns among former enemies about whether or not their rivals will abide by their promises to refrain from violence.[10] By virtue of their monitoring and enforcement capabilities, peacekeepers provide reassurance that participation in the peace process will not leave groups vulnerable to exploitation by their competitors.[11] Verifying that each group is acting in good faith as they disarm and demobilize soldiers, and offering protection should violence reemerge, peacekeepers address the security concerns of the leaders of rival groups and thus minimize the potential that they will choose to derail the peace (Walter 1997, 2002).

In short, the central finding of studies of peacekeepers is that these operations are most effective at addressing the distrust that exists between rivals in the aftermath of conflict. As our previous consideration of the motivations of adversaries to a settlement demonstrates, however, not every actor hostile to the peace process is provoked into action by suspicions about his or her enemies. Leaders of the rival groups in a conflict often are less concerned about the intentions of their competitors than about losing access to political power and resources if the war reaches a definitive conclusion. Challengers to the peace may also emerge among factions excluded from a settlement and societal actors fearful that they have been "sold out" by compromises made by their leaders. An approach to peacekeeping that focuses on allaying suspicions among rivals will thus prove insufficient when settlement opponents are motivated by priorities reaching beyond a desire for security. Third parties must therefore identify additional strategies that encourage domestic actors to behave in a manner supportive of the peace process.

A recognition of the need for intervention strategies that do more than address the destabilizing effects of distrust is apparent in many recent peacekeeping missions. Under the leadership of Secretary-General Boutros Boutros-Ghali, the United Nations radically transformed its efforts at peacekeeping during the 1990s. With these reforms, peacekeeping deployments are now organized as multidimensional operations designed to address a range of pathologies that afflict postconflict states.[12] Michael W. Doyle and Nicholas Sambanis characterize these multidimensional operations in the following terms: "In addition to monitoring and traditional peacekeeping, the key strategy was to foster economic and social cooperation with the purpose of building confidence among previously warring parties, developing the social, political, and economic infrastructure to prevent future violence, and laying the foundations for a durable peace. Multidimensional peacekeeping is aimed at capacities expansion (e.g., economic reconstruction) and institutional transformation (e.g., reform of the police, army, and judicial system, elections, civil society rebuilding)" (Doyle and Sambanis 2006, 14–15).

Although these operations have the potential to address the emergence of parties hostile to peace that are motivated by a range of issues, there is little evidence to suggest that these activities are being designed or implemented with this specific goal in mind. Efforts to reform post–civil war states' security forces constitute a case in point. One recent study finds that security-sector reforms that address the economic motivations ex-combatants may have for returning to conflict are more likely to succeed than those that do not. Ensuring that former rebel and government soldiers have a place in the new national security forces is a "low-cost way" to decrease combatants' incentives for continued or renewed fighting (Glassmyer and Sambanis 2008, 380). Although peacekeeping operations have provided assistance with a strategy of absorbing former fighters into the postwar state's security forces in countries like Mali and Mozambique,[13] those experiences contrast starkly with the case of Iraq, where the Coalition Provisional Authority disbanded the country's military and civilian internal security agencies and purged members of the Baathist party from Interior Ministry forces and the Iraqi police (Perito 2008).

Just why so little attention has been given to the question of how intervention might reshape the preferences of individuals and groups in favor of stability is unclear. Part of the explanation may have to do with a sense within peacekeeping operations that they are already overextended and would find it difficult to take on yet another task.[14] Donors may also be leery of contributing to yet another set of activities seen as necessary for stabilizing an emerging peace. Finally, many quantitative studies investigating the role of peacekeepers in post–civil war states have themselves contributed to this state of affairs by representing the efforts of peacekeepers with a simple dichotomous indicator that reflects only whether such troops were present or absent in the aftermath of conflict (see, e.g., Hartzell, Hoddie, and Rothchild 2001; Walter 2002; Fortna 2004).

In this book, our focus is on strategies that reach beyond the role of peacekeepers: restructuring institutions and soft intervention. These mechanisms give third parties the potential to complement and expand the efforts of peacekeepers to discourage the emergence of foes of the peace. In those instances in which peacekeepers are unavailable for deployment, these two strategies may serve as an opportunity for foreign states to play a positive role in the peace process at a relatively low cost.

This study also makes it possible to explore exactly how these two strategies influence the choices of citizens vis-à-vis the peace process. We examine how individuals and groups respond to third-party incentives intended to elicit behavior supportive of the emergent peace. In short, we seek to consider how successful these tactics are in transforming potential challengers to peace into stakeholders in the post–civil war order.

Restructuring Institutions

How to recast governing institutions is an issue that confronts all states in which civil wars have ended without a definitive victory for government forces. The existence of widespread violence during the war is itself a demonstration that institutions intended to manage conflict peacefully among communities have failed and the consideration of alternatives has become a necessity. In recent years, the strategy that has been most often embraced for restructuring postwar institutions is the adoption of democracy. Informed by the failure of authoritarian states during the 1990s and the attendant celebration of the "triumph of liberalism," academics and policymakers credit democratic institutions with a capacity to move competition from the battlefield to the ballot box by establishing rules for the peaceful resolution of disputes.[15] Democracy has thus increasingly been viewed as the only viable institutional option in the aftermath of civil war.

This consensus concerning the virtues of democracy is reflected in the common emphasis on elections as a final step in the peace process. In surveying peace agreements since the end of the cold war, Terrence Lyons finds that settlements "routinely featured measures to introduce a process of democratization. The legitimacy of a new, postconflict dispensation through electoral validation was essential. Even in the most difficult cases, peace agreements called for elections, as in the 1999 Lusaka peace agreement for the Democratic Republic of the Congo and the 2001 Bonn agreement to rebuild political order in Afghanistan. Iraq is another case in which elections have been regarded as necessary to manage a transitional process and end U.S. occupation" (Lyons 2005, 2–3).

Democratization and Challengers to Peace

Despite its intuitive appeal, promoting democracy as a means of restructuring institutions in the aftermath of civil war ignores the vital need to address the disruptive influence of those opposed to peace. In fact, there is a strong potential that the introduction of democracy will itself provide an incentive for the emergence of individual actors and groups who favor a return to hostilities. This is the central finding of research indicating that political liberalization preceded the renewal of conflict in the countries of Angola, Bosnia, and Rwanda (Paris 2004).[16]

Why might democracy serve as an invitation to a renewal of civil violence? A fundamental premise of democracy is that competition is a necessary and valuable aspect of the political process. This emphasis on the virtues of competition is reflected in the elections that define democratic states. In countries emerging from civil war, however, democracy's "invitation to struggle" takes place in an environment in which the norms of nonviolent dispute resolution are new and governments typically lack the capacity to ensure that political competition remains peaceful. In this context, electoral campaigns can reach beyond speeches and rallies to violence between the supporters of rival candidates.[17] Cambodia's 1992 elections, for example, have been described as taking place in a "time of poisonous politics," a reference to the threats, harassment, and acts of violence engaged in by the Khmer Rouge, cadres of the Cambodian People's Party and the state of Cambodia, and state forces (Brown 1998, 92).

The relationship between the introduction of democracy and the instigation of violence by those hostile to the peace process is further reinforced by the inherent uncertainty of electoral outcomes.[18] Just contemplating the possibility that communities will find their leadership excluded from government following an election may motivate a return to civil war. As previously described in this chapter, it was Savimbi's recognition of his fading electoral fortunes that led to his choice in 1992 to reinitiate hostilities in Angola.

To address electoral uncertainty and the motivation it provides to spoilers, post–civil war peace settlements now typically include provisions for the establishment of power-sharing institutions. These institutions are intended to provide each group with a guarantee that it will have a minimum level of representation within government. To cite one example, the Dayton Peace Accords designed to end the civil war in Bosnia make extensive use of power-sharing mechanisms. Most notably, the agreement includes the requirement that the presidency take the form of a "committee of three," made up of one representative each from the Bosniacs, the Bosnian Serbs, and the Bosnian Croats (Woodward 1999, 92). By assuring each community access to a minimum degree of state power, groups are expected to be less vitally concerned about failing to gain support among a majority of voters in an election (Lijphart 1977, 1999).[19]

At the same time, critics of power-sharing institutions warn that employing these guarantees has the potential to generate new liabilities for post–civil war states. Of greatest concern is that power sharing may reinforce existing divisions within a society by making the legitimacy of all claims to government power contingent on membership in one of the contending groups. As a result, new identities and societal cleavages that might cross-cut or supersede the most salient societal division cannot emerge. Based on this critique, the institutional alternatives to power sharing emphasize the potential for the development of structures that encourage individuals to move beyond their conflict-centered identities (Horowitz 1985, 1990).[20]

A final reason for anticipating a relationship between the introduction of democracy and the emergence of post–civil war violence relates to the issue of state legitimacy. An important justification for requiring elections in countries emerging from civil war is the belief that the process of voting for government leaders itself confers legitimacy on officeholders. By virtue of receiving electoral support, new state leaders are thought to have a justifiable claim to make decisions that are binding on citizens.

In many states emerging from civil war, however, the concept that elections legitimate the resulting government is unfamiliar. Citizens have instead tended to evaluate governments based on their capacity to provide needed resources to their societies. Among the resources in shortest supply within post–civil war states is the social stability shattered during the conflict. In isolation, elections do little to reestablish a sense of security and order that might confer legitimacy on government.

The process of elections, in the absence of tangible accomplishments by the new government on a society's highest priorities, thus creates an environment vulnerable to those willing to engage in violent challenges to the legitimacy of government. This proved to be the case following the post–civil war elections that brought Violeta Barrios de Chamorro to power in Nicaragua. The Chamorro government's financial inability to follow through on a peace settlement commitment to allocate land to demobilized Contras, coupled with deteriorating economic conditions in the countryside, contributed to a rise in rural violence and the emergence of the Recontras (former Contra troops) and the Recompas (former Sandinista Army troops) in 1991. Resolving this issue required what was effectively a second negotiation process between the government and armed groups making material and economic demands of the government, and forty-one accords were signed during a three-month period alone (Hartzell 2002).[21]

In summary, the common prescription for post–civil war states of rapidly introducing the institutions of democracy is very likely to increase the potential that individuals and groups intent on derailing the peace process will emerge. The practice of elections, in particular, heightens the risk by reigniting competition among political rivals, creating uncertainty about opportunities to participate in postwar governance, and serving as a distraction from the overriding societal concern for security.

Institutional Alternatives

In light of the liabilities associated with the common emphasis on broadening political participation in the aftermath of civil war, contributors to part 1 of the book emphasize alternative approaches to restructuring institutions. Although they advocate different types of institutions, each author identifies a means of creating incentives for domestic actors to reinforce and build upon an incipient peace.

David Lake's chapter (chapter 2), which is centered on the challenge of establishing legitimacy for post–civil war governments, calls into question the common use of elections as an avenue for securing popular support. He argues that the relative novelty and weakness of state institutions in the postwar environment virtually assure that elections will fail to produce government leadership that the postwar population will accept as legitimate. Rather than scheduling elections, Lake suggests that third parties and transitional governments should instead focus their efforts on creating the security and order that were absent during the conflict itself.

If a new social order is established with the capacity to "protect people, defend property, and adjudicate disputes," Lake anticipates that citizens will increasingly perceive the new state as legitimate and identify their own self-interest with the survival of the postwar government. As a growing number of individuals become stakeholders in the new state structures, there will be a concomitant reduction in the number of individuals with the potential to act as destabilizing forces in the postwar environment.

Philip Roeder's chapter (chapter 3) also takes issue with the conventional wisdom concerning the political structures most likely to foster stability following civil war, particularly the view that power-sharing institutions guaranteeing regional autonomy are necessary to sustain peace. He examines post–civil war states in the Caucasus, contrasting unitary and segmented states and citing instances of enduring peace in Chechnya (Russia) and Adjara (Georgia). His central finding is that stability proves most robust in unitary states. By fostering polarized societies, segmented states have made peace more fragile and recurrence of war more likely in the Caucasus.

Roeder suggests that the reason for the maintenance of peace in these cases is that unitary-majoritarian institutions strengthen the hand of the majority leadership to suppress counterelites and promote the growth of a "shared political culture and national identity." He warns that efforts to share authority with rivals will likely create a polarized society as the opposition makes use of institutional resources to continue their resistance and perhaps reinitiate civil war.

The studies by Lake and Roeder both indicate a need to fundamentally reassess the common focus on broadening participation in the immediate aftermath of civil war. Rather than emphasize a rapid effort to ensure political representation for parties engaged in the civil war, each author instead places a priority on first fostering stability. The means by which they believe institutions should be recast to accomplish this task, however, are very different. Both perspectives also hold different implications for how postwar states might meet the challenge of actors intent on derailing the peace process.

Focused on a post–civil war government's need for legitimacy, Lake's contribution emphasizes the idea of empowering the state to provide for the population's most vital needs as a means of generating popular support. Beyond empowering the reconstituted government to pursue those who engage in acts of violence, the implicit expectation is that there will be a lower likelihood of challengers to the peace emerging as citizens come to perceive themselves as having a stake in maintaining stability. In contrast, the unitary-majoritarian institutions on which Roeder focuses have the potential to contain challenges to peace by investing political power in the majority. In the absence of positions of authority, individuals and groups who might object to the peace process are starved of the resources needed to engage in meaningful resistance.

Establishing new government institutions in the aftermath of civil war is a necessary first step toward fostering a sense of security and stability among the population. At the same time, history demonstrates that post–civil war institutional reforms often have unanticipated and surprising results with implications for the durability of the peace. This important caveat is one of the central lessons that may be drawn from the chapters by Shaheen Mozaffar (chapter 4) and Timothy Sisk (chapter 5).

In recognition of the current vogue for democratization in the aftermath of civil war, Shaheen Mozaffar examines the role that electoral institutions have played in managing competition among postwar rivals. Surveying the provisions of thirteen recent peace agreements, he notes that the proportional representation electoral system (PR) was adopted in all but one of these settlements.[22] Mozaffar finds that the results associated with these agreements, despite holding this institutional arrangement in common, have varied widely. PR appeared to encourage peace in Mozambique and South Africa, but it failed to maintain stability in Angola and Rwanda.

Mozaffar argues that these differences in settlement outcome can be explained by the fact that electoral institutions serve as only one influence, among many others, in shaping the prospects for peace in a post–civil war state. Other contingencies he explores in terms of their effects on the prospects of an enduring peace are the degree of involvement by international actors, the legacies of the civil war itself (the continued presence of militias and suspicion of former enemies), and the larger institutional framework for governance. Taken as a whole, Mozaffar's chapter illustrates that selecting the most appropriate institutions for a postwar state is no guarantee of ultimate success.

Timothy Sisk's chapter adds further complexity to our understanding of the role that restructured institutions play in the aftermath of civil war. Central to his contribution is the consideration of a dilemma confronting any effort at post–civil war institutional design: the institutional structures that may be necessary to ensure an immediate end to the fighting may prove superfluous or antiquated at a later stage of the peace process.[23] For this reason, Sisk suggests that institutions created by a peace settlement may subsequently require renegotiation and substantial revision. Borrowing the words of du Toit, he describes this as the necessity of engineering "post-settlement settlements" (Du Toit 2003).

Sisk's focus on the need to revisit agreements is far removed from the conventional understanding that settlements create enduring institutions for conflict management (see, e.g., Hartzell and Hoddie 2007). Yet it is clear that reconsidering the structure of governing institutions would be necessary if institutional models such as those advocated by Lake were adopted. While popular participation may not form an immediate postwar priority, the expectation is that a transition to democracy will take place once peace is firmly in place.

Although Mozaffar and Sisk highlight the fact that there are limits to institutional reforms, neither implies that these efforts at restructuring governments are unnecessary or futile. Instead, the clear implication to be drawn from their research is that the postwar restructuring of institutions must be complemented and reinforced by additional strategies for creating an environment supportive of peace. Part 2 of the volume focuses on one critical tactic for achieving this goal: soft intervention. Our central focus there, as in part 1, is on strategies for addressing the disruptive effects that opponents of peace have on the settlement process.

Soft Intervention

The concept of soft intervention encompasses a set of tactics, each falling short of the deployment of military forces, available to outside actors seeking to influence the politics of a target state. It is the absence of an explicit military role that identifies these forms of intervention as "softer" than the use of force. In the context of this book, we are chiefly concerned with how soft intervention might be employed as a mechanism to encourage support for the peace process in post–civil war states. A critical aspect of this discussion is how these tactics of incentives and disincentives might facilitate the transformation of potential opponents of peace into supporters of an emergent order.

In contrast to the flourishing research concerning peacekeeping and democratization in post–civil war states, there has been relatively little written on the topic of soft intervention. The reason likely is that efforts at soft intervention are less dramatic than alternative forms of third-party involvement within these countries. Troops crossing an international border will always garner more attention than a transfer of money or influence. Yet it is unfortunate that these tactics have not received sustained attention, given their potential to meaningfully influence the key actors in the peace process.

We define soft intervention as explicitly nonmilitary incentives and disincentives available to third parties seeking to influence the trajectory of a peace process or the nature of the postconflict environment, or both. The choice of soft intervention tactics that third parties employ is dependent upon their motivation, their capacities, and their assessment of the potential costs and benefits associated with each action.

What makes soft intervention strategies especially intriguing is that they offer a low-cost option for third parties seeking to influence the postwar peace process. These approaches should thus prove particularly valuable in contexts in which deploying armed forces is not a viable option, due to the objections of either the target state or domestic constituencies wary of foreign entanglements. By considering soft intervention, outside actors may find that they have more tools at their disposal for facilitating peace and dealing with actors and groups hostile to peace than previously were recognized.

Our exploration of the strategies of soft intervention provides an opportunity to answer important questions about the array of means through which outside actors influence the domestic politics of post–civil war states. While we know, for example, that a positive correlation exists between levels of foreign assistance and the stability of the postconflict peace, we know little about how and why foreign aid is associated with this outcome (Kang and Meernik 2005). Do governments use the aid to repress those who might contest the peace? Is aid distributed to economic groups that use it to start businesses that generate employment and thus give some actors a stake in the peace? If aid is given to some social groups but not others, does that action strengthen the dedication of some to the peace and weaken the commitment of others? These questions highlight the point that if intervention is ever to be used as something other than a blunt-force instrument, scholars and policymakers need to discover the types of impacts it has on different social groups.

Placing a spotlight on soft intervention strategies also calls on scholars and policymakers to identify what factors and conditions we believe are most crucial to a lasting peace and the outcomes we expect from the strategies adopted by the international community. Intervention strategies, especially those focused on maintaining peace through the deployment of peacekeeping forces, may well secure groups' compliance with the terms of a civil war settlement. One may ask, however, whether compliance provides a basis for a lasting peace. Will the peace hold once third-party troops withdraw from Bosnia and Herzegovina, for example? If tolerance and reconciliation among formerly warring groups are necessary conditions for an enduring peace, can soft intervention strategies be used to foster such outcomes? Can soft intervention strategies encourage reconciliation among groups and thus promote an enduring peace? These are the issues that we explore by examining the forms and effects of soft intervention.

Tactics of Soft Intervention

As described by Donald Rothchild and Nikolas Emmanuel in chapter 6, soft intervention strategies are actions that either reward conduct supportive of the peace process or punish efforts to derail conciliation among enemies.[24] It is through a combination of incentives and disincentives that soft intervention offers a powerful means to determine the future prospects for peace.

Rothchild and Emmanuel identify the following means through which third parties engage in soft intervention to reward actors supportive of the peace process:

- *Purchase:* Providing targeted, short-term economic rewards to communities supportive of the peace process. Purchase is a tactic that has been employed by the United States during the intervention in Iraq. The *New York Times* reported that the American military made payments of approximately $300 a month to members of both Sunni and Shiite militias to "guard checkpoints and buildings and—for those who used to be insurgents—to no longer blow up American convoys and shoot American troops."[25]
- *Insurance*: Protecting the cultural and political interests of communities supportive of the peace process. An effort at providing insurance in the aftermath of civil war is apparent in the 2005 negotiated resolution to the North-South conflict in the Sudan. The US special envoy to the peace process offered foreign monitoring of the agreement to confirm that religious freedoms were being respected.
- *Legitimation:* Providing international recognition and authority to communities supportive of the peace process. Once it signed the 1999 Lomé Peace Agreement ending the civil war in Sierra Leone, the Revolutionary United Front (RUF), a group with a history of human rights abuses during the course of the conflict, received a degree of legitimation when its leaders were assigned cabinet positions in the postwar government.[26]

These items can be collectively characterized as means of influence; they are tactics by which third parties induce others to produce the desired outcome of maintaining peace (Rothchild 1997). For each of the incentives identifying rewards for current and future acts complementary to the peace process, Rothchild and Emmanuel identify an opposing disincentive that can be used to punish actors intent on undermining the peace.

- *Embargoes or Sanctions*: Imposing short-term economic harm on defectors from a peace agreement. This tactic is reflected in the Security Council's adopting of Resolution 1306 on July 5, 2000, which placed a ban on the direct or indirect import of rough diamonds from Sierra Leone through a Certificate of Origin regime. This measure was one of several employed to punish the RUF for its violations of the 1999 Lomé Peace Agreement.
- *Risk Generation*: Removing established protections for the cultural and political interests of defectors from a peace agreement. Risk generation would occur, for example, when foreign monitors are withdrawn from a postwar state. In contrast to the other strategies we categorize as soft intervention,

risk generation should rarely be employed by third parties, because the withdrawal of assistance may provide settlement opponents with even greater opportunities to engage in acts intended to derail the peace process.

- *Delegitimation*: Removing the international recognition and authority of defectors from a peace agreement. Foday Sankoh, the leader of Sierra Leone's rebel RUF, was the target of this soft intervention strategy in 2000. Secretary of State Madeline Albright had previously recognized Sankoh as an important actor in Sierra Leone's peace process with a legitimate claim to participation in the postwar government. Once Sankoh failed to fulfill his obligations as specified in the Lomé Peace Accord, however, Albright declared he had "lost his chance . . . to be a part of the system" and "he has to go."[27]

Together these different forms of soft intervention constitute a series of carrots and sticks intended to push potentially recalcitrant actors to behave in a manner supportive of the peace process. It is worthwhile to keep in mind that coercive (hard) and noncoercive (soft) means of intervention into postwar states should not be considered mutually exclusive. If peacekeepers are available for deployment to a target state, there is every reason to expect that bringing their coercive influence to bear in the aftermath of a settlement will help to foster peace. However, relying solely on foreign military coercion without simultaneously adopting soft incentives for cooperation among rivals is not a recipe for success. At best, third parties demanding peace at the barrel of a gun are likely to induce formalistic behavior among rivals who cooperate as a simple act of expediency. Soft intervention, by creating rewards for collaboration across societal divisions and punishments for hostile activities, helps rivals identify avenues of compromise and the benefits of peace. It is in recognizing these rewards that peace becomes self-enforcing and durable in the aftermath of foreign intervention.

Soft Intervention and Societal Actors

Informed by Rothchild and Emmanuel's definition of soft intervention as a set of tactics that link rewards with activities supportive of the peace process and punishments with behaving as settlement opponents, chapters 7–9 examine the actual performance of soft intervention strategies in the setting of post–civil war states. Each chapter offers a unique contribution by considering a particular segment of society and how it might be influenced by strategies of soft intervention.

In chapter 7, Terrence Lyons looks at the potential role of soft intervention in transforming the armed groups once engaged in civil war violence into entities supportive of peace. Considering several cases at the critical moment immediately following the signing of a settlement, he assesses the degree of success associated with efforts to change militias organized for the promotion of violence into political parties organized to engage in peaceful political competition. He argues that this is a crucial step in the peace process because demilitarizing political actors limits their capacity to derail the peace process.

Lyons acknowledges the significance of other influences but notes that in certain cases tactics of soft intervention played an important role in efforts to either reward or punish domestic political actors who had an influence over the peace process. In the case of Mozambique, the soft intervention tactic of purchase was central to ensuring a successful end to the conflict. Sizable contributions by both the Italian government and private companies with investments in Mozambique encouraged the rebel RENAMO organization to transform itself into a political party. These contributions were provided with the understanding that they were contingent on RENAMO's continued support of conflict resolution efforts.

Turning to disincentives targeting opponents of peace, Lyons finds that the soft intervention tactic of embargoes or sanctions was on display in the case of Liberia. Specifically, he notes that a UN-sponsored embargo on diamond exports harmed the ability of Liberian president Charles Taylor, a former rebel leader himself, to provide financial support for rebel troops in the neighboring state of Sierra Leone. This lost revenue stream contributed to Taylor's inability to contain an uprising that contributed to his fall from power in 1999. These examples suggest that soft intervention tactics have often been employed by states seeking to influence those military entities with the greatest capacity to act as enemies of an emergent peace.

While Lyons centers his analysis on a country's political elite, Michael Foley, in chapter 8, considers efforts by third parties to influence postwar civil society through the tactics of soft intervention. As noted earlier, civil-society organizations often become polarized during the conflict as competing organizations come to support different interests. Is soft intervention effective at promoting reintegration among divided communities and generating support for the peace process among civil society? Foley's analysis of three post–civil war states indicates that the historical record is decidedly mixed.

The efforts by third parties to engage postwar civil society in El Salvador provide the greatest source of optimism. In this instance, Foley notes that the US Agency for International Development played an important role in implementing the accords through the soft intervention tactics of purchase and insurance. These efforts were apparent in the funding of civil-society organizations engaged in voter registration, civic education, and the monitoring of elections. The effect was to give societal groups the opportunity to engage in activities complementary to the goal of bringing a definitive end to the violence.

The degree of success associated with soft intervention tactics in El Salvador is not apparent in the other two cases analyzed in chapter 8: Bosnia and Northern Ireland. Instead, Foley identifies a range of pathologies that have harmed efforts by third parties to engage in effective soft intervention in these post–civil war states. He warns that the civil-society organizations that emerge in the aftermath of conflict are often more adept at writing grant proposals and securing funds from contributors than at promoting a peace agenda. His research also indicates that civil-society organizations that are on the receiving end of soft incentives such as purchase and legitimation may find their motivations and patriotism questioned by government officials and citizens wary of foreign meddling in their domestic affairs.

Susan Woodward, in chapter 9, centers her analysis of soft intervention on the role that these incentives and disincentives may play in shaping support for the peace process among a country's economic interests. This is a particularly relevant topic given the recent interest in the economic bases of civil war; a growing number of studies have focused on war profiteers and civil-war-as-organized-crime.[28]

Despite the focus on the economic causes of civil war initiation, Woodward finds that there is little enthusiasm among policymakers for employing tactics of soft intervention to influence the actions of business interests once the war has ended. The international financial institutions (IFIs) that play a leading role in postconflict economic reconstruction efforts instead consistently have favored a set of policies intended to liberalize the economy and reduce the size and influence of government. These policies are adopted with the goal of creating an environment hospitable to foreign investment and local entrepreneurship. If successful at fostering economic growth, popular support for peace is expected to increase as citizens recognize a "peace dividend."

The reliance on a standard package of liberalizing policies effectively prevents IFIs and foreign governments from making their financial assistance conditional on the actions of local economic actors.[29] In effect, the price that is paid for a singular focus on promoting liberalization is limiting the leverage that foreign actors might wield over those within the state. This does not mean, however, that soft intervention could not be deployed as a means to encourage business activities complementary to the peace process.

Woodward suggests such an argument by offering a critical assessment of the effect of international economic assistance on local entrepreneurship. She finds that very little of donor funds is spent on local goods and services; instead, donor fears of corruption and low-quality products steer the vast majority of dollars toward foreign suppliers. Thus an opportunity for developing local businesses is lost. These same funds could be employed as a means to reward actors engaged in activities supportive of peace and punish those who are not. The US military's recent use of "microgrants," grants of twenty-five hundred dollars or less directed at strengthening and expanding small businesses in Baghdad neighborhoods, is an example of how funds might be used to foster a stake in the peace on the part of economic actors. Based on the premise that "better business means more jobs [and] more money in the community, and [that makes] working for terrorists to feed families" a less attractive alternative, US troops have sought to disburse microgrants to small enterprises in violence-prone neighborhoods, including some near Sadr City (Tomkins 2008, 1).

Taken together, the chapters in part 2 of the book provide a critical assessment of how soft intervention has performed in the aftermath of civil war. These authors also provide a basis for investigating how these tactics have influenced different dimensions of a postwar society: militias, civil society, and economic actors. The chapters also offer a means of initiating a consideration of how policymakers might make better use of the opportunities for influencing the peace process through the tactics of soft intervention.

Our ambition for this book is to reach beyond the common focus on peacekeeping and suggest alternative means through which post–civil war states might achieve stability. We examine in depth two approaches that have not enjoyed the same level of attention garnered by peacekeeping: restructuring institutions and soft intervention. Behind these strategies is the assumption that a central challenge confronting post–civil war countries is the need to create substantial constituencies within society who want to bring a definitive end to the violence. Restructuring institutions and soft intervention are thus intended to address the challenge of transforming potential enemies of a settlement into stakeholders in the post–civil war state.

References

Berman, Sheri. 1997. "Civil Society and the Collapse of the Weimar Republic." *World Politics* 49, 3: 401–429.

Boyce, James K. 2002. *Investing in Peace: Aid and Conditionality after Civil Wars.* Adelphi Paper No. 351. Oxford: Oxford University Press.

Brown, Frederick A. 1998. "Cambodia's Rocky Venture in Democracy." In *Postconflict Elections, Democratization, and International Assistance*, ed. Krishna Kumar. Boulder, CO: Lynne Rienner.

Collier, Paul. 2000. "Rebellion as a Quasi-Criminal Activity." *Journal of Conflict Resolution* 44, 6: 839–853.

Collier, Paul, and Anke Hoeffler. 1998. "On the Economic Causes of Civil War." *Oxford Economic Papers* 50, 4: 563–573.

Davenport, Christian, and Allan Stam. 2009. "Understanding Rwandan Political Violence in 1994." Accessed at www.genodynamics.com on August 20, 2009.

Doyle, Michael, and Nicholas Sambanis. 2006. *Making War and Building Peace: United Nations Peace Operations.* Princeton, NJ: Princeton University Press.

Du Toit, Pierre. 2003. "Why Post-Settlement Settlements?" *Journal of Democracy* 14, 3: 104–118.

Fearon, James. 1998. "Commitment Problems and the Spread of Ethnic Conflict." In *The International Spread of Ethnic Conflict*, ed. David A. Lake and Donald Rothchild. Princeton, NJ: Princeton University Press.

Fortna, Virginia Page. 2004. "Does Peacekeeping Keep Peace? International Intervention and the Duration of Peace after Civil War." *International Studies Quarterly* 48, 2: 269–292.

Gettleman, Jeffrey. 2007. "Rebel Unity Is Scarce at the Darfur Talks in Libya." *New York Times*, October 31 (Washington ed.), section A.

Glassmyer, Katherine, and Nicholas Sambanis. 2008. "Rebel-Military Integration and Civil War Termination." *Journal of Peace Research* 45, 3: 365–384.

Hartzell, Caroline A. 2002. "Peace in Stages: The Role of an Implementation Regime in Nicaragua." In *Ending Civil Wars: The Implementation of Peace Agreements*, ed. Stephen John Stedman, Donald Rothchild, and Elizabeth M. Cousens. Boulder, CO: Lynne Rienner.

———. 2009. "Settling Civil Wars: Armed Opponents' Fates and the Duration of the Peace." *Conflict Management and Peace Science* 26, 4: 347–365.

Hartzell, Caroline A., and Matthew Hoddie. 2003. "Institutionalizing Peace: Power Sharing and Post–Civil War Conflict Management." *American Journal of Political Science* 47, 2: 318–332.

———. 2007. *Crafting Peace: Power-Sharing Institutions and the Negotiated Settlement of Civil Wars.* University Park: Pennsylvania State University Press.

Hartzell, Caroline A., Matthew Hoddie, and Donald Rothchild. 2001. "Stabilizing the Peace after Civil War: An Investigation of Some Key Variables." *International Organization* 55, 1: 183–208.

Horowitz, Donald. 1985. *Ethnic Groups in Conflict.* Berkeley: University of California Press.

———. 1990. "Making Moderation Pay: The Politics of Ethnic Conflict Management." In *Conflict and Peacemaking in Multiethnic Societies*, ed. Joseph V. Montville. New York: Lexington Books.

———. 2001. *The Deadly Ethnic Riot.* Berkeley: University of California Press.

Humphreys, Macartan. 2005. "Natural Resources, Conflict, and Conflict Resolution: Uncovering the Mechanisms." *Journal of Conflict Resolution* 49, 4: 508–537.

Inglehart, Ronald, Mansoor Moaddel, and Mark Tessler. 2006. "Xenophobia and In-Group Solidarity in Iraq: A Natural Experiment on the Impact of Insecurity." *Perspectives on Politics* 4, 3: 495–505.

Kang, Seonjou, and James Meernik. 2005. "Civil War Destruction and the Prospects for Economic Growth." *Journal of Politics* 67, 1: 88–109.

Kaufmann, Chaim. 1996. "Possible and Impossible Solutions to Ethnic Civil Wars." *International Security* 20, 4: 136–175.

Ledgerwood, Judy L. 1994. "UN Peacekeeping Missions: The Lessons from Cambodia." *Asia Pacific Issues: Analysis from the East-West Center*, no. 11. Accessed at www.seasite.niu.edu/khmer/Ledgerwood/PDFAsiaPacific.htm on September 11, 2008.

Levine, Daniel. 2006. "Is Being 'Partial to the Peace Agreement' the Same as 'Protecting the People'?" Center for International and Security Studies at Maryland, College Park, MD. Accessed at www.cissm.umd.edu/papers/files/partiality_levine.pdf on February 19, 2008.

Lijphart, Arend. 1977. *Democracy in Plural Societies: A Comparative Exploration*. New Haven, CT: Yale University Press.

———. 1999. *Patterns of Democracy: Government Forms and Performance in Thirty-Six Countries*. New Haven, CT: Yale University Press.

Lyons, Terrence. 2005. *Demilitarizing Politics: Elections on the Uncertain Road to Peace*. Boulder, CO: Lynne Rienner.

Paris, Roland. 2004. *At War's End: Building Peace after Civil Conflict*. Cambridge: Cambridge University Press.

Perito, Robert M. 2008. "Iraq's Interior Ministry: Frustrating Reform." USIP Briefing, United States Institute of Peace, May. Accessed at www.usip.org/pubs/usipeace_briefings/2008/0523_iraq_interior_ministry.html on September 9, 2008.

Pickering, Paula M. 2006. "Generating Social Capital for Bridging Ethnic Divisions in the Balkans: Case Studies of Two Bosniak Cities." *Ethnic and Racial Studies* 29, 1: 79–103.

Przeworski, Adam. 1991. *Democracy and the Market: Political and Economic Reforms in Eastern Europe and Latin America*. Cambridge: Cambridge University Press.

Putnam, Robert D. 1993. *Making Democracy Work: Civic Traditions in Modern Italy*. Princeton, NJ: Princeton University Press.

———. 2000. *Bowling Alone: The Collapse and Revival of American Community*. New York: Simon and Schuster.

Quinn, J. Michael, T. David Mason, and Mehmet Gurses. 2007. "Sustaining the Peace: Determinants of Civil War Recurrence." *International Interactions* 33, 2: 167–193.

Regan, Patrick M. 2000. *Civil Wars and Foreign Powers: Outside Interventions and Intrastate Conflict*. Ann Arbor: University of Michigan Press.

Regan, Patrick M., and Aysegul Aydin. 2006. "Diplomacy and Other Forms of Intervention in Civil Wars." *Journal of Conflict Resolution* 50, 5: 736–756.

Roeder, Philip G. 2003. "Clash of Civilizations and Escalation of Domestic Ethnopolitical Conflicts." *Comparative Political Studies* 36, 5: 509–540.

Roeder, Philip G., and Donald Rothchild (eds.). 2005. *Sustainable Peace: Power and Democracy after Civil Wars*. Ithaca, NY: Cornell University Press.

Ross, Michael L. 2004. "How Do Natural Resources Influence Civil War? Evidence from Thirteen Cases." *International Organization* 58, 1: 35–67.

Rothchild, Donald. 1997. *Managing Ethnic Conflict in Africa: Pressures and Incentives for Cooperation*. Washington, DC: Brookings Institution Press.

Rothschild, Joseph. 1981. *Ethnopolitics: A Conceptual Framework*. New York: Columbia University Press.

Saldomando, Angel. 1994. "Nicaragua: Conflictos y Negociacion: La Dificil Construccion de la Paz." In *Procesos de Negociacion Comparados en Africa y America Latina*, ed. Gabriel Aguilera Peralta, Rafael Vergara, Héctor Dada, David González López, Angel Saldomando, Dinorah Azpúru de Cuestas, and Liisa North. Guatemala: Flasco.

Sambanis, Nicholas. 2006. "It's Official: There is Now a Civil War in Iraq." *New York Times*, July 23 (National Edition), section A.

Stedman, Stephen. 1997. "Spoiler Problems in Peace Processes." *International Security* 22, 2: 5–53.

Tomkins, Richard. 2008. "U.S. 'Micrograntsʼ Win Hearts, Minds, One Business at a Time." *Washington Times*, September 8, p. 1.

Walter, Barbara F. 1997. "The Critical Barrier to Civil War Settlement." *International Organization* 51, 3: 335–364.

———. 2002. *Committing to Peace: The Successful Settlement of Civil Wars*. Princeton, NJ: Princeton University Press.

Wilkinson, Steven I. 2006. *Votes and Violence: Electoral Competition and Ethnic Riots in India*. Cambridge: Cambridge University Press.

Woodward, Susan. 1999. "Bosnia and Herzegovina: How Not to End Civil War." In *Civil Wars, Insecurity, and Intervention*, ed. Barbara F. Walter and Jack Snyder. New York: Columbia University Press.

Zahar, Marie-Joelle. 2003. "Reframing the Spoiler Debate in Peace Processes." In *Contemporary Peacemaking: Conflict, Violence, and Peace Processes*, ed. John Darby and Roger MacGinty. New York: Palgrave Macmillan.

Notes

1. To a lesser extent, the Kurds have also been involved in this conflict. This community has sought, at different times, independence and autonomy from Iraq.
2. The estimate of the number of people killed in Rwanda during 1994 is drawn from Davenport and Stam 2009.
3. For a detailed consideration of spoilers, see Stedman 1997 and Zahar 2003.
4. The estimate of twenty-eight separate rebel groups in Darfur is provided by the United Nations.
5. For a discussion of the dangers associated with a polarized civil society, see Berman 1997.
6. Kaufmann (1996) notes that this division of society is an inescapable function of civil war. Pickering (2006) considers this polarization process in the context of Bosnian civil war; Inglehart, Moaddel, and Tessler (2006) document a similar outcome associated with internal conflict following the US-led invasion of Iraq.
7. There is also a parallel literature considering how foreign states might influence the outcome of civil wars through partisan intervention. See, for example, Regan 2000; Regan and Aydin 2006.
8. Fortna makes the point that a "selection effect" is taking place; for those cases that are the most difficult to resolve, there is a greater likelihood that peacekeeping forces will be deployed.
9. Statistics about UN peacekeeping missions are available from the UN Web site at www.un.org/Depts/dpko/dpko/index.asp.

10. Fears about the true intentions of rivals are known as the credible commitment problem. See Fearon 1998 and Walter 1997. For studies that demonstrate that peacekeepers contribute to an enduring peace, see Walter 1997, 2002; Hartzell and Hoddie 2003; Fortna 2004; Quinn, Mason, and Gurses 2007. Doyle and Sambanis (2006, 111–112) find that only multidimensional peacekeeping operations, rather than traditional operations centered on separating combatants, are likely to improve the prospects for peace in post–civil war states characterized by high levels of postconflict hostility and a weak economy.
11. The importance of peacekeepers to the sense of security within postwar communities is reflected in the fact that vulnerable groups often choose to cluster around the encampments of these third-party troops.
12. Two people have served as secretary-general of the United Nations since Boutros-Ghali's bid for a second term in office was vetoed by the United States in 1996. In part, the United States objected to the continuation of Boutros-Ghali's leadership because of his expansive understanding of the role of peacekeepers. This action by the United States underscores the importance of considering alternatives to peacekeeping missions, given the reluctance of third parties to commit soldiers to efforts to resolve civil wars in foreign states.
13. In each of these cases, security-sector reforms were complemented by well-funded civilian reintegration programs that offered former fighters vocational training and cash payments as a means of reintegrating them into civilian life (Glassmyer and Sambanis 2008).
14. While undersecretary-general for peacekeeping operations, Kofi Annan stated that UN operations were being "asked to do too much with too little" (Ledgerwood 1994).
15. See Paris 2004 for a detailed discussion of the promotion of democracy following civil war. In keeping with our discussion, Paris emphasizes the dangers associated with the early introduction of democracy into post–civil war states.
16. A related finding is that the leaders of nationalist parties who engage in ethnic outbidding tend to perform well in early postwar elections and that this enhances the potential for tensions between communities. Outbidding occurs when leaders compete with one another to portray themselves as the most effective at promoting their individual group's interests. For a discussion of the phenomenon of outbidding, see Rothschild 1981.
17. Horowitz (2001, 235) describes electoral campaigns as enhancing the potential for ethnic riots, although he places an emphasis on these riots in the aftermath of elections. For a further consideration of the relationship between electoral competition and political violence, see Wilkinson 2006.
18. It is in this sense that Przeworski (1991, 13) refers to democracy as "organized uncertainty."
19. Hartzell and Hoddie (2007) provide a detailed consideration of the value of power-sharing institutions in the aftermath of civil war.
20. See also Roeder 2003 on the design of postwar institutions with an eye toward encouraging individuals to move beyond wartime identities. Because these types of institutional mechanisms have rarely been employed in the aftermath of civil war, it is difficult to assess empirically whether they would have the intended effect of creating crosscutting identities.
21. Government promises to provide Recontras and Recompas with houses and land, as

well as money for the weapons they turned in, finally succeeded in bring a degree of peace to the Nicaraguan countryside. Also see Saldomando 1994.

22. The exception was the 2003 settlement intended to end the second Liberian civil war.
23. On this topic, also see Roeder and Rothchild 2005.
24. Rothchild first employed this distinction between hard and soft intervention in his book *Managing Ethnic Conflict in Africa: Pressures and Incentives for Cooperation* (1997). While Rothchild's book considered how mediators might bring civil war rivals to the bargaining table and facilitate a settlement, our focus in this book shifts to a different stage of the peace process—the fragile period immediately following the signing of an agreement. It is worthwhile to emphasize that mediation is itself not a form of soft intervention; rather, soft intervention is a set of strategies available to both mediators and other third-party actors as they seek to facilitate and maintain peace.
25. *New York Times*, August 22, 2008.
26. Legitimation of the RUF prompted the International Crisis Group to criticize the negotiated settlement on the grounds that it "placed war criminals on the same level as elected governments and international mediators" (cited in Levine 2006).
27. Jesse Jackson, interview by Cable News Network (CNN), June 18, 2000. Transcript available from the Global Security Web site, www.globalsecurity.org.
28. Several studies have found a high level of correlation between a dependence on wealth drawn from natural resources and the onset of civil war. See, for example, Collier and Hoeffler 1998, Collier 2000, Ross 2004, and Humphreys 2005.
29. See Boyce 2002 for a discussion of how conditionality might be attached to economic aid provided to post–civil war states.

PART ONE

Restructuring Institutions

TWO

Building Legitimate States after Civil Wars

DAVID A. LAKE

Angola, Cambodia, Liberia, and Somalia are all generally regarded not only as failed states but as state-building failures. The list could easily be extended. In each instance, an international trustee, typically the United Nations or a "coalition of the willing" sanctioned by that international organization, intervened to rehabilitate a state that had fallen into anarchy and chaos. In each instance, success was short-lived at best. The record of state-building by international trustees since the end of the cold war offers few reasons for optimism.[1]

Max Weber famously defined the state as "a human community that (successfully) claims the monopoly of the legitimate use of physical force within a given territory" (1948, 78). State-building after a civil war, in turn, requires the reconstruction of both the state's monopoly of violence and the legitimacy of that monopoly. As we know from the literature on civil war termination, in the absence of total victory, rebuilding a state's monopoly of force can be quite difficult. Barbara Walter describes this as "the critical barrier to civil war settlement" (1997). The disarming or merging of forces can leave groups vulnerable, hesitant to enter negotiations, and reluctant to implement agreements once reached. Most important, with coercion being their primary political instrument, disarming or merging forces implies changing the balance of power between the groups that existed at the time of agreement. Such a change fatally undermines the credibility of

The support of the Carnegie Corporation under the grant "Rebuilding Political Authority in States at Risk: International Strategies and NGOs" is gratefully acknowledged. I am indebted to Jennifer Keister for research assistance. Helpful comments were received at seminars at the University of California, San Diego; the University of California Washington Center; and the Center for the Study of Civil War at the Peace Research Center, Oslo, Norway. This chapter is dedicated to the memory of Donald Rothchild, scholar, friend, and collaborator extraordinaire.

any peace agreement. If one or another party is weakened by disarming, then the stronger party will have an incentive to violate the agreement in the future; fearing this outcome, the weaker party will refuse to make or implement the agreement. Without denying its importance, this problem of rebuilding the state's monopoly of coercive violence is relatively well understood—if still difficult to resolve.

Perhaps even tougher, however, is rebuilding the legitimacy of the state after civil war. Typically, the old political community has been torn apart by the violence. Loyalty to the state, especially if it is controlled or dominated by one group, has evaporated. Short of total victory by the state—the modal outcome of civil wars—the political differences that led to war must be accommodated by changing the prewar institutions and rules, but there is no foundation on which to build new institutions. In the anarchy that exists after an indecisive civil war or where the international community has intervened to stop the killing, groups face the enormously difficult task of rebuilding legitimacy in an environment of fear and animosity.

Legitimacy is central to nearly all political relationships. It is seldom discussed by social scientists, however, because it is "squishy," vague, impossible to define precisely or operationalize in any neat fashion. Until very recently, the concept has been largely ignored in the state-building literature (Paris and Sisk 2009, 9). Yet, restoring the legitimacy of the state's monopoly of violence is key to successful state-building.

The current model of state-building employed by the international community has been roundly criticized. Importantly, it implicitly rests on a formal-legal conception of legitimacy in which law or institutions confer authority on individuals, who then employ that authority to create a social order. But a formal-legal approach, however well suited to established states governed by a rule of law, is inappropriate in the anarchy that prevails in or after a civil war. Precisely because the prior regime has lost its legitimacy, there is no accepted legal or institutional framework that can confer authority on a nascent government, no matter how democratically constituted. In this chapter, I develop an alternative, relational conception of legitimacy drawn from social-contract theories of the state (see also Lake 2009). In this approach, authority derives from a mutually beneficial contract in which the ruler provides a social order of benefit to the ruled, and the ruled in turn comply with the extractions (e.g., taxes) and constraints on their behavior (e.g., law) that are necessary to the production of that order. The contract becomes self-enforcing—or legitimate—when individuals and groups become vested in that social order by undertaking investments specific to the particular contract, in short, when they become stakeholders to the peace. In this way, legitimacy follows from social order, not the other way around as in the current model.

This alternative conception implies that hard interventions to provide security, protect property rights, and adjudicate disputes within society should be the first step in state-building. Ironically, the social contract may require the use or threat of coercive violence by an international trustee to create an initial social order that the state can then inherit and claim as its own. Through their significantly greater resources and coercive capabilities, trustees can "lend" credibility to a newly formed state and reset expectations in more positive directions. Trustees must also legitimate their own role in the process of state-building to those whom they govern, however, and they do so most effectively not by gaining the approval of the United Nations, as is now believed, but by being an essential contributor to the re-establishment of social order. Hard and soft interventions are both necessary and complementary, and they meld together. Coercion is necessary to create social order, and social order then legitimates the state. Performance in both arenas matters.

Legitimacy

As long recognized by such philosophers as Machiavelli and Rousseau, "pure" coercive power cannot govern a society, at least not for long (Tyler 2001; Zelditch 2001). Keeping soldiers and tanks on every street corner and spies in every coffeehouse and living room is not only costly but is ultimately ineffective. Any regime that desires to endure must find some mechanism for inducing what Levi has called "quasi-voluntary compliance"—behavior that is voluntary because subjects choose to comply, but quasi-voluntary because noncompliance can in principle be sanctioned (1988, 48–70). Legitimacy is the bridge between choice and compulsion.

A state is legitimate when citizens accept that it has the right to issue certain commands and that they, in turn, have an obligation or duty to comply. Thus, a ruler is legitimate—possesses authority—when directives and laws are understood by subordinates as binding on the members of the relevant community, even if those individuals fail to comply in practice at all times. Obligation arises from the collective's belief in rightful rule. Even though I might occasionally defect from the law (e.g., exceed the speed limit) or even reject that the state has the right to enact certain laws (e.g., monitoring of phone calls and e-mail or restricting a woman's right to choose), if others accept this law or right, the state is thereby empowered to make binding decrees regardless of my beliefs or motivations and to punish me for violations. Alternatively, no matter how fervently I might believe in the rightness of a ruler, if everyone around me denies that authority and defies the law, the ruler cannot be regarded as legitimate. It is this collective belief that legitimates (and limits) a state and gives it authority over its members (Bernard 1962, 169; Lasswell and Kaplan 1950, 133).

Successful state-building, in turn, requires the (re)establishment of the legitimacy of rule, or the collective's acceptance of the state's monopoly of coercive violence. Legitimacy is a variable, not an absolute. The larger the proportion of the community that accepts its authority, the more legitimate the state. There is no threshold of legitimacy above which we would necessarily agree that state-building has been successful, or below which it has clearly failed. Success is always relative. Ideally, however, we might hold up as a normative objective that rebuilt states ought to be able to exercise sufficient authority to prevent widespread and systematic violence and to channel political demands into routine bargaining and compromise rather than continued war.

Current State-Building Practice and the Theory of Legitimacy

There is no single, well-articulated theory of state-building. Nonetheless, we can infer backward from current practice to theory and then subject that theory to critical examination. Nor is there a single practice of state-building. Each episode is unique, involving different actors who have pursued different actions in different orders. Yet, there is enough commonality across instances to posit a broad model of current state-building.[2] This model has two central features and several ancillary components.

First, an international trustee, sometimes with the assistance of residual national militaries or police, assumes responsibility for public security during the transition to a new state. This step often entails creating a secure environment for NGOs to deliver humanitarian assistance, monitoring and enforcing a cease-fire between warring factions, cantoning and disarming militias or government forces, and general policing during political reconstruction. Creating public security is intended to open up a space in which political reforms can be enacted.

Second, the international trustee also assumes primary responsibility for rebuilding the political institutions of the state on more inclusive and democratic principles. As soon as practicable after the end of hostilities, the principal parties are brought together in a constitutional convention composed of all "acceptable" groups within the country, typically excluding only those responsible for widespread atrocities or those who represent an overthrown faction (e.g., the Khmer Rouge in Cambodia). This convention is charged with writing inclusive rules of political participation and creating a new structure of democratic politics tailored to the unique historical and factional experience of the country. As part of this process, an interim government is often created. Once the constitution is ratified or validated in some manner, internationally monitored elections are held for the newly created national offices. In all cases that did not immediately dissolve into renewed fighting, all UN peace-building operations in the 1990s resulted in elections within three years (Paris 2004, 19).

In addition to reconstructing the political institutions of the state, contemporary state-building efforts may include economic liberalization and political reconciliation. Along with political liberalization, Roland Paris argues that contemporary state-builders have also sought to implement the Washington Consensus on economic policy, including reducing barriers to international trade and investment and stimulating the growth of private enterprise (2004, 19). Although descriptively correct, economic liberalization was typically not part of the formal mandate adopted by international organizations overseeing the state-building mission but was a universal policy usually grafted on by international financial institutions as a condition for (often desperately needed) development aid. For this reason, economic liberalization has only a secondary status in contemporary state-building practice.

State-builders have also recommended and often implemented some mechanism for political reconciliation, including truth commissions, war crimes trials for human rights abusers, and lustration (Teitel 2003; Chesterman 2004, chap. 5; Boraine 2005). There is more variance in reconciliation efforts and mechanisms than in democratization or liberalization, so it is difficult to regard them as a core feature of state-building, but they are nonetheless frequent enough to deserve note. Perhaps because of the wide variance in mechanisms, there is little consensus on their effectiveness (Call 2003, 2004; Horne and Levi 2004; Brahm 2007).

Formal-Legal Legitimacy

Underlying this current model is a theory of state-building that itself rests on a particular formal-legal conception of authority that is, unfortunately, inappropriate in the context of post–civil war states. It is not just that the core concept of democratization appears to be insufficient or even counterproductive in building stable states, although that may well be the case; rather, leading with the construction of *any* political institution is unlikely to produce a legitimate government after civil war.

The formal-legal approach to authority derives again from the work of Weber. In this view, lawful or duly constituted institutions confer authority on their officers, who then have the power and duty to govern according to the rules of those institutions. Legitimate authority is thus derived from prior institutions. One day, for instance, Arnold Schwarzenegger is simply a muscle-bound actor and producer, and the next he is the duly elected governor of California with all the rights and responsibilities of that office. Critically, institutions confer authority on individuals who then govern more or less well to produce a particular social order. In shorthand, the key sequencing of events is understood to be institutions ⇒ authority ⇒ order.

This theory is reflected in the current model of state-building in its emphasis on creating a new institution (the constitution) and in holding new elections. The duly ratified constitution is expected to confer authority on the individuals who are elected to the positions it creates. Once they have authority, moreover, officials are expected to govern and make the hard choices in establishing a secure social order that benefits the people and allows the officials to be reelected in the future. The period through the election is widely known as the "transition" after which a new state is born.

In many post–civil war states, however, institutions are nonexistent or weak and are not regarded as legitimate by significant groups. In the absence of a preexisting legal framework that justifies and itself legitimates institutions, there is no foundation for determining "duly constituted" authority. In the anarchy of a post–civil war state, there are by definition no legitimate institutions that can confer authority on anyone. The formal-legal approach more generally suffers from an acute "chicken-and-egg" problem. If institutions confer authority on individual office holders, who or what confers authority on those institutions? Lawful institutions cannot exist without law, but law cannot exist without institutions. In short, a formal-legal approach can never explain its own origins: law cannot emerge from the state of nature without some other catalyst. In post–civil war states, by implication, institutions and the authority they foster cannot arise spontaneously.

Under the current model, the focus is on creating a legitimate *process* by which a new government is constituted—or through which this chicken-and-egg problem can be resolved. If all groups are involved in the process of institutional design and creation, it is anticipated that all will buy into those institutions and accept the state's authority over them. This expectation very much reflects what Fukuyama described as an "end of history" ideology (1992), but it is in this sense that the democratic nature of current state-building matters. Yet, even if democracy is inherently legitimating in the West, it is far from clear that this same criterion for legitimacy is widely accepted or employed elsewhere—and especially in post–civil war states. The evidence to date, as Paris ably shows (2004), is that democratization has, at best, no impact on building effective states and may even have a detrimental effect by reifying divisions and distrust. Although it is an unquestioned article of faith in developed countries that democracy is a "good thing" and desirable for all, there has been little sustained analysis of this point, especially in post–civil war states, and there is little evidence that democracy per se can produce legitimate governments in weak or fragile states.

International Formal-Legal Legitimacy

International trustees and the international community more generally play a major role in contemporary state-building. In essence, states in civil wars are commonly assumed to be in "receivership" or to be "wards" of the international community that require a trustee to oversee their affairs until such time as they are able to assume responsibility for themselves. The international trustees, in turn, devote substantial effort to legitimating their own role in state-building. They do so in part as an attempt to avoid original sin: if the trustee is illegitimate, then no state created by that trustee can be legitimate. If the trustee is to function as a catalyst for effective state-building, it must itself be regarded as legitimate.

Much of the debate in the 1990s over peacemaking, a form of "hard" intervention in the language of this volume, can be understood as an attempt to determine when external intervention is legitimate. This problem does not arise in peacekeeping, where the international monitors are invited in by the parties to a conflict. But peace enforcement clashes with the principles of sovereignty and self-determination. Thus, over the past decades, the international community has wrestled with when and in what form external intervention is permissible and appropriate—in a word, when it is legitimate.

As with domestic institutions, a formal-legal conception of authority underlies the debate about intervention. If societies cannot create legitimacy from within the state of nature themselves, then some prior institution—in this case, the United Nations or some other international body—must confer legitimacy on the newly constructed state. The approval of a trustee by some international body, then, came to be understood by the international community as a means of conferring legitimacy on an organization or a state to govern a "failed" member of that community.

Yet, it is not obvious that international legitimacy, if it exists, can legitimate a state created or overseen by an international trustee. The international community has worried about how it legitimates its role to itself, but it has been far less concerned whether this actually legitimates the nascent state it is seeking to build. Nor is there evidence that international legitimacy matters to the population that must ultimately comply with the rule of the state. Even if the UN Security Council approves a mission or a coalition of the willing to impose stability and build a state in a territory, there is no guarantee that the people on the ground will concur. Even with international legitimacy, a large number of post–civil war states fail and do not ever obtain domestic support. The cause could be lack of effort or other sources of failure, but the record clearly suggests that international approval is not itself a sufficient condition for domestic legitimacy.

An Alternative Model of State-Building

If a formal-legal conception of authority is an inappropriate foundation for a theory of state-building after civil war, and if the policies that follow from this conception appear not to produce the desired result, we should examine alternative theories of legitimacy and their policy implications. One such alternative is social-contract theory, rooted in a relational conception of authority. This seems a particularly promising direction for inquiry precisely because it seeks to explain the emergence of authority from within the state of nature.[3]

In a relational conception of authority, legitimacy does not follow from the office or position of the ruler but from a bargain between ruler and ruled. Authority is understood as a contract in which the ruler provides the social order demanded by the ruled, and the ruled accept the authority of the ruler to exert the restraints on their behavior necessary to provide that order. If the ruler extracts too much or provides too little social order, the ruled can withdraw their consent—and the ruler's legitimacy evaporates. In this way, relational authority is contingent on the actions of both ruler and ruled.

Following Hedley Bull, a social order is "a pattern of human activity that sustains elementary, primary, or universal goals of social life," including security against violence resulting in death or bodily harm, an assurance that property will not be subject to challenges that are constant or without limit, and an expectation that promises and agreements, once made, will be kept (1977, 5). As a shorthand, then, we can think of social order as the protection of persons, property, and promises.

This relational conception of authority has three important implications. First, relational authority is inherently strategic, with both ruler and ruled integral to the contract. Indeed, the ruler does not possess authority unless the ruled acknowledge an obligation to comply with her will (Bernard 1962, 163; Simon 1976, 146). In turn, the ruler's authority and her ability to use coercion legitimately follow from the satisfaction of the ruled with the social order so produced (Bernard 1962, 164–165). Obedience springs not from authority or coercion but rather from the interest of the ruled in social order.

Second, authority is not a condition but a variable. Most important, authority varies in strength, measured by the maximum divergence between the ruler's command and the willingness of the ruled to comply. The ruler is weak when she is limited to willing only that which the ruled would do anyway. She is strong when the ruled are willing to undertake abhorrent actions at her behest. Authority is never absolute; there is always some command that the ruler could issue that the ruled would defy.

Third, a relational conception also implies that the key problem in any hierarchy is limiting abuses of authority by the ruler (Simon 1976, 134). Granting coercive power to the ruler to create and enforce a social order necessarily gives her the ability to use coercion in her own self-interest. Thus, to grant authority to a ruler, the ruled must be relatively confident that the authority will be used for the intended purpose of creating a social order. Within states, the creation of relatively more democratic institutions that diffuse power and ensure popular preferences are represented in the policy process is one common method of creating credibility—or "tying the sovereign's hands" in North and Weingast's now classic rendition of this problem (1989).

The potential for abuse might seem irrelevant in a post–civil war state where the problem is typically too little rather than too much authority, but it is often the fear of abuse that prevents individuals and groups from conferring authority on any state. Such fears of abusive authority, for instance, are critical to blocking the reconstruction of the state in Somalia today (Bradbury 2003, 15, 21; Menkhaus 2003, 408). This is also a concern for international trustees, who must also credibly commit to particular policies or courses of action as a necessary and typically prior step in any grant of authority (see below).

The Origins of Legitimacy

In this relational conception, legitimacy arises from the self-interest of actors who invest in or acquire assets that are specific to or have more value in a particular authority relationship than in others. Such "vested interests"—typically a term of opprobrium, decried by political reformers and radicals everywhere—are the foundation for the contract between ruler and ruled and essential to the group's interest in supporting a specific authority relationship. Authority becomes more robust—more legitimate—as stakeholders acquire more assets that are dependent on that hierarchy.

Constitutions within countries are authority contracts in that they specify the rights and obligations of both citizens (the ruled) and the state (the ruler). All constitutions must be self-enforcing. Although it may centralize or decentralize authority and preserve a large realm of private authority to citizens or aggrandize all rights to the state, any constitution exists only so long as the parties to that contract accept and agree to work within its rules—there is no "third party" above or outside the constitution with responsibility for enforcing it.

Constitutions become self-enforcing and persist as individuals and groups develop vested interests in the particular sets of rules outlined in the contract and the policies derived from those rules. As constitutionally derived rules create incentives for actors, the parties respond by making investments premised, in part, on those rules and their attendant outcomes. Individuals acquire property on the expectation that the state will protect their rights. They enter into contracts with one another with some confidence that constitutionally prescribed actors and rules will help enforce those private agreements. The same holds for policies that follow from those constitutionally derived rules. Individuals condition their retirement savings on state pension plans and other programs that assist the elderly—or on the absence of such plans and programs. Firms invest in plants and equipment on the expectation that property protections and particular investment incentives will continue.

As they make rule- or policy-specific investments, actors acquire new incentives to preserve the constitution that produces those rules and policies. In other words, they become stakeholders in the constitution, regard it as legitimate, and can be expected to devote political effort to defending it. American farmers, whose broad geographic dispersion gives them considerable clout within Congress and the ability to lobby effectively, are dependent on government subsidies. In turn, farmers fight hard to maintain their current subsidies and would fight even harder to preserve their disproportionate representation in Congress were it ever challenged. Similarly, because Social Security affects so many people and conditions so deeply their lifetime consumption and savings habits, the population as a whole is acutely dependent on the program and politicians can change it only at their peril. The same calculus occurs in developing countries, whether it is rural farmers adjusting to the incentives created by state marketing boards or cronies who are dependent on an autocratic leader for privileged access to government contracts and resources.[4] The greater the rule- or policy-induced investments, and the more specific those investments are to particular rules or policies, the greater the coalition in favor of preserving the extant constitution and its policy outputs even when the results may be "sub-optimal" relative to those of a constitution enacted by an ideal social planner.

Vesting may also, over time, alter the composition of groups affected by rules and policies. As the "winners" win, some fraction of their gains will be devoted to protecting their investments. Conversely, as the "losers" lose, they have less to fight with and may, at an extreme, be eliminated from the political arena (Becker 1983; Rogowski 1989; Hathaway 1998). As recent changes in tax law have contributed to increased income inequality in the United States, for instance, the wealthiest individuals have enjoyed even higher incomes and the opportunity to use their disproportionate gains to preserve beneficial policies, while the poorest Americans have lost both economically and politically. The political decimation of the losers from policy occurs in developing countries as well. Agricultural policies biased against rural farmers and favoring urban dwellers lead to increased migration to the cities, swelling the ranks and political power of the latter at the expense of the former (Bates 1981). By favoring groups or realigning incentives, rules and policies strengthen defenders and weaken opponents and thus become harder to challenge or overturn. By creating winners, then, constitutions and their derived rules and policies endogenously create their own supporters in the form of individuals or groups who have stakes in the existing order and who will act politically to protect their interests.

In this world of self-enforcing constitutions and vested interests, formal legal institutions are the reflection of authority, not its foundation. It is not the constitution itself that confers legitimacy, but the self-interest of the parties to that contract that permits the ruler to rule. As relationally specific assets accumulate and the parties become vested in a particular social order, this self-interest legitimates the ruler's authority. The ruled confer the authority on the ruler and, indeed, empower the ruler to preserve and enforce the rules under which they benefit.

State-Building in the State of Nature

This relational approach reverses the sequence of steps posited by the formal-legal conception of authority and by state-building policies premised on that conception. In a relational approach, social order encourages the vesting of individuals and groups in that order, which in turn creates stakeholders with an interest in defending that order—and supporting the ruler behind it. As vested interests accumulate specific assets, society as a collective legitimates and empowers a ruler with authority. Stable political regimes then follow from that order and authority. In shorthand, order ⇒ authority ⇒ institutions. This implies a very different theory of state-building with, at least, two key implications.

First, establishing social order ought to be the highest priority of would-be state-builders. Especially in the anarchy of a post–civil war state, social order is a prerequisite for legitimate political authority. Rather than writing constitutions and holding elections, state-builders need to demonstrate first that they can restore order. This means, at a minimum, ensuring that they can protect people and property from violence and provide general public safety so that individuals can acquire food, shelter, and basic health services. In addition, state-builders must reestablish a functioning legal system to punish criminals, adjudicate disputes over property, and enforce promises made between individuals in the course of economic exchange and their daily lives. Only once persons, property, and promises are relatively secure will individuals grant their consent to the state.[5]

Second, the social order created must be credible if it is to become legitimate. Vesting interests in a particular social order is necessary for the collective consent that makes an order self-reinforcing. To risk such investments, individuals and groups must believe that this order and not some alternative order—this set of rules and procedures and not some different set—will remain in place over time before they begin acquiring the specific assets that then bind them to that order and create incentives to support or even defend a particular regime. The problem of building order, legitimacy, and states is essentially one of establishing the credibility of that order so that individuals and groups can become, in essence, stakeholders in the peace.

In the short run, state-builders can secure a social order simply by establishing a coercive presence within a fragile state that can protect people, defend property, and adjudicate disputes. The soft intervention techniques identified by Rothchild and Emmanuel thus often require a parallel "hard" intervention to take root and to ignite the process of vesting interests (see chapter 6, this volume). Over the longer run, however, state-builders must also help the conflicting factions reconcile with one another and establish new rules on the treatment of groups and individuals, the distribution and use of property, and crime and contracts. This process necessarily involves negotiating some of the divisive issues that contributed to civil war in the first place. In the formal-legal approach, democracy is expected to address these issues by empowering new groups and "normalizing" conflicts within transparent political institutions. A relational approach suggests that underlying issues need to be addressed sufficiently so that groups "buy into" the new order established by the trustee.

Once a social order is established, state-builders can turn to creating an interim government, writing a new constitution, and holding elections, as appropriate. But contrary to formal-legal theory and current practice, institution-building is clearly a secondary concern. Indeed, it is expected that as groups become vested in the new order, institutions will tend to arise organically from the interests of the groups in preserving that order. Most importantly, in a relational approach, institutions follow rather than precede the development of a new political regime.

There is considerable evidence to support this theory of state-building. Although the formation of original states from within the state of nature is shrouded in the mists of time, a relational conception appears consistent with what we know about the process. In the anthropological literature on "contact era" Melanesia, which provides one of the few windows into "living" societies creating their first authority structures, one prominent form is the local big man, an individual who uses his comparative advantage in material accumulation to generate wealth and, in turn, to produce a local social order that earns him authority over his followers (Sahlins 2000).[6] These big-man societies are particularly interesting because they possess authority structures without any formal-legal apparatus or even the institution of hereditary chieftaincy. Similarly, based largely on archaeological evidence, Earle argues that it was the ability of chiefs to provide the public good of defense or irrigation that created and sustained their authority (1997). In discussing the rise of the ancient Mesopotamian empires, the first large-scale political units with a well-documented archaeological record, Mann points to the important role of "compulsory cooperation," first identified by Spencer, which provided a social order that led to a deeper division of labor, higher incomes, institutionalized loyalty, and greater authority for the imperial center (Mann 1986, esp. 146–155; see also Spencer 1969). In all of these cases, formal-legal institutions followed rather than drove the process. In the end, authority rests on the ruler's ability to deliver the "goods" demanded by the ruled and the latter's willingness to recognize as legitimate the status of the former.

Contemporary examples follow this same general outline.[7] In the absence of a legitimate state, it appears that groups can emerge that assume statelike powers and may, eventually, become states. By providing social-insurance benefits for their members, for instance, Hamas in Gaza and Hezbollah in southern Lebanon have grown from social-service organizations into radical Islamic groups, then quasi-states with specific areas under their control, and now into national governing parties in still fragile states (Berman and Laitin 2005, Iannaccone and Berman 2006). Maoist rebels in Nepal earned legitimacy by restoring order in the absence of the state, providing justice through "people's courts," collecting taxes, awarding contracts, providing basic health care, and aiding victims of flooding.[8] Clan elders in Somaliland, unlike those in the southern regions of Somalia, have kept the peace, rebuilt public goods destroyed by Siad Barre's regime and the civil war (e.g., airports and water supplies) and created a new governing structure that incorporates their traditional role and status (Ahmed and Green 1999, 123–124; Huliaras 2002, 160–163; Bradbury 2003, 19). On this foundation, in turn, a new constitution approved in 2002 began the process of creating a new multiparty political system—one that, surprisingly, survived its first constitutional succession of power (Bradbury, Abokor, and Yusuf 2003). In these and other cases, the first step toward legitimacy is the provision of a stable social order of value to the group's members.

Conversely, it appears that the inability to deliver basic public services is intimately connected to state failure. The State Failure Task Force studied leading indicators of state failure and concluded that infant mortality was a significant predictor (see Goldstone et al. 2000).[9] The task force lacked a good theory for why infant mortality should matter. However, in the relational approach advanced here, a state that is unable to deliver public services to mothers and young children that are sufficient to prevent escalating mortality is easily understood as failing to keep its part of the social contract. When the state is unable or perhaps unwilling to provide for its most vulnerable, the population will withdraw its support and possibly back other potential sources of authority that can deliver the necessary social order. In this sense, infant mortality is not just a leading indicator of state failure but a crucial cause.

In addition, the lessons learned from contemporary state-building efforts resonate with this relational approach (see Dobbins et al. 2007). Although the Iraq war did not originally begin as a civil war, the overriding lesson from that war is the need to provide social order early in the state-building process. Analysts now see the failure to provide adequate troops to maintain order in Iraq as the crucial mistake of the American occupation. Despite considerable efforts to build new, more inclusive, and democratic institutions, the US-led effort foundered on the inability to protect persons and property in the major population centers. Faced with widespread insecurity, groups turned inward, split along sectarian lines, and then turned on each other, fatally undermining the power-sharing institutions carefully designed by the American authorities and the Iraqis themselves. The so-called surge begun in early 2007 was designed to reverse these early mistakes by clearing, holding, and rebuilding sections of Baghdad. By providing security and restarting the delivery of public services, the United States undercut the growing insurgency and even "flipped" the loyalty of Sunni tribes in Anbar province. It remains to be seen whether this move will ultimately be effective. Yet, the Iraq case demonstrates strongly that new institutions by themselves cannot endure without a foundation of social order.

Competitors for Legitimacy

New states seeking legitimacy do not arise in a political vacuum. They face two sets of competitors for legitimacy, and both threaten prospects for success.

Domestic Competitors

Theorizing from the state of nature is a useful exercise, as it distills the problem of building legitimate states and reveals an alternative approach of greater potential. In reality, however, civil war in the modern world seldom reduces society to the anomie envisioned in the "original condition." Rather, civil war typically activates ethnic, religious, or other identity-group loyalties and renews the role of the group itself as a provider of security. In some cases, these alternative loyalties and group structures prevent the state from acquiring legitimacy (Boone 2003). But once contemporary states fall into violence, society typically reverts not to anomie but to some prior or even emergent subnational identity groups. In civil war, these groups form a "social" state of nature, or group-based anarchy. Group-based anarchy makes the process of building legitimate states more complex and difficult in three ways.

First, to transfer legitimacy from the group to the state, individuals must be convinced that the state can provide a more secure order that leaves them better off than can their group. In the anomie of the original condition, the social product permitted by any social contract with the state is likely to be very much larger than the "nasty" and "brutish" status quo. Subordinating themselves to the state appears relatively attractive to all these socially isolated individuals. In a social state of nature, however, groups that cohere and survive are typically hierarchical, authoritative actors able to organize for self-defense and the provision of at least rudimentary social services. Clans, religious groups, or ethnic groups band together to provide at least minimal protection and support for their members. Although perhaps smaller than that possible under an effective state, the social product created by the group may be significant.[10] Thus it is implied that the state cannot gain the allegiance of its citizens by providing just any social order. It must provide a better social order and a larger social product than the groups can, a more challenging task requiring even greater credibility.

Second, group anarchy creates the possibility of redistributive bargaining, which makes it harder to settle on a peaceful equilibrium. In the original condition, each person is the equal of any other, or at least does not possess so much physical strength or resources that he or she can permanently dominate others. As a result, all will share relatively equally in the benefits of the social contract. In a social state of nature, however, groups will not be equal but will likely vary in size, resources, or ability. Each will use its attributes to bargain for a larger share of the social product created by a new state. In turn, groups will cycle through alternative redistributive schemes, delaying agreement. And the longer any agreement endures, locking in a particular distribution of benefits, the more difficult it will be to arrive at a new contract (Fearon 1998).

Third, as hierarchically organized entities themselves, groups will create leaders with some measure of authority. At a minimum, leaders of groups successful enough to organize and participate in the political process will possess the ability to speak for the group and represent it to others. With this authority comes the potential for its abuse, giving leaders the opportunity to act in their own interests rather than for the group as a whole. Importantly, leaders may develop a vested interest in their positions as leaders and in the privileges and rents that follow from that status, perquisites that would not carry over into a new state either because the leaders might be excluded from power or because they might simply have to share power with other group leaders in the new central government. To the extent that leaders are vested in privileged positions within their groups and have autonomy in conducting affairs, they may undercut efforts to forge a new social contract.

In no case does competition either among groups or between groups and the state make building legitimacy easier. Rather, groups appear to make a complex and difficult process even more so. The problems of domestic competitors for legitimacy cannot be solved by building institutions earlier rather than later in the process. Writing rules for new institutions will only exacerbate the problem of lock-in and redistributive bargaining. Greater democracy may tie political power to group size, but it disadvantages groups that have resources other than sheer population. It may also threaten the position of group elites. A relational approach to authority, in contrast, suggests that the social product from a common state may still be large. In a social state of nature, the groups themselves are still limited in their opportunities for exchange and specialization and consume resources for self-protection that might be devoted to more productive activities. Building a state can still carry potentially large benefits. A relational approach suggests nonetheless that in the presence of competing groups, would-be state-builders have to work harder to both provide a more secure and robust social order and demonstrate the credibility of that order and the limits on their own authority.

International Trustees

International trustees are a second type of competitor for a nascent state. They can play a positive role in accelerating the process of state-building, thereby possibly saving lives and years of instability and suffering. Possessing reservoirs of resources and force much larger than those of any domestic group, trustees can establish a focal point around which expectations of order can converge. International trustees also serve as catalysts by facilitating a social order and expanding the social surplus that eventually leads individuals and groups to become stakeholders in a new regime. Finally, they also provide credibility for the new orders, which can then ignite the process of vesting. Trustees play an important role by creating expectations that can become self-fulfilling prophecies.

But a relational conception of authority suggests that legitimating international trustees may also undermine the legitimacy and effectiveness of the new states they are trying to create. Trustees legitimate their rule not by being duly appointed by some international body, as presently believed, but by playing a critical role in the establishment and maintenance of social order within the post–civil war state. The more crucial the services they provide in securing an order, the more legitimacy the trustees themselves will earn. Thus, the highest priority for a new trustee is to act quickly to establish a secure social order and thereby legitimate the trustee's presence.

Trustees are also likely to earn international legitimacy—even without receiving a prior multilateral imprimatur—by effectively stabilizing and creating a social order that would otherwise not exist. The ability of the trustee to provide order legitimates its role both domestically and internationally.

The core problem, however, is that the mechanism for legitimating the trustee and the nascent state is the same, the provision of a social order. As a result, when both a trustee and a state are active and order is provided, it is ambiguous, at best, which entity should get the political "credit." The more actively the trustee courts public support by extolling its contributions to reconstruction, the greater the credit it earns at the expense of the state. Although all may benefit from successful reconstruction, at the margin there is an inherent struggle between trustee and state over the apportionment of the credit and, thus, legitimacy. To alleviate this tension, the trustee must work in collaboration with the state in "shared responsibility" or, better for the long run, adopt a self-abnegating posture in which it attributes as much credit as possible to the new state—perhaps even when it is not entirely deserved.

Trustees must also legitimate themselves by limiting their power over the society they rule. As discussed above, to gain the consent of their subjects, rulers must credibly commit not to exploit the authority they acquire. In the case of international trustees, they have at least the potential for exerting extraordinary power over their subjects, owing to their greater material and political resources. To gain the consent of their subjects, trustees must credibly commit to limited rule. From the 1990s on, trustees have used two strategies to tie their own hands. First, they have acted through multilateral institutions. Whether the institution itself served as a trustee, or a single state (or coalition of states) was empowered by the institution, the effect of multilateralism has been to check the power of the trustee and open its actions to external oversight (Lake 1999, 235–245, 254–256; Thompson 2006). Any attempt by trustees to exceed their limited mandates would quickly prompt complaints and possibly censure by other states. The situation is roughly equivalent to the division of powers within countries. Second, trustees have explicitly limited the time period in which they expect to exercise their authority. Trusteeships are now intended to be transitional relationships. Although some have taken on a semipermanent status (e.g., in Bosnia), these are still regarded as anomalous. Unlike the old colonial relationships, trusteeships are created by states today with the expectation that they will be self-negating, or that the subject country will quickly return to self-rule. This understanding signals to the subject peoples that the trustee has limited ambitions. It is precisely the willingness of trustees to submit themselves to multilateral oversight and temporary governance that makes their commitment to limited rule credible to subject peoples—and helps legitimate their role in establishing new social orders and states.

This need to commit credibly to limited rule, however, undercuts or at least is in tension with the need to establish the credibility of the new social order. As I have argued, for individuals and groups to begin acquiring assets specific to a social order, they must have some expectation that the order will endure; the more confident they are in a social order, the more quickly they will become vested in that order. Trustees can help create such expectations by guaranteeing the social order and promising to remain "as long as it takes" to create a stable regime. But to credibly commit to limited rule, the same trustee must restrict the time period in which it will govern. Trustees walk a tightrope between a too long and a too short commitment. Too long, and their role may be rejected as "imperialist" and illegitimate. Too short, and they may fail to establish the necessary vesting of interests in those orders that allows them to survive. The international community has often been insensitive to this trade-off and unable to strike the right balance. As a result, the international community's concern with restricting the length of the trusteeship has in practice too often undercut the trustee's ability to produce a stable social order and regime.

State-building as an intentional process may be a peculiarly modern phenomenon. Political philosophers clearly theorized early notions of the state, but in most cases state-building itself was a natural and organic process that unfolded over decades if not generations. The idea that citizens and concerned outsiders might sit down and design and erect a state from scratch is, perhaps, unique to our age.

In pursuing state-building as a conscious process, it might seem natural to start with the success stories: states that strongly govern through and are, in turn, strongly governed by the rule of law. Thus, a formal-legal model of authority might appear to be an appropriate point of departure. Unfortunately, this view confuses the endpoint of state-building with the process of state-building. In the anarchy of a post–civil war society, a relational view that begins with the origins of authority and legitimacy seems, on reflection, likely to be superior.

This alternative approach to legitimacy leads to a very different theory and policy of state-building. It emphasizes above all that a credible social order is a prerequisite to effective institution-building. It implies that current state-builders are putting the proverbial cart before the horse by emphasizing democratization over security and that it is better for the beast to pull rather than push any vehicle over what is always difficult terrain. It also implies that state-building requires a sustained, long-term effort by participants and international trustees alike—and should not be undertaken, or is likely to fail, unless the parties are prepared to invest substantial resources in building in sequence order, authority, and only then institutions.

Finally, this alternative approach to state-building blurs the distinctions between soft and hard intervention and between political and economic and civil societies, central to this volume. Soft interventions, especially humanitarian aid and economic reconstruction, are an essential part of the state-building process. They can buy otherwise fearful factions into the social order. But such soft interventions often rely on or meld into hard, coercive intervention. Whether by the international trustee or the nascent state, restoring a measure of social order and, in turn, prosperity is necessary for legitimacy. In any ongoing civil war, coercion may be necessary to break the cycle of violence and restore expectations of social order. The policy question is not whether the international community should use soft or hard intervention, but what is the proper mix between the two sets of techniques.

References

Ahmed, Ismail I., and Reginald H. Green. 1999. "The Heritage of War and State Collapse in Somalia and Somaliland: Local-Level Effects, External Interventions, and Reconstruction." *Third World Quarterly* 20, 1: 113–127.

Bates, Robert H. 1981. *Markets and States in Tropical Africa: The Political Basis of Agricultural Policies*. Berkeley: University of California Press.

Becker, Gary S. 1983. "A Theory of Competition among Pressure Groups for Political Influence." *Quarterly Journal of Economics* 98, 3: 371–400.

Berman, Eli, and David D. Laitin. 2005. "Hard Targets: Evidence on the Tactical Use of Suicide Attacks." National Bureau of Economic Research, Cambridge, MA.

Bernard, Chester I. 1962. *The Functions of the Executive*. Cambridge, MA: Harvard University Press.

Boone, Catherine. 2003. *Political Topographies of the African State: Territorial Authority and Institutional Choice*. New York: Cambridge University Press.

Boraine, Alex. 2005. "Transitional Justice." In *Making States Work: State Failure and the Crisis of Governance*, ed. Simon Chesterman, Michael Ignatieff, and Ramesh Thakur, 318–338. New York: United Nations University Press.

Bradbury, Mark. 2003. "Living with Statelessness: The Somali Road to Development." *Conflict, Security, and Development* 3, 1: 7–25.

Bradbury, Mark, Adan Y. Abokor, and Haroon Ahmed Yusuf. 2003. "Somaliland: Choosing Politics over Violence." *Review of African Political Economy* 30, 97: 455–478.

Brahm, Eric. 2007. "Uncovering the Truth: Examining Truth Commission Success and Impact." *International Studies Perspectives* 8, 1: 16–35.

Bull, Hedley. 1977. *The Anarchical Society: A Study of Order in World Politics*. New York: Columbia University Press.

Call, Charles T. 2003. "Democratisation, War, and State-Building: Constructing the Rule of Law in El Salvador." *Journal of Latin American Studies* 35:827–862.

———. 2004. "Is Transitional Justice Really Just?" *Brown Journal of World Affairs* 11, 1: 101–113.

Chesterman, Simon. 2004. *You, the People: The United Nations, Transitional Administration, and State-Building*. New York: Oxford University Press.

Dobbins, James, Seth G. Jones, Keith Crane, and Beth Cole DeGrasse. 2007. *The Beginner's Guide to Nation-Building*. Santa Monica, CA: RAND.

Doyle, Michael W., and Nicholas Sambanis. 2006. *Making War and Building Peace: United Nations Peace Operations*. Princeton, NJ: Princeton University Press.

Earle, Timothy. 1997. *How Chiefs Come to Power: The Political Economy in Prehistory*. Stanford, CA: Stanford University Press.

Fearon, James D. 1998. "Bargaining, Enforcement, and International Cooperation." *International Organization* 52, 2: 269–305.

Fisman, Raymond. 2001. "Estimating the Value of Political Connections." *American Economic Review* 91, 4: 1095–1102.

Fukuyama, Francis. 1992. *The End of History and the Last Man*. New York: Free Press.

———. 2004. *State-Building: Governance and World Order in the 21st Century*. Ithaca, NY: Cornell University Press.

——— (ed.). 2006. *Nation-Building: Beyond Afghanistan and Iraq*. Baltimore, MD: Johns Hopkins University Press.

Godelier, Maurice, and Marilyn Strathern (eds.). 1991. *Big Men and Great Men: Personifications of Power in Melanesia*. New York: Cambridge University Press.

Goldstone, Jack A., Ted Robert Gurr, Barbara Harff, and Marc A. Levy. 2000. *State Failure Task Force Report: Phase III Findings*. McLean, VA: Science Applications International.

Hathaway, Oona. 1998. "Positive Feedback: The Impact of Trade Liberalization on Industry Demands for Protection." *International Organization* 52, 3: 575–612.

Horne, Cynthia M., and Margaret Levi. 2004. "Does Lustration Promote Trustworthy Governance? An Exploration of the Experience of Central and Eastern Europe." In *Building a Trustworthy State in Post-Socialist Transition*, ed. Susan Rose-Ackerman and János Kornai, 52–74. New York: Palgrave McMillan.

Huliaras, Asteris. 2002. "The Viability of Somaliland: Internal Constraints and Regional Geopolitics." *Journal of Contemporary African Studies* 20, 2: 157–182.

Iannaccone, Laurence R., and Eli Berman. 2006. "Religious Extremists: The Good, the Bad, and the Deadly." *Public Choice* 128, 1–2: 109–129.

Lake, David A. 1999. *Entangling Relations: American Foreign Policy in Its Century*. Princeton, NJ: Princeton University Press.

———. 2009. *Hierarchy in International Relations*. Ithaca, NY: Cornell University Press.

Lasswell, Harold D., and Abraham Kaplan. 1950. *Power and Society: A Framework for Analysis*. New Haven, CT: Yale University Press.

Levi, Margaret. 1988. *Of Rule and Revenue*. Berkeley: University of California Press.

Mann, Michael. 1986. *The Sources of Social Power*. Vol. 1, *A History of Power from the Beginning to A.D. 1760*. New York: Cambridge University Press.

Meierhenrich, Jens. 2004. "Forming States after Failure." In Rotberg 2004, 153–169.

Menkhaus, Ken. 2003. "State Collapse in Somalia: Second Thoughts." *Review of African Political Economy* 30, 97: 405–422.

North, Douglass C. 1981. *Structure and Change in Economic History*. New York: Norton.

North, Douglass, and Barry R. Weingast. 1989. "Constitutions and Credible Commitments: The Evolution of the Institutions of Public Choice in 17th Century England." *Journal of Economic History* 49, 4: 803–832.

Olson, Mancur. 2000. *Power and Prosperity: Outgrowing Communist and Capitalist Dictatorships*. New York: Basic Books.

Paris, Roland. 2004. *At War's End: Building Peace after Civil Conflict*. New York: Cambridge University Press.

Paris, Roland, and Timothy D. Sisk (eds.). 2009. *The Dilemmas of Statebuilding: Confronting the Contradictions of Postwar Peace Operations*. New York: Routledge.

Rogowski, Ronald. 1989. *Commerce and Coalitions: How Trade Affects Domestic Political Alignments*. Princeton, NJ: Princeton University Press.

Rotberg, Robert I. (ed.). 2004. *When States Fail: Causes and Consequences*. Princeton, NJ: Princeton University Press.

Sahlins, Marshall. 2000. *Culture in Practice: Selected Essays*. New York: Zone Books.

Simon, Herbert A. 1976. *Administrative Behavior: A Study of Decision-Making Processes in Administrative Organization*. 3rd ed. New York: Free Press.

Spencer, Herbert. 1969. *Principles of Sociology*. One-volume abridged ed. London: Macmillan.

Teitel, Ruti G. 2003. "Transitional Justice Genealogy." *Harvard Human Rights Journal* 16:69–94.

Thompson, Alexander. 2006. "Screening Power: The Security Council as an Informative Agent." In *Delegation and Agency in International Organizations*, ed. Darren G. Hawkins, David A. Lake, Daniel L. Nielson, and Michael J. Tierney, 229–254. New York: Cambridge University Press.

Tyler, Tom R. 2001. "A Psychological Perspective on the Legitimacy of Institutions and Authorities." In *The Psychology of Legitimacy: Emerging Perspectives on Ideology, Justice, and Intergroup Relations*, ed. John T. Jost and Brenda Major. New York: Cambridge University Press.

US Army and Marine Corps. 2007. *Counterinsurgency Field Manual*. Chicago: University of Chicago Press.

Walter, Barbara F. 1997. "The Critical Barrier to Civil War Settlement." *International Organization* 51, 3: 335–364.

Weber, Max. 1948. *From Max Weber*. Trans. H. H. Gerth and C. W. Mills. New York: Galaxy.

Widner, Jennifer A. 2004. "Building Effective Trust in the Aftermath of Severe Conflict." In Rotberg 2004, 222–236.

Zelditch, Morris J. 2001. "Theories of Legitimacy." In *The Psychology of Legitimacy: Emerging Perspectives on Ideology, Justice, and Intergroup Relations*, ed. John T. Jost and Brenda Major, 33–53. New York: Cambridge University Press.

Notes

1. I use the term *international trustee* to refer generically to external parties that exert authority over failed states. I recognize that the term is politically charged. Some object to its association with colonialism. This is particularly the case among advocates who fear that the term will alienate postcolonial states wary of their own sovereignty. Others correctly point out that *trustee* has a particular legal definition within international law and that none of the trustees I discuss below have been

appointed in that formal status. Nonetheless, all of the interventions discussed here are led by a de facto trustee that performs many of the same responsibilities as legal trustees, at least for a limited period of time. I could use a euphemism such as *external power* to describe international trustees, but I prefer the latter term precisely because it links the modern with colonial practice and emphasizes the historical continuity in the treatment of weak states.

2. On current practice, see Chesterman 2004; Paris 2004; Fukuyama 2004, 2006; Doyle and Sambanis 2006.
3. Social-contract theories of the state begin with Thomas Hobbes. Modern approaches include North 1981; Levi 1988; and Olson 2000.
4. On the topic of the incentives generated by marketing boards, see Bates 1981. Fisman (2001) discusses autocratic rulers' manipulation of access to government contracts and resources.
5. On the importance of loyalty and the role of stakeholders in state-building, see Meierhenrich 2004. For an example of this strategy in action, see US Army and Marine Corps 2007.
6. For a related conception, see Godelier and Strathern 1991.
7. On the importance of providing social services in Uganda, for instance, see Widner 2004.
8. "Judged by the People," *Economist*, October 7, 2006, 48.
9. For a related discussion, see Rotberg 2004, 20–25.
10. On the rebuilding of social life in Somalia absent the state, see Bradbury 2003.

THREE

States and Civil Societies following Civil Wars

PHILIP G. ROEDER

At the end of a civil war fought between proponents of competing nation-state projects, the strategy to prevent a recurrence of secessionist war and maintain the peace typically includes three political tasks: reconstituting the state, introducing democratic institutions and practices, and fostering the growth of civil society. In chapter 2, David Lake stresses that early introduction of democracy, particularly elections, can actually subvert the peace. In this chapter I argue that premature efforts to grow civil society may also make the peace more fragile. In particular, when the state is not yet reconstituted as a unified authoritative institution, but is cobbled together after a cease-fire as de facto jurisdictions awaiting a final agreement on the issues of independence, the attempt to grow civil society will foster attitudes and structures that further divide leaders and publics into separate communities. This outcome will deepen the conflict between competing nation-state projects and make peace more fragile and recurrence of war more likely.

In the strategy of soft intervention, more durable incentives for cooperation are often the outputs of institutions. When third parties intervene, they can manipulate incentives in order to influence the behavior of the parties to the previous civil war, but these incentives remain in place and continue to influence behavior only as long as active intervention continues. Alternatively, third parties can create institutions that in turn manipulate incentives; the likely result is that these incentives will become more permanent and will influence behavior of the parties even after the

I am much in debt to the editors of this volume, to the participants in the preparatory workshops of contributors, and to Yekaterina Oziashvili for their comments and helpful suggestions for this chapter.

third-party interveners withdraw. The structure of the state is the meta-institutional arrangement that creates incentives for cooperation or conflict in many realms of politics.

At the core of the problem of maintaining the peace is creating what Matthew Hoddie and Caroline Hartzell call stakeholders, citizens who believe that peace serves their interests. Hoddie and Hartzell point out that maintaining the peace entails not only serving the interests that the participants brought to the bargaining table but also using incentives to realign or transform their very conception of their interests. In this chapter I expand on this theme and add two points: First, maintenance of the peace requires not only that "stakeholders" believe that peace (that is, abjuring the means of warfare) is in their interest, but that a particular peace (that is, the substance of the settlement on the issue of independence) is at least as good as another peace that they are likely to achieve through renewal of warfare. Second, to consider themselves stakeholders, participants must sense not only that their interests are being served by the peace, but also that they are empowered as partial owners of the postsettlement state. The soft intervention incentives of purchase and insurance speak to serving the interests of the parties, but legitimation speaks to creating a sense of the rightness of the political outcome. A sense of ownership rather than alienation from the common-state, which is supposed to bind the parties at the end of the civil war, is essential to the legitimation and perpetuation of a peace settlement. Whether civil society fosters the growth of identities and interests that promote a sense of ownership or of alienation from the common-state will depend on the structure of the state that is reconstituted after a civil war.

Reconstituting the State, Growing Civil Society, and Peace

The analysis in this chapter presents a simple two-step causal claim. First, in building peace in a society recently torn by severe nationalist conflict between secessionists and the central government, the structure of the state shapes the structure of civil society, which in turn influences the prospects for peace (see fig. 3.1). The second step in this causal claim highlights that civil society may contribute to maintenance of the peace after a civil war, but it may also contribute to re-escalation of the conflict. The different outcomes depend on the structure of civil society, which can take at least three forms: a *hegemonic* civil society, defined by an associational life that bridges the divide by suppressing expression of the interests that fueled the secessionist attempt; a *polarized* civil society, defined by organizations that

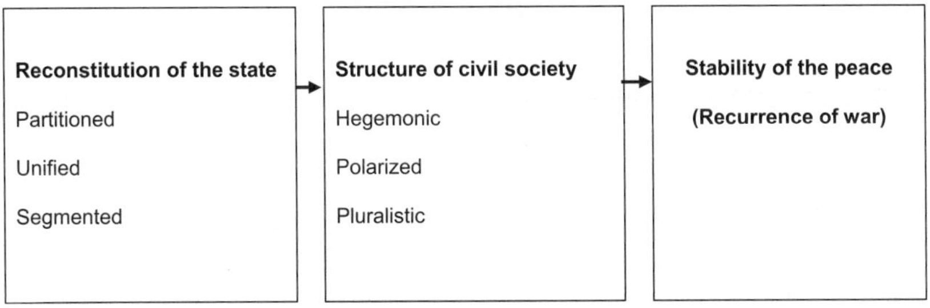

Fig. 3.1. Postwar states, societies, and peace: the causal claim.

reinforce the divide that fueled the previous war (compare Varshney 2001); and a *pluralistic* civil society that has no readily apparent dominant form of association but a multiplicity of organizations, some of which express common or segmental interests associated with the civil war divide and most of which are simply irrelevant to this divide. It is the vision of the last of these three types of civil society that is typically the foundation for calls to foster the growth of associational life after wars in deeply divided societies. Pluralistic civil society is most likely to create a sense of shared interest and shared ownership in a shared common-state that is not challenged by alternative nation-state projects.

Yet, in the aftermath of a secessionist civil war, the opportunities to create a pluralistic civil society are few, because these civil wars typically destroy previously independent centers of organizational resources, mobilize societies behind opposing sides of the war effort, and empower political and social leaders who have fashioned their careers around opposing nation-state projects. For third-party interveners, whether they recognize this or not, their options are frequently limited to fostering polarized or hegemonic civil societies. On this constrained menu of options, it is hegemonic civil society that is more likely to support the peace. In a strong civil society that is polarized, most associations enroll members from only one or the other community, reinforce a single recurring divide, and organize and mobilize each community so that it has greater capacity for a resumption of conflict. (In a polarized civil society, there may be competition within the community, but none that reaches across the boundaries of the community or challenges its separate nation-state project.) This development threatens civil peace by empowering segmental groups at the expense of the common-state and by making the center-periphery divide the single dimension along which policy for the whole common-state must be decided. The sense of shared interest and shared ownership of the common-state is likely to be challenged by the empowered secessionist leaders who fought the previous civil war. Alternatively, in a strong civil society that is hegemonic, no associations express the secessionist interests that previously tore the country apart. (If the country is kept whole, one hegemonic civil society binds the parts; if the country is partitioned, distinct hegemonic civil societies emerge in the new countries. Again, associations may contest many issues within the nation-state but not the existence of the hegemonic nation-state.) In this case the peace is more likely to be preserved, because the conflict over nation-state projects is more attenuated than in a polarized civil society. Of course, there is a cost to creating a hegemonic civil society—that is, disfranchising groups that overtly represent the (formerly) secessionist communities and requiring that the members of these communities express their interests only through organizations that affirm (or at least do not overtly contest) national unity. Nevertheless, the most efficient way to pursue issues other than the nation-state conflict is by joining associations that (on the issue of contending nation-state projects) are more likely to reinforce a sense of shared interest and shared ownership in a shared common-state.

The most important fact affecting the direction in which civil society develops is the structure of the state created at the end of the civil war. Partition creates separate independent countries (Chapman and Roeder 2007). Segmentation preserves the secessionist states as de facto or de jure jurisdictions but attempts to keep them within the larger common-state from which they sought to secede. Unification creates a single unitary state with no formal recognition of the secessionist states as jurisdictions. When the central government emerges victorious, it tends to impose a unitary state that permits the central government to foster a hegemonic civil society in which associations linked to the nation-state projects of the former secessionists are disfranchised. When secessionists are victorious, partition is likely, after which they and the rump state are likely to create two separate hegemonic civil societies within their own states. When neither the central government nor the secessionists are victorious, the compromise they are likely to accept creates segmentation that fosters a polarized civil society within the borders of one common-state. More extreme polarization is likely under segmentation because of de facto separation after a cease-fire, which leaves the secessionists in effective control of their people and territory and excludes the common-state government from any effective role in governing them until a final constitutional settlement can be arranged.[1]

After a civil war, cultivation of a pluralistic civil society is likely to require more sustained and more extensive intervention than most outside interveners are likely to want to undertake. Yet, a sure path to recurring warfare is a strategy that combines, on the one hand, premature intervention to foster a compromise to end the civil war quickly, rather than letting the war come to a conclusion in victory by one side or the other, with, on the other hand, early cultivation of civil society, in hopes of bridging the gap between parties left in power by the inconclusive civil war. This strategy is likely to result in states-within-states that foster alienation from the common-state rather than a sense of empowerment and ownership as stakeholders. In this strategy investments in civil society are more likely to result in a polarized civil society, with each constituent civil society wedded to a separate nation-state project inside its own state-within-the-common-state. As a consequence, attitudes and structures of civil society keep each constituent mobilized for a resumption of warfare over the issue of independence.

War and Peace in the Caucasus after 1991

This chapter addresses the twin issues of how the structure of the state creates incentives that shape the structure of civil society and how civil society in turn affects the prospects for peaceful politics after a settlement. Propositions concerning constraints and consequences are illustrated with examples from five cease-fires in the Caucasus region. These all followed civil wars that focused on competing nation-state projects, where one party sought to secede from an existing sovereign state. At this point these propositions must remain hypotheses awaiting tests with a much broader range of data, but four key claims emerge.

First, as shown by the Caucasus cases, civil wars typically destroy many elements that might support a pluralistic civil society after the civil war. Indeed, civil wars typically foster the consolidation of power by the political elites and movements leading the armed struggle; if these predominant elites and movements tolerate the growth of civil society during the civil war, they foster the growth of associations that offer stark alternatives of creating hegemonic or polarized societies.

Second, as the Caucasus cases illustrate, after a cease-fire the structure of civil society depends on the structure of state institutions. That is, state institutions are an overarching constraint that determines whether associations knit the parties together or keep them apart. Without extraordinary interventions, after civil war those institutions typically tend to foster extreme forms of hegemonic or polarized civil societies. On one hand, when the postwar settlement empowers de facto secessionist states (following an informal cease-fire) or autonomous regional governments (following a formal settlement), leaders at the center and on the periphery are likely to consolidate further the distinct civil societies that emerged during the civil war. This set of circumstances deepens the separation of regional societies from one another and from the larger society of which they were formerly parts and prevents emergence of either a hegemonic or a pluralistic civil society that could bring about reconciliation of the regions and the central government. Alternatively, when the postwar settlement establishes the predominance of the central government in a unitary state without regional autonomy, the outcome is more likely to be a hegemonic civil society in which no associations press the interests of the formerly secessionist groups.

Third, interveners who focus their energies on building civil society without first attending to the tasks of building a supportive political-institutional environment find that their hands are tied. In the absence of the proper political-institutional environment, outside actors have only limited opportunity to foster the development of a pluralistic civil society. When the parties are separated in a segmented state following a civil war, the actions of nongovernmental, governmental, and intergovernmental aid agencies are more likely to reinforce the development of separate societies than to create a civil society that knits together societies on opposite sides of a conflict. When the central government dominates the periphery in a unified state, this aid is likely to support the suppression of the former secessionists.

Fourth, given the importance of the structure of the state, interveners must focus on first reconstituting the state before building civil society. This may mean delaying soft intervention until a victor emerges and resolves the issue of statehood.

The civil wars in the Caucasus region were occasioned by secessionist attempts after the breakup of the Soviet Union in 1991. Seven wars of national independence have left more than one hundred thousand people dead since 1991. Included are two wars between South Ossetia and Georgia (with interim negotiated settlements in 1992 and 2008), two between Abkhazia and Georgia (with interim negotiated settlements in 1994 and 2008), one between Nagornyi Karabakh and Azerbaijan (with an interim negotiated settlement in 1994), and two between Chechnya and Russia (with an interim negotiated settlement in 1996 and an imposed settlement in 2003). Although most attention here focuses on the aftermaths of the five cease-fires, for which there is a longer record of observed consequences, two less-violent conflicts in the Caucasus that temporarily led to de facto separation of regions from the control of the successor states in the past two decades—Adjara in Georgia and the Talysh-Mugan Republic in Azerbaijan—are also compared and contrasted with the five. These comparisons are limited to secessionist conflicts, that is, conflicts in which contending nation-state projects for the creation of new states are at issue. They do not include conflicts of communal or ideological contention in which the parties fight over control of the same state.

The population of the Caucasus region has long resembled an ethnographic mosaic of many small pieces. To accommodate this ethnic diversity, the Union of Soviet Socialist Republics recognized Armenia, Azerbaijan, and Georgia as union republics (soviet socialist republics, SSRs) alongside the Russian Soviet Federated Socialist Republic (RSFSR).[2] Within the RSFSR, the Communists created separate autonomous soviet socialist republics (ASSRs) for the Chechens (with the Ingushes) and other ethnic groups. Within Azerbaijan, the Nagornyi Karabakh, populated by Armenians, became an autonomous oblast. And within Georgia, the Abkhazians and Adjarians received ASSRs and the South Ossetians received an autonomous oblast (see fig. 3.2).

The civil wars that led to the settlements of the 1990s had their immediate roots in the last four years of the USSR. Under Mikhail Gorbachev's reform program called perestroika, the central government in Moscow loosened its control over union republics. The union-republic governments of Azerbaijan, Georgia, and the RSFSR asserted greater independence and increasingly confronted the USSR government of Gorbachev. Many regional administrations that were formally subordinate to the union republics,

Fig. 3.2. Jurisdictions in the Caucasus region.

notably Abkhazia, South Ossetia, Nagornyi Karabakh, and Chechnya, saw these moves by union-republic governments as threatening their own autonomy and reacted by seeking to end their subordination to their respective union-republic governments. They elevated themselves to the status of union republics on a par with Azerbaijan, Georgia, and Russia; or petitioned for admission to another union republic (Karabakh to Armenia or Russia, South Ossetia and Abkhazia to Russia); or declared themselves independent members of the global community of sovereign states. Wars followed the breakup of the USSR in December 1991, when Armenian armies intervened to effect the separation of Karabakh from Azerbaijan, when Georgia attempted to reestablish its control over South Ossetia and Abkhazia, and when Russia tried to reestablish its control over Chechnya.

The crisis between Georgia and Abkhazia began on March 18, 1989,[3] with an Abkhaz appeal to the USSR leadership to elevate the Abkhaz autonomous republic and remove it from Georgia's jurisdiction. Failing in this appeal, the Abkhaz ASSR Supreme Soviet unilaterally adopted such a declaration on August 25, 1990, adding that henceforth Abkhazia's relations with Georgia would be defined by treaties. Following the dissolution of the USSR, Abkhazia proclaimed itself a sovereign state under its 1925 constitution. On August 12, 1992, Georgian troops crossed into Abkhazia and occupied much of the republic, but with help from volunteers mobilized by the Confederation of Mountain Peoples and from the Russian armed forces, the Abkhazians mounted a coordinated year-long counteroffensive that expelled the Georgian army. The Abkhaz army reached the republic's border with Georgia on September 30, 1993. Signature of the Moscow Agreement on May 14, 1994, formalized a cease-fire. The war produced more than 2,500 casualties and 300,000 mostly Georgian refugees from Abkhazia. The introduction of Russian peacekeepers along the border between Abkhazia and Georgia not only prevented a resumption of war but also blocked further attempts by Georgia to reverse the secession, for more than a decade. The Abkhazians used the cease-fire to develop their separate state within the Georgian common-state: on November 26, 1994, the Abkhaz Supreme Soviet adopted a new constitution that proclaimed the republic's sovereignty based on "the people's right to free self-determination" and asserted that Abkhazia was a subject of international law. The constitution created a presidency, a cabinet, a parliament, and local district governments, which the secessionist leaders used to consolidate their hold within Abkhazia. Popular elections to the People's Assembly were held again in 1996, 2001, and 2007; direct presidential elections were held in 1999 and 2004–5 (ICG 2006a). This consolidation of a state-within-a-state in opposition to the claims of Georgian sovereignty set the stage for Georgian brinkmanship and probes in the summers of 2004 and 2006 and a brief resumption of war in August 2008.

The South Ossetian crisis began on November 10, 1989, with a South Ossetian legislative appeal, but after this failed to convince either the USSR or the Georgian SSR government to elevate its status, the local soviet unilaterally proclaimed the oblast a republic on September 20, 1990. Soon after the declaration, busloads (reportedly two hundred) of Georgian activists flooded into the oblast's capital, Tskhinvali, followed by Georgian troops, and for the next two months a small civil war raged in the region. Intervention by troops of the USSR police (MVD and KGB) forced the Georgians to retreat. On November 28, 1990, South Ossetia's soviet unilaterally elevated its autonomous oblast to equal status with Georgia, with the intent of removing South Ossetia from Georgian jurisdiction altogether. With the dissolution of the USSR, the South Ossetian soviet declared South Ossetia's independence on December 22, 1991, and a referendum the next month confirmed this. On April 17, 1992, the South Ossetian soviet called on Russia to admit its territory to the Russian Federation. When Georgian forces tried to reconquer South Ossetia, fighting resumed, but Russian armed support quickly tipped the balance in favor of South Ossetia, and in the Sochi Agreement on June 24, 1992, the parties agreed to a cease-fire. This war produced at least 2,000 casualties and 30,000 refugees from South Ossetia. The presence of a Russian peacekeeping force after July 1992 kept South Ossetia independent in fact, if not in the eyes of Georgia or the international community. Although the secessionist government controlled only some villages within the former autonomous oblast after 1992, it consolidated its control within these areas, holding presidential elections in 1996, 2001, and 2006. A new referendum on independence on November 12, 2006, turned out an overwhelming vote in the areas it controlled, confirming the government's claim to sovereignty, but the secessionist government also continued to press for admission to the Russian Federation. This consolidation of a state-within-a-state in opposition to Georgian claims of sovereignty set the stage for new conflict: Georgian attempts to resolve the issue by force in July and August 2004 led to a new but limited conflict between Georgia and South Ossetia, in which 22 died. On August 7, 2008, Georgia launched an attack to reestablish its control over South Ossetia, but in the subsequent renewed civil war, it lost all control over the secessionist region. Despite a cease-fire on August 12, military operations continued until October 10, when Russia withdrew its troops from Georgia proper and positioned them to defend South Ossetia.

The Nagornyi Karabakh crisis was engaged on February 20, 1988, when the legislature (soviet) of the Nagorno-Karabakh Autonomous Oblast appealed to transfer the oblast to the jurisdiction of Armenia. Failing to elicit a favorable response from the USSR, the oblast soviet voted on July 12, 1988, to secede from Azerbaijan and join Armenia on its own. As the Soviet Union crumbled, the Azerbaijan Supreme Soviet voted to revoke the autonomous status of the oblast, but troops from Armenia prevented any attempt at forceful reintegration of the Karabakh by Azerbaijan. Armenia invaded Azerbaijan's territory in January 1992; by mid-1992 Armenian armed forces controlled the Karabakh and the Lachin corridor that linked it with Armenia. The Bishkek cease-fire agreement on May 12, 1994, left the Armenian armed forces in place and kept Nagornyi Karabakh outside the control of Azerbaijan. Within Nagornyi Karabakh the State Defense Committee, under the chairmanship of Robert Kocharyan, assumed effective control and institutionalized itself as a government with a parliament and armed forces. Direct presidential elections were introduced in 1997 and held again in 2002 and 2007. A popular referendum in December 2006 ratified a new constitution, codifying the republic's claim to be a sovereign state.

In what became Chechnya, a festering conflict between the leadership of the Chechen-Ingush ASSR and Boris Yeltsin's reformist government of the RSFSR became a secession crisis after the Chechen National Congress (CNC) staged a successful coup in the republic's capital, Groznyi. Elections coordinated by the CNC then elected its leader Dzhokhar Dudaev as president of the republic, and on October 27, 1991, Dudaev declared the republic's independence. The first civil war began with a Russian drive to regain Chechnya on December 11, 1994. The result was an indecisive and bloody war that continued for two years. Peace talks in the late summer of 1996 led to the Khasavyurt Agreement of August 30, 1996—a compromise permitting the Chechens to claim that their republic was independent and Moscow to claim that Chechnya remained a subject of the Russian Federation (Lieven 1998; Gall and de Waal 1998; Evangelista 2002). The second war began in late September 1999 when Russian air forces resumed bombing of strategic targets within Chechnya. On October 1 Prime Minister Vladimir Putin announced that Russia would commence ground operations, and by the beginning of February 2000 Russian troops had taken control of the last rebel strongholds within Groznyi. In 2003 the Moscow-imposed administration conducted its first elections for a president who would incorporate Chechnya within the Russian federal system. Six years later (April 2009) the Chechen government announced a successful conclusion of its counterterrorism operations.

The Legacies of the Caucasian Wars and Settlements

Postwar societies are, of course, unfavorable environments for any civil society and particularly unfavorable for pluralistic civil societies with multiple limited-purpose associations (also called nongovernmental organizations or NGOs) that link individuals across the nation-state divide that produced the previous civil war. Indeed, the war is likely to have destroyed much of the civil society that bound together members of the community on opposite sides of the conflict and to have left a legacy of distrust of that part of associational life. Mobilizational pressures during the war are likely to have pushed society toward the hierarchical, monopolistic, nonvoluntary organizations typical of a society mobilized for combat. After the war, NGOs are hampered by shortages of materiel such as office supplies, transportation, and communications; shortages of personnel, particularly volunteers, since few families can spare time after long hours spent keeping their members fed, clothed, and housed; and shortages of public support, since opinion is often hostile to such associations. In Nagornyi Karabakh, for example, the International Crisis Group (ICG) reported more than a decade after the cease-fire that only about eight NGOs were significant players (ICG 2005b, 11). Active NGOs tended to be extensions of international NGOs (INGOs) that focused on humanitarian relief, such as mine removal (the Halo Trust), refugees (Red Cross), and health care (Medecins Sans Frontières). Few, if any, NGOs actively engaged citizens in cooperation across the national divide. For example, the ICG noted, "no visits of homes, cemeteries, or religious or cultural monuments have been organized across the ceasefire line" (ICG 2005a, 27; also see Orudzhev 2004). The Azerbaijani and Armenian communities did not even maintain direct communication, such as telephone connections, with one another. Civil society was similarly weak inside Abkhazia, Chechnya, and South Ossetia. In Abkhazia in 2006, for example, only about thirty NGOs were active and these tended to be led by members of the nationalist movement that emerged in the late 1980s. Although NGOs participated in second-track negotiations with Georgians, none challenged the separation of Abkhazia from Georgia: They remained "advocates of a democratic, plural but also independent Abkhazia" (ICG 2006a, 15).

In all of these societies, the political culture shaped by the recent experience of the civil war has been a serious obstacle. Like the now proverbial insurgents who would renew conflict, associations seeking to promote accommodation also must operate like fish in a pond, but these ponds provide little oxygen to sustain accommodation. According to Avaz Hasanov and Armine Ishkanian, "with those societies reproducing ever more antagonistic visions of the conflict and its future, it is unrealistic to expect that [across the divide] civil-society actors should be close to one another in their thinking" (2005). Tony Vaux and Jonathan Goodhand report that in Armenia, Azerbaijan, and Karabakh peace groups "have little claim to any constituency" (2002, 28). Indeed, the war created its own supporting constituency: for example, in Armenia itself, according to Thomas de Waal, after 1994 "the veterans' group Yerkrapah . . . became the most powerful organization in the country" (2003, 244; see also Cornell 2001, 247; Wilhelmsen 2005).

The manner in which the state was reconstituted at the end of the civil wars shaped the motivations (identities and interests) and the capabilities (means and opportunities) of political elites and civil associations. First, unitary and segmental institutional arrangements empowered political leaders differently. Segmental states empowered secessionist political leaders with the means and opportunities to coerce other political actors within the secessionist regions, to establish their hegemony within these separate jurisdictions, and to suppress unionist counterelites in the regions. Alternatively, unitary institutions empowered unionist leaders to suppress separatist counterelites, including replacing political and associational elites within the regions who were not loyal to the nation-state project of the central government.

Second, state-institutional arrangements shaped political cultures and particularly national identities, with profound implications for whether the citizens felt they shared identities and interests in a common-state. Segmental institutions preserved and even hardened the political cultures and national identities that separated parties at the end of the civil war. Leaders empowered within separate regions by de facto separation nourished national identities that further alienated their people from the larger common-state society of which they were only formally a part (Tishkov 2004, 199–201; Campana 2006). Alternatively, unitary institutions tended to foster growth of a new shared political culture and national identity. A central government was given a monopoly to propagate an identity that stressed the commonalities among peoples previously divided by the war.

Third, these state institutional arrangements shaped the associations of civil society. In segmental states, associations seeking policies and patronage naturally focused on decision-making centers located *within* the separate jurisdictions. Elites within the separatist regions reinforced this natural tendency; they ensured privileged access to resources and policymaking for particularistic associations that focused on these jurisdictions and supported the separatist leaders' agendas; they suppressed or at least placed obstacles around associations with unionist agendas. Alternatively, unitary states favored associations that emphasized issues cutting across the civil war divide and that denied the separatist claims of individual regions. Common-state leaders suppressed or placed obstacles around associations that threatened separation.

Consequences of a Segmented State

Segmented states resulted from the Sochi Agreement of 1992 (Georgia-South Ossetia), the Moscow Agreement of 1994 (Georgia-Abkhazia), the Bishkek Agreement of 1994 (Azerbaijan-Nagornyi Karabakh), and the Khasavyurt Agreement of 1996 (Russia-Chechnya). The segmented states preserved and fostered the development of polarized civil societies. The civil wars had already encouraged the emergence of civil societies in which political and social organizations had become increasingly monopolistic rather than competitive, reinforcing rather than crosscutting, hierarchically controlled rather than autonomous, and compulsory or mobilizational rather than voluntary. During the civil wars, elites used this capacity to mobilize the community for warfare; the community developed a hierarchical command structure that enabled the elites to mobilize combat resources more extensively and more rapidly.

After the civil wars, segmentation left these elites and their supporting associations in place. These political leaders within each community had the incentives, the means, and the opportunities to foster a political culture that conflicted with the nation-state claims of the other side and an "official" civil society dominated by government-organized NGOs (GONGOs). Regional leaderships could be autocratic or democratic and might even sustain competitive elections that offered choice along other dimensions of policy such as economic reform, but on the issue of the separation of the region from the jurisdiction of the former central government, there was little toleration of dissent. In the Caucasus, governments mobilized the media and schools to reinforce their message of independence and separation. For example, the Nagornyi Karabakh government unleashed propaganda in schools and the media that propagated what de Waal called "an official hate narrative" (2003, 274–275; Hasanov and Ishkanian 2005).

"Front" organizations reinforced the agendas of the elites to block the growth of a civil society that would cut across the cease-fire lines. In Armenia, Azerbaijan, and Karabakh, according to Vaux and Goodhand, "we see a re-emergence of the kind of quasi-statal 'NGOs' that existed in Soviet times, such as mass organizations of youth, women, workers, etc." (2002, 18; also see Hasanov and Ishkanian 2005; de Waal 2003, 251, 257). Thus the emergence of a civil society that could link Karabakh Armenians to Azeris became even less likely.

These hegemonic elites have given particular attention to the suppression of those associations and second-track contacts that might reach across the nationalist divide. For example, South Ossetian authorities arrested an Ossetian in Tskhinvali for organizing youth groups to take summer trips along the Georgian coast, fearing that this project might foster a constituency for compromise with the Georgians (ICG 2004, 13). In the Karabakh conflict, Azerbaijan's President Heydar Aliev announced in 1999 that "for as long as we have not signed a peace agreement with Armenia there is no need for cooperation between our NGOs and Armenians" (quoted in Hasanov and Ishkanian 2005; also see ICG 2005a, 27). Aliev's government blocked direct meetings between Azeri and Karabakh civil-society leaders and even resorted to intimidation to prevent NGOs from meeting with Armenians.

Particularly among the displaced persons of the Caucasus, state leaders have been careful to mobilize the populations and preclude emergence of alternative associations that might reduce the pressure from this constituency for a return to the status quo ante bellum. In Azerbaijan the Karabakh Azeris were still kept in camps more than a decade after the end of the war. Within these camps Azerbaijan's president appointed leaders of "Executive Committees in exile" to govern the refugee communities in a manner that preserved the administrative jurisdictions for Karabakh and the seven surrounding districts that are under Armenian occupation. Azerbaijan prevented these refugees from resettling in the cities and integrating within Azerbaijan society and blocked the emergence of independent NGOs to represent the interests of the displaced persons. The only highly visible NGOs operating among the displaced persons were militant organizations backed by the authorities—such as the Karabakh Liberation Organization and the Karabakh Guerrillas—calling for an instant military solution to the problem (ICG 2005b, 21, 23). Similarly, after Mikhail Saakashvili became president in late 2003, the government of Georgia expanded its efforts to promote governments-in-exile for Abkhazia and South Ossetia as the official spokespersons for displaced Georgians and for Georgians living within the two regions.

This civil society often comes back to tie the hands of politicians and make it more difficult for politicians to compromise on the nation-state issue. In the Caucasus the first movers in the unfolding nation-state crises were the leaders of the governments of the union republics and autonomous regions. The first acts that proclaimed nation-state crises were appeals and declarations by the soviets (legislatures) of Abkhazia, South Ossetia, Nagornyi Karabakh, and Chechnya concerning the status of their jurisdictions within the Soviet ethnofederal hierarchy. Yet, once nation-state crises developed, the most active associations on both sides of the conflict in these polarized civil societies tended to take still more radical positions on the nation-state issue, to use still more extreme measures than the leaders, and to block any moves toward compromise on the issue that had produced the previous civil war (Lieven 1998, 58–60, 67–69; Matveeva 2004). Many arguments for the role of civil society in sustaining peace see civil society as a check on the radicalism and militancy of political leaders. This view is based on a strong (and often unstated) assumption that civil society is more moderate than the political leaders on the issues that divide the larger state. Yet, the Caucasus cases show a decidedly sadder outcome: civil wars fostered both the rise of radical political leaders and the growth of radical associations; these leaders and associations served as checks on moderation on the part of one another and posed redundant threats to the peace.

Even when an individual political or social leader stepped forward to urge reconciliation, other leaders worked together to restrain the rebel so that radical and militant political leaders checked more moderate political leaders, radical and militant political leaders monitored and sanctioned moderate elites in civil society, and a radical and militant civil society monitored and sanctioned moderate political leaders. Indeed, in four of the seven governments that were parties to these civil wars (Armenia in 1998, Azerbaijan in 1992, Georgia in 2004, and South Ossetia in 2001), more radical and militant associations actually toppled more moderate political leaders and replaced them with their own spokespersons. For example, in Armenia and Azerbaijan, nongovernmental organizations became obstacles to peaceful compromise over the Karabakh issue. In Azerbaijan the Azeri Popular Front (APF) was formed in July 1989 and, according to Svante Cornell, "drew its popularity from an increasingly rigid stand on the Karabakh question" (2001, 88). The APF seized power in a June 1992 coup, following mounting nationalist frustration after the first round of Azerbaijani losses in the war with Armenia. In Armenia, after the cease-fire, as negotiations dragged out and at least one leader on the Armenian side began to entertain the idea of compromise with Azerbaijan, still more radical members of civil society, empowered by the civil war, stepped in to stop the compromisers. On September 26, 1997, President Levon Ter-Petrosyan publicly announced his conclusion that international recognition of a change in the status of Karabakh was unlikely and that the diplomatic and economic isolation of Armenia was costing his country dearly. In private he had also worried that the revival of Azerbaijan's oil industry and consolidation of political order would give Azerbaijan a diplomatic and military advantage in a new round of warfare. Thus, Ter-Petrosyan announced that his government would be more open to finding a compromise with Azerbaijan. Yet, civil society rose up against him. Cornell records that practically all political parties, except the ruling Armenian National Movement, rallied in opposition by mid-November "and increasingly virulently condemned his position on the conflict" (2001, 117; also see de Waal 2003, 259–260). On February 3, 1998, a "palace revolt" toppled Ter-Petrosyan and appointed the former president of Karabakh, Robert Kocharyan, as Armenia's president.

Similarly, in South Ossetia the nationalist movement Ademon Nykhas backed the autonomous oblast's moves for separation from Georgia, but when South Ossetia's leadership began to discuss compromises and reconciliation with Georgia, the NGO turned against the region's leadership. The more conciliatory position of the South Ossetian government of Ludvig Chibirov led the Ademon Nykhas to brand the government a Georgian puppet. In December 2001 elections, the radicals defeated Chibirov and elected Eduard Kokoity as president of South Ossetia. Kokoity refused further discussions of compromises with the Georgian government and immediately proposed integration of South Ossetia into the Russian Federation (Cornell 2001, 195; ICG 2004, 8, 13).

Consequences of a Unitary State

Three nationalist conflicts in the Caucasus ended in victory for the common-state government—the conflicts over the self-determination attempts of Chechnya (Russia), Talysh-Mugan (Azerbaijan), and Adjara (Georgia). Only one of these had escalated to the intensity of a civil war, however. In all three cases, victory by the common-state government brought imposition of central rule and a rapid shift from segmented to unitary institutions. This victory also resulted in the suppression of local secessionist elites and the appointment of unionist leaders within each region. These actions also brought an end to polarized societies and the beginning of hegemonic civil societies. The new political leaders in the regions suppressed separatist organizations, including political parties and associations, and fostered new political parties and associations that linked the region to the rest of the country.

Although Chechnya is still a work in progress and could reverse course toward renewed civil war, since 1999 the government of the Russian Federation has replaced the secessionist leadership with a new unionist government in Groznyi (Nichol 2006). Despite continuing terrorist attacks, the Russian government conducted elections for a Chechen president on October 5, 2003. Moscow's candidate, Akhmad Kadyrov, won handily, but terrorists assassinated him seven months later, and new presidential elections had to be held in August 2004. Moscow's next candidate, Alu Alkhanov, the former minister of interior for the republic, was elected, but Moscow soon eased Alkhanov from office and secured regional legislative approval of Putin's appointment of Kadyrov's son, Ramzan, to the republic's presidency in April 2007. Kadyrov moved quickly to consolidate his control over governmental agencies within the republic, easing from office any challengers. Although civil society is weak in all of Russia's provinces, and particularly so in Chechnya following the wartime destruction of the capital, nongovernmental organizations from Moscow, including such human rights watchdogs as Memorial, began to operate within Chechnya (Cook and Vinogradova 2006; Fuller 2007a, 2007b). What civil society does exist increasingly links Chechnya to, rather than separating it from, the larger Russian society. Politics is dominated by Putin's party, Unified Russia, which won 33 of 58 seats in the November 27, 2005, elections to Chechnya's legislature. In public utterances, such as responses to public opinion polls, Chechens now increasingly emphasize their civic identities as Russians (*rossiiskie*). In short, within a brief time the shift in political institutions has changed the dominant elites, associations, and public discourse from separatism to unionism. This change, of course, does not mean that Chechens deep in their hearts do not prefer independence over union, but under current institutional conditions they find it much more difficult than under previous institutional arrangements to act upon any preferences for independence.

The Talysh-Mugan Republic lasted only sixty-four days, beginning with the coup by Colonel Ali Akram Hummatov in Lenkoran, Azerbaijan, on June 21, 1993, and the declaration of a republic; it came to an end on August 24, when Azerbaijani units forced Hummatov to flee. Azerbaijan's president now appoints heads of government in the districts that were claimed by the Talysh-Mugan Republic, and the republic itself disappeared as a jurisdiction. This unionist leadership has ensured that organizations have been unable to mobilize Talysh identity in opposition to Azerbaijan. Although the sixty-four-day republic still forms the critical rallying point for the current Talysh nationalist movement, this nation-state project survives largely among expatriates linked by the Internet. Talysh nationalists lament that a national awakening has not yet taken place within the population that remains in Azerbaijan (Ter-Abrahamian 2005). So-called separatist violence since 1993 has been limited to such sporadic incidents as the robbery and failed kidnapping of six villagers on a shopping trip in 1999 (BBC Monitoring Trans Caucasus Unit 1999). Azerbaijan's Justice Ministry has refused to register the Talis People's Party, and so the party has sought to refashion itself as the Equality of Peoples of Azerbaijan Party, reaching out to other minorities such as Kurds and Lezgins and working within the system premised on the territorial integrity of Azerbaijan. In Azerbaijan's recent elections, Talyshes competed against other Talyshes over issues that cut across ethnic divides and worked within common institutions, like the New Azerbaijan Party of President Ilham Aliev, in order to press their local interests (BBC Monitoring Trans Caucasus Unit 2002; Kennicott 2005). The Azerbaijan government has cultivated an official Talysh cultural establishment but has monitored this closely and has come down hard on any hint of a nation-state project, as attested by the arrests of Novruzali Mammadov and other leaders of the Talysh Cultural Center and editors of the newspaper *Talyshi Sado* in February 2007 (Bakinsky and Muradova 2007). In short, the shift in institutional arrangements has brought a shift in locally predominant elites and associational life toward unionism. It has apparently prevented the cultivation of a separatist nation-state project among the majority of the Talysh population.

A similar shift is apparent in the case of Adjara, but still more becomes apparent in this case if we juxtapose the Adjarians to the Armenian and Azeri minorities within Georgia. The importance of the distinction between segmented and unitary institutions is thus underscored: the former can foster the growth of elites with separatist agendas who then cultivate a separate associational life within the region, but the latter can lead to domination of the central government and its associational life over the regions and former separatists. (Indeed, this cross-sectional comparison and the longitudinal change in Adjara approximate a natural experiment.) If primordial ethnographic differences from the Georgian majority were the primary factor affecting the creation of separate predominant elites and separate civil societies among the minorities, then Georgia's Azeri minority should have been most completely mobilized by leaders and associations that separated Azeris from Georgians. Georgia's Adjarian and Armenian minorities should have been less mobilized by elites and associations that separated them from the Georgians. (The Azeris are separated from Georgians by both language and a religion that belongs to a different civilization, as Samuel P. Huntington defines this term; the Armenians are separated from Georgians by language and a religion that belongs to the same civilization; and the Adjarians are separated from Georgians by a religion that belongs to a different civilization but not by language [see Derluguian 1998; Huntington 1996].) Alternatively, because it is political institutions that are most important, the Adjarians were most completely mobilized by leaders and associations that separated them from the larger Georgian polity and society. Among these minorities, only the Adjarians had a regional government within Georgia, and within this jurisdiction local elites consolidated their own predominance and privileged associations that emphasized their separation from Georgia. From 1991 to 2004 Adjara was controlled by the ultimate monopolistic political machine: Aslan Abashidze populated government with his close relatives, who by 2000 occupied 57 percent of senior executive posts and 54 percent of the seats in the legislature. Adjara maintained patronage through the rents collected at the Batumi port and the Georgia-Turkey road link at the Sarpi border crossing. Abashidze's government used violence to prevent parties from Tbilisi from gaining a foothold in the republic and to ensure the predominance of Abashidze's Democratic Revival Union Party (ICG 2003, 13–14).

By contrast, in the same years the Armenians and Azeris in Georgia lacked official homelands and so lacked leadership and strong associations to press their interests. Armenians in the Samtskhe-Javakheti region have been fragmented and, as one NGO leader told ICG researchers, "do not speak with one voice" (ICG 2006b, 15). The Azeris of the Kvemo-Kartli region are even less well organized. During the late Soviet period, Armenian leaders fostered a movement, Javakhk, that sought an autonomous region, but Georgian officials disrupted this after independence. Indeed, in July 2003 Tony Vaux reported that "the so-called 'Javakh' separatist movement is so weak that it can hardly be called a movement at all. It consists of a number of opportunistic individuals who want to make enough trouble to be rewarded with government posts" (2003, 22; also see ICG 2006b, 17). What little organization exists is largely a consequence of foreign support. Owing to their inclusion in the unitary state of Georgia, Armenians and

Azeris must pursue their political fortunes through institutions that they share in common with other citizens of Georgia.

Since the Georgian government toppled Abashidze in May 2004 by a show of force, the status of the Adjarians more closely resembles the status of Armenians and Azeris in Georgia. Leadership within Adjara is now appointed by the government in Tbilisi, with the governor serving as a prefect representing the center. Regional political parties are now banned, and so the political arena is dominated by parties organized from Tbilisi. Adjarians have rapidly integrated within the larger Georgian society: Perhaps the most remarkable symbol of their integration is the rapid conversion from Islam to the Georgian Orthodox Church reported by a sizable proportion of the Adjarian population.

State Institutions Constrain Interveners as Well

In cases of seemingly intractable divides in nationalist conflicts, there has been a tendency to call in the deus ex machina of third parties to bring the desired denouement. In the development of civil society, interveners have been urged to play a still more active role to foster the growth of associational life in the separate societies as a way to bridge the gap following a cease-fire and to move toward a final agreement on state borders. Yet, the Caucasus cases suggest caution: a rush to fund civil society without first reconstituting the state through either partition or unification may end up consolidating polarized civil societies. In aiding civic organizations in Abkhazia, South Ossetia, and Nagornyi Karabakh, third parties have actually reinforced the separation of the communities from the larger common-state community. Aid to Azerbaijan and Georgia has helped central governments consolidate hegemonic control within the rump state. This polarization has made agreement on a compromise settlement less likely, the peace more fragile, and recurrence of war more likely. Indeed, after de facto settlements, the Russia-Chechnya civil war recurred in 1999, the Georgia-Abkhazia war in 2008, and the Georgia–South Ossetia war in 2008 as well; only the Azerbaijan-Nagornyi Karabakh civil war has not recurred, and in this case there is no clear movement toward a compromise on the nation-state issues that began the first civil war and were left unresolved in the de facto settlement.

After a civil war, the separatist political cultures cultivated in segmented states have resisted international pressures for accommodation through civil societies. In Abkhazia, for example, there is strong resistance to attempts to put issues of accommodation on the agenda of local community discussions. Vaux notes that some civic activists complain that international aid is available only for "conflict resolution." "In the Gali region . . . some NGOs complained of being made to discuss conflict rather than their immediate problems of feeding the destitute and getting their children into school" (2003, 25). In fact, most INGO activities in Abkhazia do focus on simple humanitarian relief; it is the local resistance to even opening a discussion of reintegration of Abkhazia within Georgia and of displaced Georgians within Abkhazia that leads to these exaggerated complaints.

Because INGOs and the aid agencies of intergovernmental organizations and foreign governments tend to operate within the boundaries of the de facto segmental jurisdictions, such as Karabakh, Abkhazia, and South Ossetia, interveners tend to reinforce the separation of these regions. They create a cadre and network of cooperation within the jurisdiction (such as Abkhazia) but separate from the larger society (such as Georgia). Even purely humanitarian intervention often creates civil societies, but each is bounded by the segmental divides that emerged or deepened in the civil war. In this institutional environment, interveners in effect reinforce polarization.

While such institutionalization of polarization is often unintentional, sometimes it is quite deliberate. In the Caucasus some of the most active INGOs have been the Armenian relief agencies operating in the Karabakh and radical Muslim organizations operating in Chechnya. These often offer not only humanitarian relief but state-building assistance for the de facto states. By providing funds, materiel, and skills training, they tend to strengthen associations that seek to push the spectrum within the leadership and civil society toward still more radical positions and more militant forms of resistance on the independence issue (Hasanov and Ishkanian 2005).

In the Western view, civil society, as Alexis de Tocqueville underscored almost 175 years ago, can be a key ingredient in the success of democracy when a pluralistic associational life makes individuals better citizens of a common nation-state (1835 [1966], vol. 2, chap. 5). It can also make a unique contribution to maintaining civil peace. In a pluralistic civil society, multiple autonomous, competitive, voluntary, limited-purpose associations knit together individuals in a dense network of crosscutting ties. Crosscutting, but limited-purpose, associations multiply the number of identities that compete with national identities as the bases for political action, so citizens enter politics not only as members of their different nation-state communities but at other times as laborers and managers, teachers and parents, producers and consumers, environmentalists and extractors, and so forth. Multiple crosscutting identities prevent a single common-state identity from becoming hegemonic except in a narrow range of policy issues—such as defending the borders of the common-state from foreign invasion. Potential separatist identities and interests are salient to only a narrow range of policy issues and must compete with alternative crosscutting identities and interests for policy outcomes. In a pluralistic civil society, coercive capabilities—such as the capacity to call a strike or to threaten to withhold votes in a nation-wide election—are dispersed among these multiple associations. Each association has limited capacity to disturb the peace on its own, and because the divides created by associations do not reinforce but crosscut one another, coalitions of associations that unite in common action to disturb the constitutional order are less common.

In the conditions following civil war, the creation of a pluralistic civil society requires extensive and sustained effort to impose compromises and intensive micromanagement to foster growth of specific associations. Just a brief review of these tasks suggests how unlikely it is that most interveners will undertake this project. The centerpiece of any intervention must be institution-building, for political institutions constitute the most powerful incentives for citizens to form the types of associations that will not simply replicate the deep divide that produced the previous civil war. Donald Rothchild and I suggested a power-dividing or multiple-majorities strategy for building such political institutions (Roeder and Rothchild 2005). First, the power-dividing strategy seeks to give civil society room to grow separately from the state by limiting the decision-making authority of all governments within the state. In this way the strategy places a premium on constitutional limits that say the government shall make no law in some areas, such as establishing religion. Yet, few leaders of societies after civil war are willing to limit their governments in this way; instead they tend to want an activist state that reconstitutes state, nation, economy, and society. Interveners' attempts to impose such restraint are likely to encounter significant resistance.

Second, in what remains of government decision-making, the power-dividing or multiple-majorities strategy devolves power both horizontally and vertically to multiple, often overlapping, functionally specific organs and jurisdictions. Governmental decision-making is not concentrated in one, two, or three common-state institutions at the center or balanced between these and a single layer of general-purpose homeland administrations. At the common-state level, decisions are dispersed among multiple organs, such as an independent central bank, a national water authority, and a higher education board, each of which is empowered to make policy in a narrow realm. Rather than look for a single best norm of representation, the power-dividing strategy seeks to employ diverse norms of representation for the various decision-making organs. Variation in these norms of representation seeks to guarantee that the majority in each common-state decision-making organ is not defined by the same, recurring social divide. In devolving decision-making to lower jurisdictions, power-dividing avoids placing all devolved powers in the same hands, such as provincial governments. Power-dividing seeks to disperse these powers among separate and independent jurisdictions, such as school districts, police districts, water districts, and street and transportation districts. These jurisdictions cut across one another and particularly across any jurisdictions left from the civil war. Because these jurisdictions do not all focus on the same divides and are not simply nested, majorities and minorities on issues are less likely to become cumulative or recurring. Powers in other policy realms cannot easily be used as leverage to win on key issues at the heart of contention between nation-state projects. And the pork and patronage generated in diverse policy realms cannot all be invested in political machines supporting contending nation-state projects: Secessionist politicians have fewer opportunities to convert such decision rights as control over sewage disposal and water delivery into means to cement political machines and to pressure other communities. Yet, this costly institution-building strategy is unlikely to be embraced by interveners after a civil war. Central and regional leaders are likely to resist empowerment of competing centers of power. After a civil war, multiple-majority institutional arrangements to promote a pluralistic civil society are likely to be less efficient than hierarchically organized institutions.

Yet, in the experience of other societies, it is power-dividing institutions that most increase the likelihood that multiple autonomous limited-purpose associations will form in crosscutting patterns that compete with divides over competing nation-state projects. In these associations many members of regional or ethnic minorities are members of a policy majority on some issues—not a majority defined by their membership in an alternative nation, but a majority defined by some other identity that these individuals carry in diverse repertoires of identities and interests. The logic is that associations form in a pattern that reflects the configuration of interests privileged within political institutions. Thus, in order to employ the most efficient means to influence decisions in agencies that balance creditors against lenders or upstream versus downstream river-basin dwellers, associations will form on either side of these divides and seek to maximize their memberships by including all that share their interest on that narrow issue. Pork and patronage available to the leaders in these diverse organs will not disappear, but they are more likely to be used to support associations defined by the narrow divides of that organ rather than some recurring divide over competing nation-state projects. Investment in civil society after civil war is unlikely to produce this type of pluralistic society except through extensive, intrusive, and enduring intervention to remake the state and civil society.

In the absence of such undertakings to transform states and societies after civil wars, before investing in civil society, practitioners of soft intervention must first consider the structure of the state at the end of a civil war. Inconclusive outcomes to civil wars on the central nation-state issues of the previous civil war can lead to segmented states that foster polarized civil societies that subvert the postsettlement peace. Thus, it may be prudent for practitioners of soft intervention to delay intervention until these issues have been resolved on the battlefield and then use soft intervention to reinforce the new status quo rather than to transform the status quo left by a cease-fire and search for a compromise.

References

Bakinsky, Khazri, and Mina Muradova. March 5, 2007. "Azerbaijan: US-Iran Tensions Cause for Minority Arrests?" Interfax; transcribed by Eurasianet; Radio Free Europe/Radio Liberty Newsline, April 10, 2007.

BBC Monitoring Trans Caucasus Unit. 1999. "Azeri Paper Links President's Absence to 'Bullying' by Separatist Supporters." *Sharg* (Baku), June 7.

———. 2002. "Azeri Security Ministry Unconcerned about Ethnic Minority Party's Activity." *Ekho* (Baku), August 31, 4.

Campana, Aurélie. 2006. "The Effects of War on the Chechen National Identity Construction." *National Identities* 8, 2: 129–148.

Chapman, Thomas, and Philip G. Roeder. 2007. "Partition as a Solution to Wars of Nationalism: The Role of Institutions." *American Political Science Review* 101, 4: 677–691.

Cook, Linda J., and Elena Vinogradova. 2006. "NGOs and Social Policy-Making in Russia's Regions." *Problems of Post-Communism* 53, 5: 28–41.

Cornell, Svante E. 2001. *Small Nations and Great Powers: A Study of Ethnopolitical Conflict in the Caucasus*. London: Routledge Curzon.

Derluguian, Georgi M. 1998. "The Tale of Two Resorts: Abkhazia and Ajaria Before and Since the Soviet Collapse." In *The Myth of "Ethnic Conflict": Politics, Economics, and "Cultural" Violence*, ed. Beverly Crawford and Ronnie D. Lipshutz, 261–292. International and Area Studies Research Series, No. 98. Berkeley: University of California Press.

De Tocqueville, Alexis. [1835] 1966. *Democracy in America*. Translated by George Lawrence, edited by J. P. Mayer. Garden City, NY: Doubleday.

De Waal, Thomas. 2003. *Black Garden: Armenia and Azerbaijan through Peace and War*. New York: New York University Press.

Evangelista, Matthew. 2002. *The Chechen Wars: Will Russia Go the Way of the Soviet Union?* Washington, DC: Brookings Institution Press.

Fuller, Liz. 2007a. "Chechnya: Kadyrov Completes First 100 Days in Office." Radio Free Europe/Radio Liberty, Prague, July 11.

———. 2007b. "Chechnya: Rights Situation May Be Improving." Radio Free Europe/Radio Liberty, Prague, June 24.

Gall, Carlotta, and Thomas de Waal. 1998. *Chechnya: Calamity in the Caucasus*. New York: New York University Press.

Hasanov, Avaz, and Armine Ishkanian. 2005. "Bridging Divides: Civil Society Peacebuilding Initiatives." In *The Limits of Leadership: Elites and Societies in the Nagorny Karabakh Peace Process*, ed. Laurence Broers. Accord Series, No. 17. London: Conciliation Resources.

Huntington, Samuel P. 1996. *The Clash of Civilizations and the Remaking of World Order*. New York: Simon and Schuster.

International Crisis Group (ICG). 2003. "Georgia: What Now?" Europe Report No. 151, Tbilisi/Brussels, December 3.

———. 2004. "Georgia: Avoiding War in South Ossetia." Europe Report No. 159, Tbilisi/Brussels, November 26.

———. 2005a. "Nagorno-Karabakh: A Plan for Peace." Europe Report No. 167, Tbilisi/Brussels, October 11.

———. 2005b. "Nagorno-Karabakh: Viewing the Conflict from the Ground." Europe Report No. 166, Tbilisi/Brussels, September 14.

———. 2006a. "Abkhazia Today." Europe Report No. 176. Tbilisi/Brussels, September 15.

———. 2006b. "Georgia's Armenian and Azeri Minorities." Europe Report No. 178. Tbilisi/Brussels, November 22.

Kennicott, Philip. 2005. "Mushy Fruit Has a Meaning for Azerbaijani Democracy." *Washington Post*, October 3, A09.

Lieven, Anatol. 1998. *Chechnya: Tombstone of Russian Power*. New Haven, CT: Yale University Press.

Matveeva, Anna. 2004. "Minorities in the South Caucasus." United Nations Office of the High Commissioner for Human Rights, Central Asia Seminar, Working Paper 3, October, Bishkek.

Nichol, Jim. 2006. *Bringing Peace to Chechnya? Assessments and Implications*. CRS Report for Congress Updated March 31, 2006. Washington, DC: Library of Congress, Congressional Research Service.

Orudzhev, R. 2004. "International Alert—za dialog mezhdu liderami obshchestvennosti Azerbaidzhana, Armenii, i Nagornogo Karabakha." *Ekho* (Baku), August. Available online at www.consortium-initiative.org.

Roeder, Philip G. 2007. *Where Nation-States Come From: Institutional Change in the Age of Nationalism*. Princeton, NJ: Princeton University Press.

———. 2009. "Ethnofederalism and the Mismanagement of Conflicting Nationalisms." *Regional and Federal Studies* 19, 2: 203–219.

Roeder, Philip G., and Donald Rothchild (eds.). 2005. *Sustainable Peace: Power and Democracy after Civil Wars*. Ithaca, NY: Cornell University Press.

Ter-Abrahamian, Hrant. 2005. "On the Formation of the National Identity of the Talishis in Azerbaijan Republic." In *Iran and the Caucasus (Research Papers from the Caucasian Centre for Iranian Studies, Yerevan)*, 9.1: 121–44. Leiden: Brill.

Tishkov, Valery. 2004. *Chechnya: Life in a War-Torn Society*. Berkeley: University of California Press.

Varshney, Ashutosh. 2001. "Ethnic Conflict and Civil Society: India and Beyond." *World Politics* 53, 3: 362–398.

Vaux, Tony. 2003. "Strategic Conflict Assessment: Georgia." Humanitarian Initiatives, Conflict Studies 3. Report for the Global Conflict Prevention Pool, UK Government.

Vaux, Tony, and Jonathan Goodhand. 2002. "War and Peace in the Southern Caucasus: A Strategic Conflict Assessment of the Armenia-Azerbaijan Conflict." Humanitarian Initiatives, Conflict Studies 1. Report for the Global Conflict Prevention Pool, UK Government.

Wilhelmsen, Julie. 2005. "Between a Rock and a Hard Place: The Islamisation of the Chechen Separatist Movement." *Europe-Asia Studies* 57, 1: 35–59.

Notes

1. For further discussion of the consequences of de jure autonomy arrangements, see Roeder 2009.
2. In fact, until 1936 the Armenian, Azerbaijani, and Georgian republics were part of the Transcaucasian Soviet Federated Socialist Republic, which was on juridical par with the RSFSR. Many of the other autonomous regions described in this paragraph also did not emerge in their final form until after many experiments with alternative ethnographic and territorial configurations in the design of ethnofederal jurisdictions.
3. The next paragraphs are based on Roeder 2007.

FOUR

Electoral Rules and Post–Civil War Conflict Management: The Limitations of Institutional Design

SHAHEEN MOZAFFAR

A central challenge confronting post–civil war states is the transformation of actors and organizations of armed combat (soldiers and militias) into actors and organizations of "normal" politics (voters and political parties). One key indicator of a successful postconflict transformation is society's embrace of routinized patterns of political interactions that conform to institutional incentives, including the prescriptions embodied in the electoral systems that are negotiated in peace settlements. Routinized patterns of political interactions conforming to these prescriptions obtain when political actors recognize that the benefits they derive from playing by the new rules outweigh the cost of returning to armed combat (Shugart 1992; Rothchild 1997). The accrued benefits they derive from playing by the newly established rules subsequently enhance the confidence of political actors in the new institutions. This confidence helps to shape the political actors' strategic calculations in favor of the new postwar rules rather than returning to combat.

Electoral institutions (or electoral systems) have the potential to help foster peace by encouraging political actors in postconflict societies to make this strategic calculation.[1] In examining this role of electoral institutions, I stress the importance of a context-sensitive approach, which avoids the reflexivity of structural accounts in the literatures on both civil war resolution and electoral systems and instead draws attention to the interaction of agency and structure in shaping the role of electoral systems in postconflict states. Structural accounts view successful civil war resolution as stemming

Don Rothchild exemplified the phrase "a gentleman and a scholar." He was also a friend. I dedicate this chapter as a memorial to him. I will miss the many illuminating conversations we had at our regular early breakfasts at the American Political Science Association meetings and the numerous e-mail exchanges that influenced my thinking on the role and the limits of institutions in conflict management.

ineluctably from such factors as post-cold-war changes in the international system, the presence of multiple actors and "spoilers," the availability of "lootable" resources such as diamonds, a supportive regional environment, and the role of third parties (Walter 1999; Collier 2000; Downs and Stedman 2002; Lyons 2005). In contrast, a context-sensitive approach, without denying the significance of structural factors, draws attention to the importance of contingencies and strategic choices associated with the nature, conduct, and termination of civil wars, and especially with the politics and process of regime transitions in shaping the behavior of political actors within the postwar state.

A context-sensitive approach is thus important in clarifying the role of both nonstate and state actors in postconflict countries, a central concern of this book and this chapter. As the editors note in their introduction, transforming the behavior of nonstate actors in ways that sustain peace is the principal goal that third-party peacekeepers and new or redesigned institutions seek to achieve after the termination of civil wars. But the goal of a peace agreement is also to transform the behavior of state actors in peaceful directions. Government actors were also engaged in military combat with nonstate actors during the civil war, and without any demonstrable transformation of government actors' behavior toward peace, nonstate actors will have no incentive to transform theirs.

What makes the achievement of this dual behavioral transformation so difficult, and hence the prospects for establishing a sustainable peace so uncertain, is that the key state and nonstate actors who are expected to change their behavior in peaceful directions when wars end are the very actors who employed violence, fear, and extremist rhetoric during the war. Structural conditions, the presence of third-party peacekeepers, and the design of political institutions negotiated in peace settlements are necessary but insufficient to secure the requisite behavioral transformation of nonstate actors. Analysis must also focus on the variables associated with the legacies of civil wars—militarized organizations, the role of fear as an instrument of political control, and the associated balance-of-power relations among former combatants and between them and state actors—that typically define the contingencies surrounding regime transitions following the implementation of peace agreements (Lyons 2005, 9). Sources of great uncertainty and turbulence, these legacies and contingencies will shape the strategic calculations of both state and nonstate actors during the implementation of peace agreements, and these calculations will determine whether former combatants will change their behavior based on the use of violence to behavior based on norms of reciprocity and cooperation.

Closer attention to the continuing impact of the legacies and contingencies of civil wars also helps to avoid the notion of a zero-sum tradeoff between democracy and stability in postconflict societies. However, this notion, which derives from the often-destabilizing effects of rapid democratization in postconflict societies, is misconstrued because it presupposes that democratic institutions negotiated in peace settlements will automatically transform the behavior of former combatants toward peaceful interactions. A context-sensitive approach helps to clarify the apparent incompatibility between democracy and stability in the aftermath of civil wars by highlighting (a) the mediating influence of civil war legacies and contingencies on new democratic institutions in securing peace in postconflict societies and (b) the need to calibrate the design of these institutions to the specificities of varying civil war contexts.

In the comparative literature on electoral systems, institutional and sociological approaches also advance reflexive explanations in which political outcomes are ineluctably traced either to the institutional design of electoral systems or to social structural factors.[2] A context-sensitive approach, instead, stresses the importance of specifying the conditions under which the electoral systems and contextual factors separately and jointly shape political outcomes. This specification is especially crucial in clarifying the role of electoral systems in facilitating the transition to sustainable peace for three reasons. First, the choice of the institutional design of electoral systems in peace agreements is only one component of the overall institutional framework negotiated in peace settlements for the democratic governance of postconflict societies. Key aspects of this broader institutional framework, such as whether the postconflict regime is a presidential or a parliamentary system, or whether parliamentary and presidential elections are held concurrently or separately, will influence the operation and impact of electoral systems. Further, since the operation and impact of electoral systems will shape the strategic calculations of former combatants about whether to continue playing by the new electoral rules, the influence of the larger institutional context on electoral systems requires systematic analysis. A context-sensitive approach accomplishes this goal.

Second, as noted above, the immediate contingencies surrounding the termination of civil wars and regime transition through the implementation of peace agreements will shape the strategic calculations of both state and nonstate actors. These contingencies will thus compete with the new political institutions generally and with electoral systems in particular, as alternative sources of incentives and opportunities for political actors to organize their election campaigns and mobilize votes. Hence, any analysis must also clarify the extent to which these contingencies shape electoral outcomes independently and jointly with the new electoral systems. A context-sensitive approach also facilitates this objective.

Finally, the exclusive preference for a proportional representation (PR) formula for converting votes into seats in the institutional design of electoral systems negotiated in peace agreements over the past quarter century is motivated by both strategic rationality and practical considerations. The mathematical formula that translates votes into seats in PR systems allocates seats in the national legislature to political parties in approximate proportion to the votes won by the parties. Former combatants are thus assured of inclusion and representation in the new democratic polity. However, the routine adoption of PR electoral systems has not led inexorably to successful conflict management. The success or failure in maintaining post–civil war stability thus seems to be independent of the PR systems adopted in peace agreements. How electoral systems secure peace after civil wars end thus remains a puzzle. A context-sensitive approach helps to solve this puzzle.

I begin with a brief review of the central theoretical arguments advanced in support of the choice of PR electoral systems as a key institutional mechanism of conflict management in post–civil war societies, and I point to reasons why these arguments do not adequately address the strategic contingencies surrounding the choice of electoral systems in peace agreements and their impact on sustaining peace in postconflict societies. I then elaborate elements of an alternative approach that underscores the importance of electoral systems in conflict management, but in the context of (a) the historical antecedents and the associated structure, dynamics, and outcomes of civil wars, (b) the resulting social configuration, morphology, and patterns of group interaction, and (c) the choice of the overall institutional design of democratic governance enshrined in peace settlements. I provide illustrative examples from several countries in Africa and elsewhere in support of this approach. I conclude with a discussion of the theoretical and policy implications of the analysis.

The Selection of Electoral Systems in Peace Agreements

Central to the reliance on democratization as the principal means of terminating civil wars in the past quarter century is the inclusion of elections as a key provision of negotiated civil war settlements (Kumar 1998; Lyons 2002, 2005). The "bullets to ballots" logic that drives the routine inclusion of elections as a key instrument for transforming polities torn by civil

Table 4.1 The adoption of electoral systems in peace agreements

Countries	Peace agreements	Formula for legislative elections*	Formula for presidential elections*
Angola	Bicesse Peace Agreement, 1991	List-PR	TRS
Bosnia-Herzegovina	Dayton Agreement, 1995	List-PR	FPTP
Cambodia	Paris Peace Agreement, 1991	List-PR	
El Salvador	Chapultepec Peace Accords, 1992	List-PR	TRS
Iraq	2005	List-PR	
Liberia	Abuja II Accords, 1996	List-PR	TRS
Liberia	Accra Accords, 2003	FPTP	TRS
Mozambique	Rome Peace Agreement, 1994	List-PR	TRS
Namibia	1989	List-PR	TRS
Nicaragua	August Political Accord, 1989	List-PR	TRS
Rwanda	Arusha Agreement, 1993	List-PR	FPTP
Sierra Leone	Abidjan Accords, 1996	List-PR	TRS
South Africa	1994	List-PR	

*List-PR = a proportional representation system in which voters vote for a list of candidates, equal to the number of seats in the electoral constituency, submitted by each party. FPTP = a first-past-the-post system in which a candidate receiving a plurality of the votes cast is the winner. TRS = a two-round majority system in which a winning candidate must receive an absolute majority of the votes cast; if no candidate receives an absolute majority, the top two finishers in the first round compete in a second round, and the winner is decided by an absolute majority of votes cast.

wars into polities structured by peaceful electoral competition is explicitly reflected in the choice of the institutional design of electoral systems, the sets of rules that convert votes into seats, in peace accords. This choice routinely involves the adoption of a proportional representation (PR) formula aimed at securing the participation of and facilitating, without guaranteeing, the victory of all the major erstwhile civil war combatants in postconflict elections.

Table 4.1 displays the adoption of electoral systems for both legislative and presidential elections in select peace agreements signed to terminate civil wars in the 1990s, along with Namibia in 1989 and Iraq in 2005. For legislative elections, there is an overwhelming preference for PR systems (twelve out of thirteen cases). Only the Accra Accords of 2003 that ended the second Liberian civil war adopted the first-past-the-post (FPTP) plurality electoral system. I discuss below the reasons for and implications of this choice in comparison with the choice of the PR system in the Abuja II Accords of 1996 that ended the first Liberian civil war.

With respect to the formula for presidential elections, eight of the ten countries with directly elected presidents opted for a two-round system in which an absolute majority (50% + 1) of the valid votes cast is required to win. If no candidate secures an absolute majority in the first round, a second-round contest is held between the two top finishers in the first round, with the winner decided by an absolute majority. The other two countries with directly elected presidents, Bosnia and Herzegovina and Rwanda, opted for the FPTP plurality system (like the one used in US presidential elections), in which a winning candidate must secure a plurality (or simple majority) of the votes cast. Cambodia and Iraq are parliamentary systems, while the president in South Africa is elected by the national legislature. In the next section I elaborate on the reasons for examining presidential electoral systems as well as electoral systems for legislative elections.

There are important strategic and practical motivations for the adoption of PR systems for legislative elections in peace settlements negotiated to end civil wars. First, it is consistent with theoretical expectations and empirical evidence concerning the mechanical effects of electoral systems (Duverger 1962; Taagepera and Shugart 1989; Lijphart 1994, 1999; Cox 1997). Majoritarian formulas such as the FPTP plurality and the two-round absolute majority formulas that are usually employed in single-member districts (SMDs) tend to favor larger, well-organized political parties over smaller ones and increase the disproportionality between their respective vote and seat shares. In contrast, electoral systems based on PR formulas, which are usually employed in large multimember districts (MMDs), tend to provide opportunities for more parties to participate in government by allocating them legislative seats in approximate proportion to their share of votes. As a condition for power sharing and the formation of an all-inclusive postwar unity government, or in reinforcing the separately negotiated power-sharing agreements and unity governments, the adoption of PR formulas in peace accords helps to encourage the participation of former civil war combatants in peaceful electoral competition. Second, by enhancing the opportunity for electoral victory of previously warring groups, PR systems help to reduce the inherent uncertainty of outcomes that attend all democratic elections and diminish groups' fear of being excluded from the new democratic dispensation. Proportional electoral systems thus underscore the importance of elections in signaling the end of civil war and the beginning of democratic transition and validate their legitimacy as an instrument of peaceful conflict management in a democratic polity. Finally, the adoption in peace accords of PR systems with large MMDs stems from the accurate recognition of the practical difficulties in war-torn societies of delineating constituency boundaries to create SMDs in which seats are allocated by the FPTP plurality formula. This understanding was one of the important reasons for the adoption of PR formulas in postconflict elections in Zimbabwe (1980), Liberia (1997), and Sierra Leone (1996).

Has the adoption of PR electoral systems in negotiated civil war settlements led to conditions associated with sustainable peace, that is, to the transformation of soldiers and militias into voters and parties and the routinization of peaceful political interactions through regular democratic elections? Empirical evidence from recent postconflict elections offers mixed results. The adoption of PR electoral systems was an important, albeit not the only, reason for the successful termination of protracted and violent civil conflicts and the sustained transition to democracy in El Salvador, Namibia, Nicaragua, Mozambique, and South Africa.

However, the use of PR electoral systems in postconflict elections did not prevent the resumption of civil war in Angola and Liberia, even though in Angola the proportional results of the legislative elections conformed to theoretical expectations. Elsewhere, the impact of PR electoral systems has been more ambiguous. In Zimbabwe, the use of the PR system in the 1980 and the 1985 elections helped establish a single dominant-party regime.[3] In Namibia and South Africa, as well, the PR systems negotiated to end the protracted civil war in the former state and the extended violent struggle to end apartheid in the latter state are two of the most proportional of PR systems, yet they have helped to entrench single dominant-party systems in both countries. In the case of Bosnia and Herzegovina, the PR system helped to end the civil war and facilitated a successful democratic transition, but the election results also entrenched political parties led by radical ethno-chauvinists who continued to rely on the organizational structures of civil war to coerce and intimidate the opposition, thus undermining the consolidation of democracy.

These mixed results of PR systems adopted in peace accords stem in part from the multiple and contradictory goals postconflict elections are expected to achieve: war termination, democratic transition, international legitimation of peace accords, and the disengagement of major and regional mediators (Lyons 2002, 216–219). More significantly, however, they reflect intrinsic problems linked to (a) the different effects of similar electoral systems in varied social, political, and institutional contexts and (b) the reflexive, as opposed to a strategic and contingent, view of institutional effects that frames both scholarship and policy prescriptions about the choice of electoral systems design in emerging democracies generally, and in postconflict democracies in particular.

Since Duverger's classic study (1962), the independent effects of different electoral systems on vote-seat distribution and the associated effects on party systems have become widely accepted in comparative scholarship. Proportional representation systems typically reduce vote-seat disproportionality and foster multiparty systems, while majoritarian systems typically increase vote-seat disproportionality and foster two-party systems. Yet it is now also widely accepted in comparative scholarship that contextual variations mitigate these typical effects of electoral systems design. Thus India and Canada, both of which use plurality FPTP formulas in SMDs, feature fragmented multiparty systems owing to the pattern of unified voting by spatially concentrated blocks of ethnic voters (Riker 1962). Lijphart's pioneering study established the importance of PR systems and associated institutional mechanisms of consociationalism, power sharing in oversized cabinets, and federalism in securing democracy in culturally plural societies (1977). But empirical evidence from some longstanding democracies with high levels of cultural fragmentation, such as India, Mauritius, and Trinidad and Tobago, show that the reliance on executive power sharing and oversized cabinets result not from the use of PR systems, but from the interaction of plurality FPTP formulas, which all of them use, with variations in the number, size, and spatial distribution of ethnic groups (Reilly and Reynolds 1999; Reilly 2005).

Electoral systems thus do not produce electoral outcomes reflexively. They do so contingently. The contingencies that mediate the effects of electoral systems derive from both the larger social structural settings (e.g., the configuration of ethnopolitical cleavages) and the overall institutional framework of democratic governance (e.g., whether the regime is parliamentary, presidential, or hybrid and whether presidential and legislative elections are held simultaneously) in which electoral systems remain embedded. In postconflict elections, moreover, additional contextual factors directly linked to the origin, trajectory, and termination of civil wars also mediate the direct effects of electoral systems. Among these civil-war-linked contextual factors are the competing interests and priorities of international actors who broker peace agreements, the information deficits of political actors about the incentives and expected effects of electoral systems, and, in particular, the legacy of fear and the need for security. Concerns for safety are more immediate rational considerations than the strategic response to the incentives of electoral rules that motivate voters to "vote for peace" in postconflict elections (Lyons 2005). In the next section, I offer a conceptualization of electoral systems as embedded institutions that highlights the importance of these factors. Illustrative examples from Africa and elsewhere are included to show this view's analytical utility and empirical relevance in clarifying the varied and contingent ways electoral systems play a role in facilitating a sustainable peace after civil wars end.

Embedded Electoral Systems and Conflict Management

In peace settlements, the choice of new democratic institutions generally, and of electoral systems in particular, reflects solutions to political conflicts rooted in structurally determined power relations of erstwhile combatants. But that choice is fundamentally about political outcomes in the post-settlement political dispensation and is thus informed by the combatants' mutual expectations and calculations about these outcomes. Civil war legacies and contingencies, in other words, constrain but do not determine the choice and design of new institutions. Civil war terminations and democratic transitions are moments of crisis and fundamental political change that diminish the influence of structural constraints and heighten the salience and autonomy of agency in shaping institutional design. The time and political capital that actors invest in institutional bargaining are also themselves crucial measures of the importance they attach to the prospective consequences of new institutions. Finally, the sunk costs of institutional bargains underscore the uncertainty of renewed negotiations and, combined with the pervasiveness of coordination problems in political life, tend to reinforce the stickiness of new institutions.[4]

Analytically sound explanations of postwar peace, however, require privileging neither electoral systems nor context. For electoral systems chosen in peace settlements remain embedded in wider social settings, civil war environments, and institutional frameworks of governance that define the strategic context in which they organize electoral competition, structure the behavior of political actors, and influence election results (Grofman et al. 1999; Bowler and Grofman 2000; Mozaffar 2004). This approach leaves open the question of whether electoral systems have independent effects or whether those effects are contextually mediated.[5]

The concept of embedded electoral systems helps to clarify the importance of factors both specific to postconflict environments and generic to routine democratic politics that, individually and jointly, condition the effects of electoral systems on political outcomes. Among the specific postconflict environmental factors are the role of international actors and the legacies of civil war manifested in the continued presence of armed militias and the role of fear in motivating the "peace vote." Among the generic factors in routine democratic politics are the overall institutional framework of governance and the prevailing configuration of social cleavages, especially ethnopolitical cleavages. Accounting for the mediating effects of these factors enables theoretically nuanced and empirically relevant analysis and understanding of the role of electoral systems in post–civil war conflict management.

The Role of International Actors

One factor the concept of embedded electoral systems helps to highlight is the role of international actors in shaping the conditions for the success or failure of elections and electoral systems in postconflict societies. The different priorities and levels of involvement and commitment of international actors, for example, contributed to the failure of the peace agreement in Angola in 1992 but to the success of the peace agreement in Mozambique in 1994, even through the PR electoral systems negotiated to end the civil wars in both countries were virtually identical and produced virtually identical results that conformed closely to theoretical expectations. Table 4.2 displays data on the electoral systems, the results of the

Table 4.2 Results of first postconflict elections in Angola (1992) and Mozambique (1994)

Legislative election indices	Angola	Mozambique
Electoral formula	List PR (d'Hondt)	List PR (d'Hondt)
Size of legislature	220	250
Average district magnitude	Provincial = 5	Provincial = 23
	Nationwide = 130	(5% legal threshold)
Number of parties	18	14
Vote percentages	53.62 (MPLA)	44.61 (FRELIMO)
	34.02 (UNITA)	38.02 (RENAMO)
Seat percentages	58.64 (MPLA)	51.60 (FRELIMO)
	31.82 (UNITA)	44.80 (RENAMO)
ENEP*	2.47	2.88
ENLP*	2.24	2.14
LSQ-index*	4.02	7.52
Presidential election indices	**Angola**	**Mozambique**
Electoral formula	Two-round majority	Two-round majority
Number of candidates	11	12
Vote percentages	49.57 (Santos)	53.30 (Chissano)
	40.07 (Savimbi)	33.73 (Dhlakma)
ENPRES*	2.45	2.50

*ENEP (effective number of electoral parties) and ENLP (effective number of legislative parties) are the Laakso-Taagepera indices of party systems that measure the degree of multipartism based, respectively, on the actual vote and seat shares of political parties (Laakso and Taagepera 1979). The LSQ-index is the least-squares index of disproportionality that measures the degree of deviation from proportionality between votes and seats (Gallagher 1991). ENPRES (effective number of presidential candidates) is the extension of the Laakso-Taagepera index that measures the degree of competitiveness in presidential elections based on the vote shares of candidates in the first round of presidential elections. See also Lijphart 1994; Cox 1997.

first postconflict elections in Angola and Mozambique during 1994, and various indices that are widely employed in the comparative electoral systems literature to measure the structure of electoral party systems (ENEP), the legislative party systems (ENLP), the disproportionality between votes and seats (LSQ-index), and the degree of competition among presidential candidates (ENPRES).

The data show that the electoral systems, both legislative and presidential election results, and the values of the various indices are remarkably similar in the two countries. Both countries adopted list-PR with the highest average d'Hondt formula, which is the least proportional of PR formulas and typically favors larger parties. In Angola, this discriminatory effect is reinforced by the allocation of 90 of the 130 legislative seats in 18 provinces with an average district magnitude of 5 seats. An average district magnitude of 5 seats is typically considered to favor smaller parties, but in Angola the two major parties, the MPLA and UNITA, reinforced their regional civil war positions by dominating the elections in the provinces. However, the allocation of the remaining 130 legislative seats in a single nationwide district produced a low mathematical threshold of 0.34%, which enabled three of the better-organized smaller parties to win multiple seats with less than 3% of the votes each, while also enabling seven other parties to win at least one seat with less than 1% of the vote. Overall, the mechanical effect of the electoral system combining the d'Hondt formula with the two-tiered seat allocation helped to reduce the disproportionality between votes and seats, as reflected in the low LSQ-index of 4.02. This low vote-seat disproportionality is also indicative of the relative proportionality in the vote and seat shares of the MPLA and UNITA. The 20% advantage in the MPLA's vote share and the 27% advantage in its seat share over UNITA stem from its incumbency advantage and the overestimation by UNITA of its electoral support, but their combined vote and seat shares relative to the combined vote and seat shares of the smaller parties attest to the emergence of what, in effect, is a two-party system, as reflected in the low ENEP and ENLP indices of 2.5 and 2.2, respectively.

The electoral system, in other words, combined with the relative military strengths of the two civil war combatants to continue their political dominance of Angolan politics after the first postconflict elections. This dominance was reinforced by the results of the presidential elections, in which the ENPRES value of 2.45 reflects the relatively even electoral strength of the two main candidates. Yet, Savimbi refused to accept these results, precipitating the collapse of the peace agreement and the resumption of civil war.

In Mozambique, the adoption of list-PR with the d'Hondt formula was coupled with the allocation of the 250 legislative seats in eleven provinces, resulting in a high average district magnitude of 23 seats. But the adoption of a 5% legal threshold effectively prevented smaller parties from winning any seats.[6] As a result, FRELIMO and RENAMO shared 83% of the votes and 96% of the seats between them. Only one party, the Democratic Union, was able to overcome the 5% threshold and win 9 seats (4%). The LSQ-index of 7.52 is slightly higher than Angola's, reflecting the failure of the eleven other parties to win more than 12% of the vote among them, but it is consistent with the theoretical expectation of a list-PR system. In particular, it reflects the relative proportionality of vote and seat shares of FRELIMO and RENAMO. The values of the party system indices, ENEP = 2.88 and ENLP = 2.14, suggest the greater electoral fragmentation among smaller parties and their inability to win seats because of the almost insurmountable 5% threshold, and the corresponding dominance of FRELIMO and RENAMO. The results of the presidential elections and the associated ENPRES index of 2.5 replicate this continued political dominance of the two civil war combatants.

Given the similar election results in both countries, especially since the results politically validated the relative military strengths of the two major combatants in both countries, why did peace persist in Mozambique but collapse in Angola? An important answer lies in the greater diplomatic and financial involvement of the international community in Mozambique than in Angola. The international actors were instrumental in demilitarizing Mozambican politics through joint decision-making and a consultative process involving FRELIMO, RENAMO and major donors under the chairmanship of the special representative of the UN secretary-general in such interim institutions as the Supervisory and Monitoring Commission and the Cease-Fire Commission, as well as in specialized commissions such as the one dealing with the demobilization and the reintegration of former combatants in civilian life. These instruments provided former combatants with crucial opportunities for negotiations and discussions that helped to alleviate their fear of each other, engendering trust and recognition of their mutual self-interest in preventing a return to violent combat and in sustaining the new democratic dispensation. These opportunities were also buttressed by the creation of an independent electoral commission staffed and administered exclusively by Mozambicans that helped considerably in dealing with charges of fraud and other irregularities in the first post-conflict elections, thus legitimating these elections as crucial instruments for ending violent conflict, facilitating peaceful conflict management, and beginning a successful process of democratization (Turner, Nelson, and Mahling-Clark 1998; Lyons 2002, 222–226; 2004; 2005).

The absence of such instruments and opportunities in Angola undermined the prospect of cooperation and the development of mutual trust and norms of reciprocity between MPLA and UNITA. That this failure precipitated the breakdown of the Bicesse Peace Accords and Savimbi's decision to return to the battlefield to advance his interests even in the face of successful election results that validated the relative political parity of the two combatants suggests that electoral systems alone are unlikely to foster a sustained transition to democracy.

The Legacies of Civil War

The failure of the Angolan peace agreement also draws attention to how the competing priorities of the international community shape the extent to which two crucial legacies of civil war—the continued presence of armed militias and the role of fear in determining voting behavior—compromise the expected effects of even the most carefully designed electoral systems in postconflict elections. In Mozambique, for example, the international community spent $95 million to demobilize the soldiers who fought in the civil war and reintegrate them into civilian life (a form of the soft intervention strategy of purchase), thus diminishing the prospect of resumed fighting in case the election results were unacceptable to either party (Lyons 2005, 153).

No such efforts were undertaken by the international community in Angola. The Bicesse Accords called for the creation of a new, integrated national army composed of equal numbers of MPLA and UNITA soldiers, but only a small proportion of troops from both sides were integrated, leaving Savimbi in control of a substantial number of troops with which to resume fighting after his exaggerated expectations of winning the presidential elections were dashed (Lyons 2005, 156–157). Angola thus shows that the failure to demilitarize postconflict societies severely vitiates the role of electoral systems in fostering peace even when they produce successful results.

The continued presence of armed militias underscores the urgent issue of the security environment in which the first postconflict elections take place. A secure environment enables voters and candidates to focus on substantive policy issues and the future development of postconflict societies. An insecure environment heightens the importance of a second legacy of civil war—fear—in shaping voting behavior and in compromising the effects of electoral systems and hence their role in securing peace. Fear influences voting behavior as the combined result of a credible commitment by militias or the state to provide security to in-groups against attack from out-groups, and the potential for emerging conflict spirals (Lyons 2005, 50). This logic of fear played a crucial role in the 1997 postconflict elections in which the voters went to the polls to "vote for peace" in response to Charles Taylor's unsubtle campaign of resuming armed conflict in case he lost the elections. That he maintained a fully operational militia during the elections and was in control of large swaths of the country gave him added leverage, both with voters and with international mediators, such as the Nigerian-led Economic Community of West African States Monitoring Group (ECOMOG) (Harris 1999; Lyons 1999).[7]

Fear-induced voting severely distorted the expected effects of the PR electoral system under which the 1997 presidential and legislative elections were held in Liberia. The institutional design of the electoral system—the whole country serving as a single electoral constituency to allocate the sixty-four seats of the national legislature by the largest-remainder formula, one of the most proportional of PR formulas[8]—should have produced a multiparty system. As indicated in table 4.3, however, the 1997 election

Table 4.3 Results of 1997 and 2005 postconflict elections in Liberia

Indices of legislative elections	1997	2005
Electoral formula	List-PR	Plurality
Assembly size	64	64
Number of electoral districts (district magnitude)	1 (64)	64 (1)
Number of parties competing	13	24
Number of parties winning seats	6	12
Number of independent candidates competing	0	18
Number of independent candidates winning seats	0	7
Vote % of largest (second largest) party	75.33 (9.58)	16.67 (14.15)
Seat % of largest (second largest) party	76.56 (10.94)	23.44 (12.50)
ENEP*	1.72	10.03
ENLP*	1.66	7.59
LSQ-Index*	2.02	7.41
Indices of presidential elections	**1997**	**2005**
Electoral formula	Two-round majority	Two-round majority
Number of candidates	13	22
Winning vote % (first round)	75.33	28.27
Winning Vote % (second round)		59.40
ENPRES* (first round only)	1.72	6.35

*ENEP = effective number of electoral parties; ENLP = effective number of legislative parties; LSQ-Index = least-squares index of disproportionality; ENPRES = effective number of presidential candidates. See also notes to table 4.2.

results gave Charles Taylor an overwhelming victory in the legislature, with 75% of the votes and 77% of the seats, and an equally decisive first-round victory in presidential elections, with 75% of the votes. His dominance was reinforced by the lack of any meaningful challenge launched by the smaller parties, resulting in the virtually complete absence of a competitive party system, as reflected in the ENEP value of 1.72, the ENLP value of 1.66, and an ENPRES value of 1.72. Strikingly, the low value 2.02 for the LSQ-index of disproportionality between legislative votes and seats is consistent with the theoretical expectations of the PR system used for the 1997 elections, but it also accurately reflects the proportional distribution of votes and seats between Taylor's National Patriotic Party (NPP) and the insignificant smaller parties.

The Institutional Framework of Democratic Governance

A central insight in comparative research is that the overall institutional framework of democratic governance, specifically, the electoral formula governing presidential elections and whether presidential and legislative elections are held concurrently or separately, mediates the impact of electoral systems for legislative elections on the resulting party system and the associated pattern of political representation in the legislature (Shugart and Carey 1992; Jones 1993, 1995; Mainwaring 1993; Cox 1997, 187–190, 203–221; Mozaffar and Vengroff 2002; Mozaffar, Scarritt, and Galaich 2003).

This insight has special resonance in postconflict societies, since most of them have adopted presidential systems in which presidential elections are decided by the two-round majority formula (see table 4.1). The two-round majority formula typically encourages the formation of minimum winning coalitions in the second round if no candidate wins an absolute majority in the first round, and it is therefore useful in accommodating the conflicting interests of warring parties in postconflict elections. This advantage, however, is offset in most postconflict presidential elections because they are held concurrently with legislative elections, mainly to avoid the cost of holding two separate elections. The coattail effects of these concurrent elections are reinforced by the characteristic problems of postconflict democracies, such as limited experience with competitive elections, information deficits about the extent of electoral support, and personal ambition, which prevent weaker candidates and smaller parties from coordinating in favor of a single candidate. Strong presidential candidates and their political parties are thus enabled to win by wide margins in the first round. For instance, only two postconflict presidential elections in Africa have been decided in the second round, the 1996 election in Sierra Leone and the 2005 election in Liberia. Jose Eduardo dos Santos's vote margin of 49.57 in the 1992 presidential election in Angola would probably have necessitated a second round had Jonas Savimbi not opted to return to the battlefield.

This tendency of concurrent presidential and legislative elections to distort the first-round margin of victory for presidential candidates in postconflict elections was exaggerated even further in the 1997 postconflict elections in Liberia. In those elections, the winners in the presidential and legislative elections were determined, curiously, by a single ballot.[9] Voters were required to cast only one ballot, and the votes were accumulated to determine both presidential and legislative winners. With Charles Taylor making open and credible threats to resume violence should he lose the elections, and the fear of resumed conflict motivating voters, the lopsided victory of the NPP, even with the use of a highly proportional electoral system design for the legislative elections, was virtually preordained.

The absence of a fused ballot, combined with the absence of a threat of resumed violence, produced dramatically different results in the 1996 postconflict elections in Sierra Leone, which were held under electoral systems that were in all other respects identical to the ones used in Liberia in 1997. As in Liberia, Sierra Leone's legislative elections were held in a single nationwide constituency, because of the practical difficulties of drawing constituency boundaries in a civil war environment. The sixty-eight seats were allocated by the PR formula, while the presidential elections were held under a two-round majority formula. The dramatically different results of the Sierra Leone elections were consistent with the theoretical expectations of the institutional design of electoral systems. The largest party won 36% of the votes and 40% of the seats, with the second-largest party winning 22% of the votes and 25% of the seats. The ENEP value of 4.75 and the ENLP value of 3.81, combined with an LSQ-index of 5.38, indicate a competitive multiparty system. Presidential election results also indicated a competitive system: the ENPRES value was 4.65 and the winning candidate received only 36% of the vote in the first round, producing a second round of competition in which the winning margin was 60%. The use of separate ballots to determine winners allows voters to engage in strategic voting by splitting their votes between one party in the presidential election and another in the legislative election; thus there is greater opportunity for the representation of all parties.

The Spatial Organization of Elections

The concept of embeddedness of electoral systems also highlights the role of elections as spatially organized and spatially delimited processes. Elections are spatially organized because votes are counted and seats allocated in geographically delimited constituencies. District magnitude is the central feature of the spatial organization of elections prescribed by the institutional designs of electoral systems, the feature that determines the structure of constraints and opportunities in electoral competition and influences election results. District magnitude, defined as the size of the electoral district as measured by the number of seats per electoral district, can range from a single nationwide district in which all legislative seats are allocated (Liberia in 1997, Namibia in 1989, Sierra Leone in 1996), to provincial districts with their numbers of seats allocated in proportion to their population (Mozambique in 1994 and Zimbabwe in 1980), to combined provincial and nationwide districts with seats allocated in varied proportions (Angola in 1992 and South Africa in 1994), to small single-member districts (Liberia 2005). District magnitude represents an important source of information that shapes the strategic coordination of voters, parties, and candidates over votes and seats (Cox 1997).

District magnitude, however, shapes electoral outcomes interactively with the configuration of social cleavages, especially the ethnopolitical cleavages, that serve as alternative sources of information shaping the strategic coordination of voters, candidates, and parties over votes and seats (Ordeshook and Shvetsova 1994; Cox 1997; Mozaffar, Scarritt, and Galaich 2003). In postconflict elections, this interaction is distorted by the legacies of civil war and the urgency of reducing violence through elections. Thus, in the 1997 elections in Liberia, the role of fear and the threatened resumption of violence, the pragmatic creation of a single national constituency to allocate all legislative seats, and the use of an unorthodox single ballot to determine the winners of both legislative and presidential elections combined to severely undermine the role of ethnopolitical cleavages in structuring the strategic choices of voters and shaping the campaign strategies of smaller parties.

Against the background of resumed armed conflict, the internationally brokered Comprehensive Peace Agreement (CPA) between the government, rebel forces, and political parties deliberately opted for the use of a plurality formula in SMDs in Liberia's second postconflict elections, held in 2005. These elections produced not only the first female president in Africa but also the second divided government on the continent (Malawi being the first), in which one party controlled the presidency, with a second-round winning margin of 59%, and a coalition of parties (including the party that won the presidency) controlled the legislature. Moreover, as table 4.3 shows, these elections also produced one of the more competitive and fragmented party systems in Africa, which fact is reflected in the high ENEP and ENLP values of 10.03 and 7.59, respectively, and a relatively low LSQ-index of 7.41 (compared to the low ENEP and ENLP values of 1.72 and 1.66, respectively, and a low LSQ-index of 2.02, in the 1997 elections held under a PR system).

Several contextual factors account for these very unusual results in the 2005 elections. First, armed militias, a ruthless "warlord" and the associated threat of resumed violence, and hence fear among the voters, were absent in the 2005 elections. Second, the installation of an interim government, the National Transitional Government of Liberia, despite its rocky two-year tenure, enabled former rebel forces, government officials, and civil-society groups to negotiate the provisions of the CPA under international auspices (Harris 2006). Third, the deleterious consequences of relying on hurriedly arranged elections based on a badly designed electoral system (a single nationwide district with PR allocation and a single ballot to determine winners in both presidential and legislative elections) apparently motivated the careful consideration of a new electoral system design for the 2005 election. Fourth, in previous elections in Liberia and elsewhere in Africa, the interaction of ethnopolitical cleavage patterns and SMDs with plurality formulas has helped to mitigate excessive party-system fragmentation (Mozaffar, Scarritt, and Galaich 2003). But after almost fifteen years of armed violence, the resumption of democratic politics occurred in a context in which voters, candidates, and parties suffered from a severe information deficit concerning the organization of electoral campaigns, the extent of electoral support, and the associated calculations about winning and losing extent. As a result, voting patterns in the 2005 elections reflected a combination of strategic voting in the presidential elections, because of the competition between a prominent female candidate and an international soccer star, and localized voting that tended to favor local candidates and parties in legislative elections (Harris 2006). The winning margin in the first round of the presidential elections was thus only 28%, requiring a second round, while twelve parties secured enough votes to win seats legislative seats (compared to six in 1997).

Electoral institutions have discernible systematic effects that are now well established in comparative scholarship. Duverger's Law succinctly captures these effects. But Duverger showed that these effects are the results of two related processes, one mechanical and one psychological. The mechanical effects of electoral systems involve the straightforward mathematical conversion of votes into seats in which district magnitudes and electoral formulas are the critical determinants. The psychological process involves political actors' response to this conversion as reflected in their behavioral adjustments to both the expected and the unexpected outcomes of the mechanical effects (Duverger 1962). Electoral systems, in other words, structure strategic coordination in democratic elections not by their mechanical effects but by the cognitive responses and associated behavioral adjustments of political actors to these effects. Electoral systems thus produce their expected results over several elections.

Both scholarship and policy prescriptions, however, tend to adopt a mechanistic view of electoral systems' effects and to view voters and candidates as disembodied actors responding reflexively to the institutional incentives of electoral systems. In this chapter, I have stressed the need to take a more nuanced view of both electoral systems and political actors that draws attention to the importance of context in shaping the strategic calculations and associated behavior of political actors, but without rejecting the role of electoral systems.

The notion that electoral systems are embedded suggests that, even when electoral systems are adopted in peace agreements through strategic bargaining between self-interested actors unimpeded by diminished structural constraints, the context of violent civil conflict, the heightened uncertainty of reconstituting war-torn societies, and the overall institutional framework of democratic governance adopted in peace agreements will shape their role and impact on the trajectory of the peace process. The routinization of behavior conforming to the institutional incentives of electoral systems as a measure of successful transition to sustainable peace results from political actors' strategic calculations about the prescriptions of electoral rules and their mutual expectations of similar responses to these prescriptions.

Electoral systems, in other words, are sources of strategic coordination among voters and candidates over votes and seats. But political actors' strategic calculations and mutual expectations assume a level of knowledge and understanding of the prescriptions embodied in electoral rules that is difficult to sustain in most new democracies because the strategic implications of new electoral systems are neither well known nor well understood. In postconflict elections, in particular, political actors are unlikely to respond reflexively to the institutional incentives of newly designed electoral systems. They are more likely to compensate their information deficit concerning the strategic implications of new electoral systems by relying on more cost-effective sources of information to coordinate their behavior over vote and seat shares. In the immediate postconflict settings, the militarized organizations of civil wars are likely to remain important sources of such information. But sustainable postconflict peace depends on the demilitarization of these organizations and their conversion into instruments of peaceful electoral competition, such as political parties (Lyons 2005). Where such conversion fails to occur, even the most inclusive PR electoral systems adopted in postconflict elections will simply reinforce the power of militarized groups and threaten the process of maintaining peace, as vividly demonstrated by Angola in 1992, Sierra Leone in 1996, and Liberia in 1997.

To stress the importance of electoral systems as embedded institutions is to caution against unrealistic expectations about the capacity of electoral systems to secure peace in postconflict societies on their own. Democratization as a means of securing peace is about transforming the political game from violent to peaceful interactions. Democratization is thus fundamentally about crafting new institutions that will organize the new game. Since elections remain the principal instrument by which large numbers of people participate peacefully in the game of democracy, the choice of electoral systems in civil war settlements is a crucial one. The choice is principally dictated by the now widely recognized patterns of outcomes associated with different electoral systems and the relevance of these outcomes to postwar conflict management. However, as I have suggested in this chapter, and as the examples Angola in 1992, Liberia in 1997, and Sierra Leone in 1996 show, electoral systems, even when they produce the expected outcomes, by themselves cannot transform war-torn societies into peaceful ones. Moreover, a comparison of Angola and Mozambique also shows that similar electoral systems producing similar outcomes may or may not lead to sustainable peace. What lessons, then, do these anomalous cases hold for analysis and understanding of the role of electoral systems in fostering peace?

The now widely acknowledged Duverger outcomes and their modifications based on contextual variations assumes a level of political stability that does not obtain in postconflict elections, especially the first postconflict elections. In these elections, basic issues of survival and eliminating the threat of violence are more salient concerns than the more mundane concerns of "normal" politics. Thus, in the 1997 Liberian elections, voters supported Charles Taylor because they correctly anticipated that his defeat would lead to violence. Electoral systems in these situations are weak instruments for converting warring actors into cooperative players. Larger and more basic concerns of controlling violence and securing law and order motivate the choice of rational voters. Hence, other factors independent of electoral systems, such as external mediators, financial assistance, and demilitarization of warring groups and civil war structures become more significant for establishing the initial conditions for the return to "normal" politics animated by routinized interactions that conform to institutional incentives.

In such extreme cases, even the most carefully designed electoral systems are likely to be overwhelmed by the imperative of reestablishing law and order and personal and collective security and stability in the immediate aftermath of the termination of violent conflict. One possible way out of the dilemma is to envision the initial choice of electoral systems as an interim measure. In most cases, this approach will entail the choice of inclusive PR systems that foster broad-based representation and can serve as a learning mechanism for previously warring groups to engage in peaceful electoral competition, buttressed by other institutional mechanisms for securing stability and intergroup accommodation. It is difficult, of course, to establish a timeline for changing the initial choice of an electoral system. In the Lancaster House Agreement that ended the civil war in Zimbabwe in 1980, for example, negotiators agreed to impose a ten-year limit for their initial institutional choice, which included (a) a parliamentary system, (b) the population-based proportional allocation of 80 of the 100 parliamentary seats to the provinces, (c) the election of these 80 seats by the PR formula by voters registered on Common Roll of African and White voters, and (d) the creation of a separate coequal legislative chamber comprising 20 seats reserved for election by White voters. The 1980 and the 1985 elections were held under this institutional design. Beginning with the 1990 elections, the parliamentary system was replaced by a presidential system, and the 80-seat parliament elected by Common Roll voters and the 20-seat separate legislative chamber elected by White voters were eliminated and replaced by a 120-seat parliament elected by the plurality FPTP formula in SMDs.[10]

Yet the prospect that the initial institutional choice may become permanent cannot be discounted, given the sunk cost of that choice, the inherent "stickiness" of institutions, and the cost of renegotiating new institutions. Moreover, since institutional choices tend to be quintessentially political choices, groups benefiting from the initial institutions are unlikely to entertain the idea of reforming them. This is precisely what happened in 2003 in South Africa, when the ruling African National Congress rejected the electoral-system reforms recommended by the Electoral Task Team that it had appointed, because these reforms would have introduced smaller new electoral constituencies (while retaining the existing single nationwide constituency but with a smaller seat allocation than the current 200 seats) that would have diluted its support in many parts of the country and weakened its control over its parliamentary members.

Nevertheless, just as there is now growing recognition that power sharing and oversized cabinets may be useful interim measures to stabilize postconflict settings, consideration of the choice of electoral systems as an interim measure may be warranted, at least in the most extreme cases of particularly violent and destructive civil conflict.[11] One option for considering the criteria that should inform such an interim measure is the short-term and long-term goals that electoral systems are designed to achieve. Reilly and Reynolds offer a list of "ideal qualities" for electoral systems linked to their short-term goals in transitional democracies and long-term goals in consolidated democracies that can serve as a preliminary basis for thinking about the choice of electoral systems to stabilize immediate postconflict settings and about their subsequent reform and political consequences beyond the initial postconflict elections. An ideal electoral system in transitional democracies will be inclusive, simple for voters to understand, fair in its results (meaning proportional outcomes), simple to run, and transparent. It will also minimize areas of conflict and will favor grand or oversize coalitions. In contrast, an ideal electoral system in consolidated democracies will be accountable and responsive to the electorate. It will enable voters to express a more sophisticated range of choice, have the ability to "throw the rascals out," promote a sense of "ownership" of the political process among voters, and favor "minimum winning" coalitions or single-party governments (Reilly and Reynolds 1999, 55).

These descriptions, even though framed in ideal terms, offer useful insights into the contingencies that define the challenges and opportunities of post–civil war conflict management, and thus they point to the strengths and limits of relying exclusively on electoral institutions to transform war-torn societies into peaceful ones. The ideal qualities of electoral systems in transitional democracies underscore the imperative of dealing with the "extreme" politics of immediate post–civil war environments. The desirable qualities identified for electoral systems in consolidated democracies highlight the importance of other institutional and noninstitutional factors in transforming post–civil war environments into environments that can sustain "normal" politics.

References

Boix, Charles. 1999. "Setting the Rules of the Game: The Choice of Electoral Systems in Advanced Democracies." *American Political Science Review* 93, 3: 609–624.

Bowler, Shaun, and Bernard Grofman (eds.). 2000. *Elections in Australia, Ireland, and Malta under the Single Transferable Vote: Reflections on an Embedded Institution*. Ann Arbor: University of Michigan Press.

Carey, John M. 2000. "Parchment, Equilibria, and Institutions." *Comparative Political Studies* 33, 6–7: 735–761.

Collier, Paul. 2000. "Rebellion as a Quasi-Criminal Activity." *Journal of Conflict Resolution* 44, 6: 839–853.

Cox, Gary W. 1997. *Making Votes Count: Strategic Coordination in the World's Electoral Systems*. Cambridge: Cambridge University Press.

Downs, George, and Stephen John Stedman. 2002. "Evaluation Issues in Peace Implementation." In *Ending Civil Wars: The Implementation of Peace Agreements*, ed. Stephen John Stedman, Donald S. Rothchild, and Elizabeth M. Cousens, 43–69. Boulder, CO: Lynne Rienner.

Duverger, Maurice. 1962. *Political Parties*. Translated by Barbara North and Robert North. New York: Wiley.

Goodin, Robert E., and Charles Tilly (eds.). 2006. *The Oxford Handbook of Contextual Political Analysis*. Oxford: Oxford University Press.

Grofman, Bernard, Sung-Chull Lee, Edwin A. Winckler, and Brian Woodall (eds.). 1999. *Elections in Japan, Korea, and Taiwan under the Single Non-Transferable Vote: The Comparative Study of an Embedded Institution*. Ann Arbor: University of Michigan Press.

Harris, David. 1999. "From 'Warlord' to 'Democratic' President: How Charles Taylor Won the 1997 Liberian Elections." *Journal of Modern African Studies* 37, 3: 431–455.

———. 2006. "Liberia 2005: An Unusual African Post-Conflict Election." *Journal of Modern African Studies* 44, 3: 375–395.

HMSO. 1980. "Southern Rhodesia: Report of the Constitutional Conference, Lancaster House, London, September–December 1979." Command Paper No. 7802. Lancaster House, London, December 21, 1979.

Jones, Mark P. 1993. "The Political Consequences of Electoral Laws in Latin America and the Caribbean." *Electoral Studies* 12, 1: 59–75.

———. 1995. *Electoral Laws and the Survival of Presidential Democracies*. South Bend, IN: University of Notre Dame Press.

Kumar, Krishna (ed.). 1998. *Postconflict Elections, Democratization, and International Assistance*. Boulder, CO: Lynn Rienner.

Laakso, Markku, and Rein Taagepera. 1979. "'Effective' Number of Parties: A Measure with Application to Western Europe." *Comparative Political Studies* 12, 1: 3–27.

Lijphart, Arend. 1977. *Democracy in Plural Societies: A Comparative Exploration*. New Haven, CT: Yale University Press.

———. 1994. *Electoral Systems and Party Systems: A Study of Twenty-Seven Democracies, 1945–1990*. New York: Oxford University Press.

———. 1999. *Patterns of Democracy: Government Forms and Performance in Thirty-six Countries*. New Haven, CT: Yale University Press.

Lipset, Seymour Martin, and Stein Rokkan. 1967. "Cleavage Structures, Party Systems, and Voter Alignments." In *Party Systems and Voter Alignments: Cross-National Perspectives*, ed. Seymour Martin Lipset and Stein Rokkan, 1–64. New York: Free Press.

Luong, Pauline Jones. 2000. "After the Break-up." *Comparative Political Studies* 33, 5: 563–592.

Lyons, Terrence. 1999. *Voting for Peace: Postconflict Elections in Liberia*. Washington, DC: Brookings Institution Press.

———. 2002. "The Role of Postsettlement Elections." In *Ending Civil Wars: The Implementation of Peace Agreements*, ed. Stephen John Stedman, Donald S. Rothchild, and Elizabeth M. Cousens, 215–235. Boulder, CO: Lynne Rienner.

———. 2004. "Postconflict Elections and the Process of Demilitarizing Politics: The Role of Electoral Administration." *Democratization* 11, 3: 1–27.

———. 2005. *Demilitarizing Politics: Elections on the Uncertain Road to Peace*. Boulder, CO: Lynne Rienner.

Mainwaring, Scott. 1991. "Politicians, Parties, and Electoral Systems: Brazil in Comparative Perspective." *Comparative Politics* 24, 1: 21–43.

———. 1993. "Presidentialism, Multipartism, and Democracy." *Comparative Political Studies* 26, 2: 198–229.

McFaul, Michael. 1999. "Institutional Design, Uncertainty, and Path Dependency during Transitions: Cases from Russia." *Constitutional Political Economy* 10, 1: 27–52.

Mozaffar, Shaheen. 1997. "Electoral Systems and Their Political Effects in Africa: A Preliminary Analysis." *Representation* 34, 3–4: 148–156.

———. 2004. "How Context Mediates the Effects of Electoral Institutions on the Structure of Party Systems in Africa's Emerging Democracies." Working Paper No. 72, Center for Social Science Research, University of Cape Town, August.

Mozaffar, Shaheen, James Scarritt, and Glen Galaich. 2003. "Electoral Institutions, Ethnopolitical Cleavages, and Party Systems in Africa's Emerging Democracies." *American Political Science Review* 97, 3: 379–390.

Mozaffar, Shaheen, and Andreas Schedler. 2002. "The Comparative Study of Electoral Governance—Introduction." *International Political Science Review* 23, 1: 5–27.

Mozaffar, Shaheen, and Richard Vengroff. 2002. "A 'Whole System' Approach to the Choice of Electoral Rules in Democratizing Countries: Senegal in Comparative Perspective." *Electoral Studies* 21, 4: 601–616.

Ordeshook, Peter C., and Olga Shvetsova. 1994. "Ethnic Heterogeneity, District Magnitude, and the Number of Parties." *American Journal of Political Science* 38, 1: 100–123.

Rae, Douglas. 1971. *The Political Consequences of Electoral Laws*. Rev. ed. New Haven, CT: Yale University Press.

Reilly, Benjamin. 2005. "Does the Choice of Electoral System Promote Democracy? The Gap between Theory and Practice." In *Sustainable Peace: Power and Democracy after Civil Wars*, ed. Philip G. Roeder and Donald Rothchild, 159–171. Ithaca, NY: Cornell University Press.

Reilly, Benjamin, and Andrew Reynolds. 1999. *Electoral Systems and Conflict in Divided Societies*. Washington, DC: National Academy Press.

Reynolds, Andrew. 2000. "Majoritarian or Power-Sharing Government." In *Democracy and Institutions: The Life Work of Arend Lijphart*, ed. Markus M. L. Crepaz, Thomas A. Koelble, and David Wilsford, 155–196. Ann Arbor: University of Michigan Press.

Riker, William H. 1962. *The Theory of Political Coalitions*. New Haven, CT: Yale University Press.

Roeder, Philip. 2003. "Clash of Civilizations and Escalation of Domestic Ethnopolitical Conflicts." *Comparative Political Studies* 36, 5: 509–540.

Rothchild, Donald, 1997. *Managing Ethnic Conflict in Africa: Pressures and Incentives for Cooperation*. Washington, DC: Brookings Institution Press.

Shugart, Matthew Soberg. 1992. "Guerrillas and Elections: An Institutionalist Perspective on the Costs of Conflict and Cooperation." *International Studies Quarterly* 36, 2: 121–52.

Shugart, Matthew Soberg, and John M. Carey. 1992. *Presidents and Assemblies: Constitutional Designs and Electoral Dynamics*. New York: Cambridge University Press.

Taagepera, Rein, and Matthew Shugart. 1989. *Seats and Votes: The Effects and Determinants of Electoral Systems*. New Haven, CT: Yale University Press.

Turner, J. Michael, Sue Nelson, and Kimberly Mahling-Clark. 1998. "Mozambique's Vote for Democratic Governance." In Kumar 1998, 153–175.

Walter, Barbara F. 1999. "Designing Transitions from Civil War: Demobilization, Democratization, and Commitments to Peace." *International Security* 24, 1: 127–155.

Waterbury, John. 1997. "Fortuitous By-Products," *Comparative Politics* 29, 3: 383–402.

Notes

1. The electoral institutions examined in this chapter refer to the set of rules that convert votes into seats. A related set of electoral institutions, not examined in this chapter, refers to election administration, the configuration of structures and procedures that govern the organization and conduct of elections. On the role of election administration in securing peace in postconflict societies, see Lyons 2004; 2005, 114–123. On the relationship between the two types of electoral institutions, see Mozaffar and Schedler 2002.
2. On the role of institutional design, see Duverger 1962. Lipset and Rokkan (1967) examine the influence of social structural factors.
3. After the 1985 elections, Zimbabwe introduced the FPTP plurality formula in SMD, according to the provisions of the 1980 Lancaster House Agreement, which ended the country's civil war. The plurality system only served to entrench a single-party dominant regime that led to the gradual erosion of democracy and the current political crisis.
4. This paragraph summarizes the insights of a large comparative literature, a select sample of which includes Rae 1971; Mainwaring 1991; Jones 1993; Lijphart 1994; Cox 1997, esp. 24–27, 20–23; Mozaffar 1997, 2004; Waterbury 1997; Boix 1999; McFaul 1999; Carey 2000, 751–755; Luong 2000; Reynolds 2000.
5. For an excellent collection that emphasizes the importance of context in systematic political analysis, see Goodin and Tilly 2006.
6. A threshold is the minimum number of votes required to win one seat. A threshold can be derived though several mathematical formulas; the most common and the most proportional of them involves dividing the number of valid votes cast by the district magnitude (the number of seats available for allocation in the electoral district). A threshold can also be legally set, with 5% being the universal norm. In Mozambique, the 5% legal threshold requires that a party win at least 5% of the valid votes cast in one of the eleven provinces that serve as an electoral district to win one of the seats allocated to that province.
7. Nigeria's decision to withdraw from ECOMOG after seven futile years of peacekeep-

ing led to the hurried arrangements for the 1997 elections without any attempt at demobilizing the armed militias or creating a secure environment.

8. Because of the civil war, the practical difficulties of drawing constituency boundaries precluded the adoption of single-member districts with seats allocated by plurality formula, the electoral system used in Liberia in prior elections and in 2003, and contributed to the choice of a single, nation-wide electoral constituency.
9. The reason for the choice of a single ballot is unclear, but it may have been dictated by the need to reduce the cost of printing different ballots. This appears to be the only time a single ballot has been used to determine the winners in both the presidential and legislative elections.
10. For the provisions of the Lancaster House Agreement, see HMSO 1980.
11. There is, of course, the option of eschewing competitive elections altogether as a mechanism for ending civil wars in these extreme situations.

FIVE

Sustaining Peace: Renegotiating Postwar Settlements

TIMOTHY D. SISK

Experience with the civil wars of the 1990s and the early 2000s has yielded an important lesson: there are, under some circumstances, real pathologies associated with the settlement pacts that have been employed to end these conflicts. The normative, strategic, and practical challenges of peace agreements are many and complex, but the principal problem is that the war-ending peace agreement itself—to stop the immediate fighting—may well be counterproductive to long-term peace. A common and well-earned criticism of war-ending settlements, such as Bosnia's Dayton Accords, is that they "freeze" the lines of conflict and entrench subsequent potential institutions along the sharp and sensitive lines of ethnicity, religion, or sect, thereby perpetuating and reinforcing the underlying drivers of conflict.[1] But reification of the lines of conflict in society is but one common problem with war-ending peace agreements. Additionally, such pacts are typically based on a narrow elite consensus and may easily fall prey to "disruption from below" by discontented spoilers, leading in turn to war recurrence in the worst cases and "post-accord violence" in others.[2]

Many countries that have come out of civil war in recent years desperately need to fundamentally revisit these dysfunctional war-ending pacts through negotiating new settlements; however, as we know from seminal research, once political institutions are in place, they can develop their own inertia as the incentives for their perpetuation become reinforced.[3] Thus, a principal puzzle is how to overcome the pathologies of war-ending pacts that may now frustrate the attainment of longer-term peace. This chapter

The author gratefully acknowledges the support of the Carnegie Corporation of New York Program in International Peace and Security for its support of "Sustainable Peacebuilding" (co-principal investigator Roland Paris) on which this essay is based.

explores a critical question: How can societies wracked by civil war transform their political institutions over time, so that deep-rooted social conflicts can be ameliorated through nonviolent means? Among the issues to consider in responding to this pivotal yet multifaceted question are the processes and logics of choosing political institutions in war-ending negotiations and the ways in which such pacts and their institutional structures, once in place, can potentially mitigate—or potentially perpetuate—conflicts among social forces, especially those organized around ethnicity or religious identity.

In the post-cold-war era, it has become increasingly clear that civil wars very often end at the negotiating table rather than on the battlefield, meaning that violence is brought to an end through war-ending pacts.[4] This is not to say that military victory is impossible, as the arguably Pyrrhic victory over the Liberation Tigers of Tamil Eelam by the government of Sri Lanka in 2009 attests, but rather to assert that negotiated settlements are a common pattern of war termination. Although international "peacemaking" did not work in Sri Lanka, it has borne success in many cases in the post-cold-war period. The increased frequency of negotiated outcomes in civil wars (historically, seemingly rare) can be attributed to the improvement in practice and effectiveness of top-level international envoys as mediators leveraging the parties into peace accords.[5] Settlements in civil wars today typically feature a power-sharing agreement through which conflicts on the battlefield or the street are ended via the sequenced introduction of democracy: elections, parliamentary politics, independent judicial institutions, and the revival of civil society, all underpinned by a process of "demilitarization" through security-sector reform (Jarstad and Sisk 2008).[6]

However, in some longstanding instances, there is a widespread concern that power-sharing agreements do not necessarily lay the foundation for a truly lasting peace. Often cited is the vulnerability to recurrent violence of confessional power sharing in Lebanon or the continued inability of a power-sharing solution to reconcile the divisions of Cyprus.[7] Indeed, the record of power sharing's failure is as strong as its record of success. Jarstad distinguishes between ethnic and nonethnic power sharing and suggests that "the main functions of power-sharing agreements—inclusion, elite-oriented regulations, international guarantees, and the leveling of power between groups—can have negative consequences for peacebuilding as well as on democratization" (Jarstad 2008, 112–113).

Today, in Afghanistan, Burundi, Iraq, and South Sudan, for example, initial war-ending power-sharing agreements and the institutions they created are coming under challenge by armed groups or recurring political violence. Moreover, recent instances of internationally brokered power sharing after election-related violence in Kenya and Zimbabwe, agreements that seem to reward the perpetrators of violence with preservation of their power, have raised anew some of these longstanding concerns about power sharing as a means of ending violence. In these cases, power sharing may reward those culpable for the violence in the first place by assuring their continued place in power. Thus, although power sharing does seem to provide an exit from violence, it may not necessarily address the underlying causes of the conflict. In short, power-sharing institutions may not lead to the creation of "stakeholders for stability" that is the central theme of this volume.

I argue that, initially, power-sharing pacts may well be essential for urgently ending the scourge of modern civil wars; however, over time, certain features of power sharing (grand coalitions, electoral system choices, and territorial divisions of power, especially) tend to frustrate the pursuit of sustainable peace. As time passes, they need to be renegotiated. The need for flexibility and fluidity in war-ending settlements was well appreciated in the early research of Donald Rothchild in his seminal *Racial Bargaining in Independent Kenya*: namely, for lasting peace in divided societies after civil war, there must be opportunities for ongoing, iterative bargaining over the terms of the social contract, which in turn requires ongoing renegotiation of the initial transitional pact over time.[8]

This enduring insight, reinforced by recent research and experience, points to the essential conclusion that initial war-ending pacts need to be replaced later, through ongoing bargaining and institution building, with agreements that more closely approximate democratic social contracts based on reciprocal rights and mutual interdependencies and especially cross-communal political parties and civil society. These findings have important implications for policymakers as they wrestle with the ways to structure post-peace-agreement peace-building processes in ways that can see power-sharing pacts not necessarily as long-term solutions to the challenges of living together after civil war—whereby the terms of agreement have to be continually complied with for fear of reigniting war—but perhaps as a necessary first step along a journey of repeated renegotiation toward a sustainable and enduring conflict-ameliorating institutional structure.

Exiting Civil Wars through Pacted Transitions

The urgency of ending civil wars remains at the top of the international community's agenda at the very highest levels of the United Nations and in the debates over intervention that occur in the international community's leading states.[9] It also resonates in current UN country-level challenges such as responding to insurgency in Afghanistan, ending atrocities in Darfur, preventing renewed violence in Kosovo, building a state in Liberia, and securing the eastern region of the Democratic Republic of the Congo (DRC). Thus, civil war conflict management is principally about negotiating and mediating settlements and ensuring their implementation. When civil wars cannot be won on the battlefield militarily, the way from violence to peace is found in a settlement that outlines the route from war to living together in a common state (see Darby and MacGinty 2008). Settlements define transition pathways and also set the stage for the basic set of rules that seek to guide the peace-building phase (Rothchild 2002).

The bias against partition of existing states in the international system is one reason why international mediators prefer to promote power sharing, but it is not the only one (Chesterman, Farer, and Sisk 2001).[10] The other justification is that partition in itself does not solve the problem of how contending social groups can live together peacefully. Thus, the move toward democracy and power sharing after war is an imperative even when prior historical legacies have led to newly independent states, such as Bosnia under international suzerainty or Kosovo in its presently quasi-independent status. War-termination today is principally about building functioning, secure, stable, and democratic states, however problematic this approach may be (Paris 2004; Barnett 2006; Call 2008; Paris and Sisk 2009).

Thus, to provide protagonists exits from war, international mediators and parties in conflict alike often turn to power-sharing institutions as an interim step (for example, in transitional regimes) or a more permanent constitutional solution to the challenges of democratization after civil war. Because power-sharing agreements are mutual security pacts, they seek to democratize while at the same time constraining the elements of contestation that may lead to instability, violence, or a return to war. Power-sharing settlements in civil wars reflect the convergence point of the parties' preferences over new rules structures, or institutions, for the state once arms have been laid down. Importantly, settlements do not end conflicts; they are simply agreements to continue bargaining under consensually defined rules of interaction. In the course of formal substantive negotiations, parties formulate their positions based on their expectations of how the structure of the new institutions will serve their interests at the moment of their adoption; they exercise, in peace negotiations, "analytical imagination" about the costs and benefits of alternative institutions, such as the electoral system (Sisk 1995). Therefore, settlements do not definitively end civil wars; they are *promises* to end conflicts by creating new rules of the game to which all parties at the table can, at the moment of war termination, agree.

In many instances today, such as in Burundi, Nepal, and South Sudan, power-sharing accords have in fact brought relative peace in the immediate aftermath of conflict after decades of war, although, as these examples suggest, such mechanisms are prone to crisis and collapse. Such settlements typically contain multiple power-sharing measures, now generally understood to include a much broader array of features than those first associated with Lijphart's consociational model but nonetheless constituting a pattern of power-sharing type that closely fits his original four elements or manifestations (grand coalition, mutual veto, proportionality, and territorial or group autonomy) (Lijphart 2004). Research on cross-national experience finds that indeed war-ending power-sharing agreements do help end bloody civil wars and yield an initial peace.[11]

Typically, this approach envisages that conflicts on the battlefield can be ended through the sequenced introduction of initial steps to first "demilitarize" politics (for example, through disarmament, demobilization, and reintegration coupled with security-sector reform) and to subsequently introduce democracy.[12] In policy terms, the "essential task matrix" approach to postwar "stabilization and reconstruction" carefully itemizes a process-and-substance approach to a linear pathway of democratization and peace.[13] While the matrix has been described as rigid, it does a good job of categorizing key objectives and tasks. As Ben Reilly appropriately observes, "In any transition from conflict to peace, the creation or restoration of some form of legitimate authority is paramount. . . . The support of the citizenry must be tested and obtained. . . . The overarching challenge of peacebuilding is to construct a sustainable democratic state that can function without international involvement" (Reilly 2003, 174; see also Reilly 2006). However, implementing power-sharing agreements does not seem to be enough; indeed, as suggested in the introduction to this chapter, under some conditions such pacts may fail to sufficiently address the underlying dynamics of conflict.

Pathologies of War-Ending Pacts: Problems of Power Sharing

As long-time critics have argued, power-sharing institutions can well contain intrinsic pathologies.[14] There are three principal concerns. First, elites may see incentives to exacerbate conflict, not ameliorate it, by appealing to nationalism to win out over rivals within their own group. Second, the mutual veto is a recipe for deadlock and, in the worst cases, constitutional crises that can precipitate a return to war. Third, as noted above, while power-sharing institutions might be necessary for transitional periods, over the long term they are not sustainable in many of the most conflict-afflicted divided societies because, at least in some instances (for instance, in Bosnia, Lebanon, and Northern Ireland), they may serve to reinforce an underlying social basis of the conflict in cementing identity as the basis of the state.

The possible perversity of elite incentives has been the Achilles heel of power sharing in many situations. Traditionally, scholars who evaluate peace-agreement settlements in civil wars have explained that the prevalence of power sharing as the most common negotiated outcome of war was a result of the "self-negating prediction" (Lijphart 1977; du Toit 1989). That is, protagonists in civil wars, when they bargain for peace, often agree to share power through settlements because they deeply fear that the *failure* to do so—to continue to pursue a military victory or to ramp up violence—could mean something worse: the potential for further, costly escalation that is ultimately or potentially self-injurious. In essence, *fear of the costs of failure to conciliate* is the underlying motive driving the parties to clinch and abide by settlements to share power as a means to escaping bloody strife. Power-sharing institutions, because they guarantee representation and rights to groups and limit democracy, are essentially mechanisms for institutionalizing fear: fear of each other (thus the need for hard-and-fast guarantees of minority rights, for example) and fear of the failure to conciliate (avoiding a worse alternative). However, there is little evidence to support the view that such fear of avoiding a worse outcome is a sufficient condition for long-term peace, especially if the institution gives elites economic, electoral, or survival incentives to mobilize their constituencies rather than convince them to be accommodating.[15]

The relationship between the adoption of grand coalition cabinets, mutual vetoes, and recurrent crises of governance is very much a problem of commitment. Power-sharing pacts are problematic because they inevitably require protagonists to give up their maximalist aims in the war—not exactly conceding defeat but foregoing aims such as territorial independence on which they have mobilized for war. When parties in conflict concede to power sharing, they thus often lose their own constituents' *credibility.* For protagonists in conflict (generally, governments and rebel forces), democratization yields fundamental problems of credibility, commitment, and security, and the uncertainties about the future suggest that international efforts to reassure "losers" in elections that they will not face existential extinction are usually not enough. As Barbara Walter has artfully shown, the long shadow of the future creates a classic security dilemma for civil war protagonists over time, one that a transitional pact may not be sufficiently powerful to resolve durably (1999).[16]

For these reasons, postwar countries are especially vulnerable to transition-related violence because of the social enmities inflamed by conflict, the incentives for mobilizing along conflict lines (often ethnic or religious/sectarian) for elections, and the ready availability of small arms and light weapons in conflict-affected countries. Transitions to democracy—even with power-sharing protections—are perilous and often are accompanied by deep vulnerability to violence: genocide in Rwanda in 1994 erupted in the context of the post–Arusha Agreement transition that unfolded in late 1993 and the early months of 1994 (Suhrke and Adelman 1999). Further, the problems that original pacts create are sometimes not experienced until many years later, when changing conditions and power relationships allow stronger protagonists unilaterally to vitiate them (as in Zimbabwe, where the terms of the Lancaster House Agreement were eventually overturned in unilateral amendments to the constitution by the ruling regime of President Robert Mugabe). As Wallensteen has observed, crises in postwar democratization often occur much further down the road in postwar societies, when the attention of the international community has turned elsewhere and where efforts to prevent the recurrence of violence are often unfulfilled (2008).

Finally, the case against power sharing as a longer-term solution is especially strong in those cases where war-ending agreements codify and entrench ethnic representation in institutional rules. Beyond the example of Bosnia cited in the introduction to this chapter is the instance of Burundi, where a lauded 1994 agreement may have set the stage for future strife. The 1994 pact has been criticized as an ill-considered power-sharing formula that heightened ethnic differentiation and that set up a longer-term, zero-sum game between the protagonists. Lemarchand has argued that the Burundi pact "carried the logic of power sharing to an extreme . . . and with extremely dysfunctional consequences. Rather than cohesion, the result had been to foster paralysis at every level of government" (2006, 9). Even so, when a more durable agreement was reached in 2004 after considerable violence, it, too, featured extensive ethnic-group-based power sharing, and Burundi through 2008 continued to see spoiler challenges to the agreement.

Renegotiating Pacts: Reopening Pandora's Box?

Traditionally conceived power sharing, which saliently features *guarantees* of representation on a party political, ethnic, or other identity basis, thus appears to be at best a limited and short-term means of promoting sustainable peace after civil war. In the long term, as Rothchild penned in the 1970s with regard to postindependence regimes, transitional pacts need to be gradually reformed to introduce ongoing incentives for more fluid bargaining that allows for the development of political coalitions that crosscut the lines of conflict over which war was fought. Both in the immediate end to civil wars and in the longer-term aspects of peace-building, third-party intervention seems essential to moving beyond initial power-sharing pacts to the longer-term sustainability of peace.

Such a process, however, raises a dilemma. How can the certainty and guarantees needed to end violence be reconciled with the countervailing demand for flexibility and the potential redesign of political institutions later in the postwar period?[17] Revisiting the terms of war-ending pacts is akin to reopening Pandora's box, since doing so raises anew fundamental questions about the relative balance of power among parties; in addition, the power-sharing institutions themselves have gained inertia in the period following the war. Thus, a central puzzle concerning the ending of civil wars is how to replace fear as the underlying motive for self-enforcing peace accords and move toward a more durable set of alternative political institutions. As Rothchild observed, "In some cases, the very incentives required to reassure weaker parties and gain commitment to a bargain in the initial period can cause political instability later on, if rigid power-sharing institutions come into conflict with the need to concentrate power at the political center in a unitary state structure" (2002, 135).

War-ending pacts *are* often limited in their ability to allow for the revising of the fundamental institutional relationships. For this reason, as du Toit has argued with regard to South Africa, the constitutional deals made at the time of transition may well undermine the ability to sustain the peace over time; consequently, he calls for "post-settlement settlements" to allow for the kind of ongoing bargaining over institutional design that Rothchild identified as the institutional key to sustaining peace some three decades before (2003). Such settlements would require a gradual negotiation change from the rigidities of power-sharing pacts to ostensibly more integrative solutions, a cultural shift from a rigid ethnic identity to fluid identities, a move toward "cosmopolitanism," which is a logical outcome of the evolution of the normative structure of the international system of human rights protections. Whether this alternative of shifting away from the rigidities is toward "cosmopolitanism" or perhaps toward "interculturalism" is a matter of terminology, but it is clear that, over time, approaches that lead to more integrated institutions and indeed cross-ethnic or broad-based political parties are essential.[18]

This principal alternative to rigid power sharing has been identified as an integrative formula. Ben Reilly demonstrates how the key to such integrative approaches (or "centripetalism," because it tries to give a center-oriented spin to political dynamics) is the electoral system; its strongest possible effect is to engender the development of multiethnic political parties (2001). The integrative approach to institutional design after violence eschews ethnic groups as the building blocks of a common society and thus is closely associated with political institutions that more fully provide an array of incentives to promote cosmopolitan solutions (Sisk 1996). As a distinct set of options for power sharing, integrative measures are intended to avoid the definition of specific groups as the building blocks of society. They also purposefully seek to integrate society along the lines of division, to create incentives for political leaders to be moderate on divisive ethnic themes, and to enhance minority influence in majority decision-making (Horowitz 1985). The elements of an integrative approach include electoral systems that encourage preelection pacts across ethnic lines, nonethnic federalism that diffuses points of power, and public policies that promote political allegiances that transcend groups.

The integrative approach to managing social conflicts emphasizes the critical role of cross-communal political parties, transethnic representative structures, and alternative methodologies for determining distribution of opportunity. Such measures, especially when coupled with increasing integration of civil society, seem to be the essential elements for sustaining peace in divided societies through democratic institutions (Varshney 2001). But it is also argued that the use of incentives to promote conciliation will run aground in the presence of deep-seated enmities that underlie ethnic disputes and that are hardened during the course of a brutal civil war; and, absent the operation of such incentives, some institutional forms of integrative models may be conflict-inducing because they tend toward winner-take-all contests (Reilly 2001; Lijphart 2004).

Regrettably, there are few cases in which, after an initial war-ending pact, the protagonists over time eschewed the promises of consociationalism for integrative solutions. South Africa may be one case; however, its experience is arguably sui generis.[19] Perhaps there are so few such cases because institutions, once in place, tend to endure. Otherwise, the question still remains: How can postwar countries move from the initial settlements that end the fighting to a longer-term set of institutions that promote and reward cooperation? In multiethnic Fiji, for example, a four-year expert review of the country's political system produced a set of recommendations for a recently adopted constitution that combines measures to guarantee a minimum level of traditional Fijian (as opposed to Indo-Fijian) representation in parliament (a group building-block option) with measures to promote the formation of political alliances across group lines (an integrative option). The Fiji experience illustrates how a well-conceived process, featuring a balanced panel of experts with firm political support, can arrive at creative solutions specifically tailored to a unique set of problems (see Constitutional Review Commission 1996). The Fiji case is instructive precisely because the efforts of spoilers to disrupt integration along ethnic lines was only temporarily successful; as Fiji recovers from the attempted coup d'état of 2000, it has returned to an integrationist formula for resolving its ethnic tensions.

Because of the paucity of current empirical examples of integrative alternatives at work in the aftermath of war, the processes of change from pacts to ostensibly more durable solutions remains underexplored.[20] At least one avenue is to move beyond perceiving power sharing as a fixed recipe (the consociational bargain) and instead see sharing power after war as a much wider range of opportunities for dialogue and shared identity building in deeply divided societies. At the end of war, power-sharing pacts are guarantees, and parties will often demand these provisions in peace negotiations. Over time, these guarantees can be sustained only if the harder edges—ethnic formulas, "mutual vetoes," and electoral incentives to mobilize by identity—are replaced through the broadening of dialogue, dialogue that is both vertical (through elites and civil society) and horizontal (at different levels and localities of governance).

From Power Sharing to Integrative Solutions

There is already an acute awareness of the problems of war-ending settlements in ending today's civil wars. To date, scholarship and policy practice tend to focus on the initial agreements to end war and the importance of their full implementation as the basis for peace-building; more recently the imperatives of state-building have been emphasized (Stedman, Cousens, and Rothchild 2002; Doyle and Sambanis 2006; Call 2008). Beyond implementation, however, there needs to be a greater understanding of how to move beyond the initial war-ending pact and adopt a more integrative and "cosmopolitan" democracy as a system of sustainable conflict management. Thus, at least one answer to the puzzle of sustaining peace after civil war has to do with the eventual ability of postconflict countries to renegotiate the terms of war-ending pacts over time and the willingness of the international community to stay engaged over the long term (through mechanisms of soft intervention) in overcoming the fears that such renegotiation may induce. Beyond the state-society social contract described in chapter 2 by David Lake, it is clear that sustainability of peace will require political institutions that reward moderation and induce crosscutting political coalitions.

Some initial experience suggests that at least one way to resolve the problem is to negotiate, in the first place, sunset clauses whereby the more fixed or rigid elements of power sharing expire over time (Samuels 2008). Alternatively, international policymakers are admonished to pay more attention to integrative options in war-ending pacts at the outset and avoid rigid power-sharing agreements in efforts to leverage the parties into peace (Simonsen 2005). It would appear that interim power-sharing or transitional governments, coupled with electoral processes that lead to constitution-making assemblies (as in South Africa or Nepal) may be an especially useful transitional way to build flexibility into institutional frameworks in the immediate emergence from civil war. While these are useful approaches, they do not sufficiently solve the fundamental dilemma of overcoming fear and replacing the certainty of war-ending power-sharing pacts with the uncertainty inherent in the renegotiation of institutional alternatives that move away from the rigidities of power-sharing bargains.

More optimistically, it should be clear to all by now that postwar transition pathways do not conform to simple models, especially those that are placed on unrealistic timetables and "task matrices" or that are driven primarily by outside agendas. Pathways away from civil war are highly varied, and for each situation, various sequences and settlement institutions may or may not be more appropriate than others. Rather than whether power sharing is or is not desirable as a general rule in ending civil wars, the debate should center on how power sharing may or may not affect short-term exigencies for stopping the war. Because the road leading away from war is usually found in peace agreements, this is primarily a consideration for mediators who must help the parties think through the consequences of various ways of crafting peace agreements.

It remains one of the critical challenges of the next generation of scholarship on postwar transitions to identify avenues toward revising pathologically dysfunctional war-ending pacts and to demonstrate how the dilemma of institutional change has been tangibly addressed in contemporary conflicts. In the meantime, the essential teleological goal of sustaining peace should be seen in the fostering in postwar countries of institutions that provide ongoing incentives for bargaining and moderation and that proliferate points of bargaining throughout political institutions and the social fabric. Unfortunately, a full understanding of the processes and pathways through which war-ending settlements can be transformed into these more promising institutional arrangements in war-torn societies remains elusive.

References

Barnett, Michael, 2006. "Building a Republican Peace: Stabilizing States after War." *International Security* 30, 4: 87–112.

Belloni, Roberto. 2007. *State Building and International Intervention in Bosnia.* London: Routledge.

Call, Charles T. (ed.). 2008. *Building States to Build Peace.* New York/Boulder, CO: International Peace Institute/Lynne Rienner.

Chesterman, Simon, Tom Farer, and Timothy Sisk. 2001. "Competing Claims: Self Determination and Security in the United Nations." An International Peace Academy Policy Brief. New York: International Peace Institute (formerly the International Peace Academy).

Constitutional Review Commission. 1996. *The Fiji Islands: Toward a United Future.* Suva, Fiji: Government Printer.

Darby, John (ed.). 2006. *Violence and Reconstruction.* South Bend, IN: University of Notre Dame Press.

Darby, John P., and Roger MacGinty (eds.). 2008. *Contemporary Peacemaking: Conflict, Violence, and Peace Processes.* 2nd ed. London: Palgrave.

Doyle, Michael W., and Nicholas Sambanis. 2006. *Making War and Building Peace.* Princeton, NJ: Princeton University Press.

Du Toit, Pierre. 1989. "Bargaining about Bargaining: Inducing the Self-Negating Prediction in Deeply Divided Societies: The Case of South Africa." *Journal of Conflict Resolution* 33, 2: 210–230.

———. 2003. "Why Post-Settlement Settlements?" *Journal of Democracy* 14, 3: 104–118.

Guttieri, Karen, and Jessica Piombo (eds.). 2007. *Interim Governments: Institutional Bridges to Peace and Democracy?* Washington, DC: United States Institute of Peace Press.

Harbom, Lotta, Stina Högbladh, and Peter Wallensteen. 2006. "Armed Conflict and Peace Agreements." *Journal of Peace Research* 43, 5: 617–631.

Hartzell, Caroline, and Matthew Hoddie. 2007. *Crafting Peace: Power-Sharing Institutions and the Negotiated Settlement of Civil War.* University Park: Pennsylvania State University Press.

Horowitz, Donald. 1985. *Ethnic Groups in Conflict.* Berkeley: University of California Press.

Human Rights Watch. 1995. *Playing the Communal Card: Communal Violence and Human Rights*. New York: Human Rights Watch.

Jarstad, Anna. 2001. "Changing the Game: Consociational Theory and Ethnic Quotas in Cyprus and New Zealand." Ph.D. diss., Uppsala University.

———. 2008. "Power Sharing: Former Enemies in Joint Government." In Jarstad and Sisk 2008.

Jarstad, Anna K., and Timothy D. Sisk (eds.). 2008. *From War to Democracy: Dilemmas of Peacebuilding*. Cambridge: Cambridge University Press.

Lemarchand, René. 2006. "Consociationalism and Power Sharing in Africa: Rwanda, Burundi, and the Democratic Republic of Congo." *African Affairs* 106, 422: 1–20.

Lijphart, Arend. 1977. *Democracy in Plural Societies*. New Haven, CT: Yale University Press.

———. 2004. "Constitutional Design for Divided Societies." *Journal of Democracy* 15, 2: 96–109.

Lyons, Terrence. 2005. *Demilitarizing Politics: Elections on the Uncertain Road to Peace*. Boulder, CO: Lynne Rienner.

Mack, Andrew. 2008. "Human Security Brief 2007." Human Security Project Report, Simon Fraser University.

North, Douglass C. 1990. *Institutions, Institutional Change, and Economic Performance*. Cambridge: Cambridge University Press.

Paris, Roland. 2004. *At War's End: Building Peace after Civil Conflict*. Cambridge: Cambridge University Press.

Paris, Roland, and Timothy Sisk (eds.). 2009. *The Dilemmas of Statebuilding: Confronting the Contradictions of Post-War Peacebuilding*. London: Routledge.

Reilly, Benjamin. 2001. *Democracy in Divided Societies: Electoral Engineering for Conflict Management*. Cambridge: Cambridge University Press.

———. 2003. "Democratic Validation." In *Contemporary Peacemaking: Conflict, Violence, and Peace Processes*, ed. John Darby and Roger MacGinty. London: Palgrave.

———. 2006. "Political Engineering and Party Politics in Conflict-Prone Societies." *Democratization* 13, 5: 811–827.

Rothchild, Donald. 1973. *Racial Bargaining in Independent Kenya: A Study of Minorities and Decolonization*. New York: Oxford University Press.

———. 1997. *Managing Ethnic Conflict in Africa: Pressures and Incentives for Cooperation*. Washington, DC: Brookings Institution Press.

———. 2002. "Settlement Terms and Post-Agreement Stability." In Stedman, Rothchild, and Cousens 2002.

———. 2005. "Reassuring Weaker Parties after Civil Wars: The Benefits and Costs of Executive Power-Sharing Systems in Africa." *Ethnopolitics* 4, 3: 247–267.

Samuels, Kristi. 2006. "Post-Conflict Peace-Building and Constitution-Making." *Chicago Journal of International Law* 6, 2: 663–683.

Simonsen, Sven Gunnar. 2005. "Addressing Ethnic Divisions in Post-Conflict Institution-Building: Lessons from Recent Cases." *Security Dialogue* 36, 3: 297–318.

Sisk, Timothy D. 1995. *Democratization in South Africa: The Elusive Social Contract*. Princeton, NJ: Princeton University Press.

———. 1996. *Power Sharing and International Mediation in Ethnic Conflicts*. New York: Carnegie Commission on Preventing Deadly Conflict, Carnegie Corporation of New York.

———. 2009. *International Mediation in Civil Wars: Bargaining with Bullets*. London: Routledge.

Sisk, Timothy D., and Christoph Stefes. 2005. "Power Sharing as an Interim Step in Peace Building: Lessons from South Africa." In *Sustainable Peace: Power and Democracy after Civil Wars*, ed. Philip G. Roeder and Donald Rothchild. Ithaca, NY: Cornell University Press.

Stedman, Stephen John, Donald Rothchild, and Elizabeth Cousens (eds.). 2002. *Ending Civil Wars: The Implementation of Peace Agreements*. Boulder, CO: Lynne Rienner.

Suhrke, Astri, and Howard Adelman, eds. 1999. *The Path to Genocide: The Rwandan Crisis from Uganda to Zaire*. New Brunswick, NJ: Transaction.

Taylor, Rupert. 2009. "The Injustice of a Consociational Solution to the Northern Ireland Problem." In *Consociational Theory: McGarry and O'Leary and the Northern Ireland Conflict*, ed. Rupert Taylor. London: Routledge.

Varshney, Ashutosh. 2001. "Ethnic Conflict and Civil Society: India and Beyond." *World Politics* 53, 3: 362–398.

Wallensteen, Peter. 2008. "International Responses to Crises of Democratization in War-Torn Societies." In Jarstad and Sisk 2008.

Walter, Barbara. 1999. "Designing Transitions from Civil War: Demobilization, Democratization, and Commitments to Peace." *International Security* 24, 1: 127–155.

Wilson, Robin. 2009. "From Consociationalism to Interculturalism." In *Consociational Theory: McGarry and O'Leary and the Northern Ireland Conflict*, ed. Rupert Taylor. London: Routledge.

Zahar, Marie-Joëlle. 2005. "Power Sharing in Lebanon: Foreign Protectors, Domestic Peace, and Democratic Failure." In Roeder and Rothchild 2005.

Notes

1. See Roberto Belloni's account of the dysfunctions of Dayton in addressing the longer-term challenges of state-building in Bosnia in Belloni 2007, esp. 42. See also chapter 1 of this volume.
2. For the data and arguments on recurrence, see chapter 1 of this volume. The problem of postagreement violence is explored in Darby 2006; some of the country case studies of post–peace pact violence explored in that book deal with Israel-Palestine, Guatemala, El Salvador, and Northern Ireland. See also Rothchild 2005.
3. For the arguments on institutional inertia, see North 1990.
4. For the data on war termination and negotiated settlement versus other outcomes (e.g., cease-fire without settlement, or military victory), see Mack 2008, 35; Harbom, Högbladh, and Wallensteen 2006.
5. I make this argument in Sisk 2009, 35–37 and 195–199.
6. As chapter 2, by David Lake, in this volume illustrates, this formula of democratization is highly problematic, leading to his and other calls that democratization be deferred until state capacity is strengthened.
7. On power sharing in Lebanon, see Zahar 2005; on Cyprus, Jarstad 2001.
8. I would like to acknowledge the deep debt I owe to Donald Rothchild for his support, mentorship, and camaraderie over the formative years of my career development. Don demonstrated what it means to be a guiding light for those who might later follow in his footsteps.
9. The continued salience of the peace-building agenda is reflected in the May 20, 2008, Security Council debate on the organization's role in postwar recovery and

the emergent outcome that the Secretary General was invited to report back to the Council in one year with a comprehensive set of findings and recommendations.

10. The independence of Kosovo, it appears, is a glaring exception and may well lead to an erosion of the bias against new states as an outcome of war in nondecolonization settings, but whether this case is sui generis or a new trend is still uncertain. Earlier cases that may appear like new states arising from the ashes of war were either the dissolution of empires or federations (as in the Balkans) or the resolution of prior decolonization-era disputes (such as Timor Leste and Eritrea).
11. See Hartzell and Hoddie (2007, 43–145), who argue in favor of power-sharing pacts and suggest that full implementation of the military integration elements of power-sharing agreements is an important element in preventing a returned to armed conflict.
12. On demilitarization prior to democratization, see Lyons 2005.
13. See the US Department of State's (S/CRS, Office of the Coordinator of Reconstruction and Stabilization) "Post-Conflict Reconstruction Essential Task Matrix," 2005, at www.crs.state.gov.
14. For a sampling of criticisms as applied to the Northern Ireland case, see Taylor 2009.
15. Indeed, there is good evidence to the contrary, namely that elites when pressed with political, economic, or social stress may instead foment conflict. For cross-national analysis of elite incentives toward conflict, see Human Rights Watch 1995. For earlier critiques of the elite incentives for mobilization in consociational arrangements, see Horowitz 1985.
16. The protagonists' dilemmas of democratization are these: democratization may be a feasible formula for escaping the war, but it poses new risks of inherent uncertainty about the future. "Losing" in the future is a real possibility: sometimes such losses lead to a return to war, as in Angola in 1992, while at other times (as in Liberia in 2005) victors are magnanimous and avert a return to violence, thereby mitigating the dilemma of uncertainty.
17. There is often reliance on interim governments as a temporary bridge between war-ending pacts and long-term peace. See Guittieri and Piombo 2007.
18. For a further exploration of the critical role of cross-communal political parties, see Reilly 2001, 2006.
19. For an analysis of this case, see Sisk and Stefes 2005.
20. For how such a transition could occur in Northern Ireland, see Wilson 2009. She writes, "It is time to break with the consociational paradigm. . . . I sketch out an emergent 'intercultural' alternative to consociationalism . . . with wider real-world traction to tackle Northern Ireland's deep-seated divisions" (221). She then goes on to specify a set of possible governance arrangements that closely approximates the integrative or centripetal model described in Reilly 2001 in terms of the development of cross-communal coalitions.

PART TWO

Soft Intervention

SIX

Soft Intervention in Africa: US Efforts to Generate Support for Peace

DONALD ROTHCHILD AND NIKOLAS EMMANUEL

> The only options besides coercion are bargaining and persuasion. Persuasion is often limited in its effectiveness. And those forms of persuasion that are effective are not always desirable. That means that some form of bargaining often will be the only effective method available—usually incentives.
>
> —Ruth W. Grant, "Ethics and Incentives: A Political Approach," 38

An incentives approach seeks to manage conflict and maintain peace by means of political bargaining. A third-party actor uses incentives and disincentives to influence the policy decisions of parties or movements, attempting to influence their choices in what the sending actor regards as a positive direction. Such an approach is broader in its implications than a realist focus might suggest. Scholars in the realist tradition of international relations, concentrating largely on the material capabilities of states and their power relationships, tend to be more concerned with the tangible dimensions of hard power (military intervention) than with the means of soft intervention (pressures and incentives) to change the behavior of target states and movements. Treating states and ethnic groups as unitary actors, realists downplay the fluidity and heterogeneity of these entities. This tendency often obscures possibilities for learning, change, and new alliance partners, as civil associations and ethnic factions respond to innovative ideas from external and internal sources. Power is much more complex than military muscle alone, for its relevance depends very much on the context in which it is employed.

In this chapter, we seek to shift the traditional perception of power rela-

Nik Emmanuel thanks the late Don Rothchild for his unending enthusiasm and support.

tions in order to look at the ways great powers make use of incentives to encourage negotiation, ethnic reconciliation, and continued cooperation after the achievement of peace. The thrust of the analysis is how an external actor, primarily the United States, can use incentives and disincentives, broadly conceived, to promote change of behavior on the ground in an effort to facilitate the process of negotiating and implementing peace agreements, thereby reducing the possibility of continued intense internal conflict.

In international relations, pressures and incentives are a form of intervention whereby a sending country intrudes for constructive or destructive reasons into the internal affairs of a receiving country. The relationship is potentially risky, yet at times it may be justified when the intervening party meets the following conditions on when and whether to intercede and how to employ force. First, when invoking coercive incentive strategies, the intervening party should seek to promote legitimate purposes—those that encourage peaceful relations and the protection of vulnerable peoples. Second, the intervention, as far as practicable, should be internationally sanctioned and monitored. Unilateral action, particularly by neighboring states, risks the possibility of favoritism for coethnics and of self-aggrandizement. Hence, international-organization approval and oversight becomes a necessary means in certain circumstances to assure that the cause of intervention remains a just one. Third, the action should be multinational whenever feasible, thus facilitating international approval and oversight. Multilateral intervention may not be practical in all cases, but when it is possible, it avoids inevitable charges of favoritism between the adversaries. Fourth, international interveners should strive to react to the provocations of state or subnational actors in a proportional manner (ICISS 2001, 37). At times, interveners have made politically astute calculations to respond disproportionately to a violation of international norms, usually in an effort to deter further infringements. Although such a calculation may be logical, it is not necessarily justifiable. Fifth, interventions should be justified in terms of the expectations of interveners that they will achieve their objectives in a reasonable period of time. Sensible doubts arise, as in the intervention by the Economic Community of West African States Cease-Fire Monitoring Group forces in Liberia in the 1990s, when the costs in human life appear to approximate or exceed the number of lives saved. To promote benevolent outcomes, it is essential that these conditions serve as the general standards for appropriate action.

We focus on soft intervention generally and incentive strategies in particular, in an effort to link ideals related to facilitating an end to civil wars and continuing peace after conflict, as well as protecting vulnerable peoples, on the one hand, with the pragmatism of a strategy that is risk- and cost-effective, on the other hand. Neither avoidance nor military intervention can be viewed as justified in most cases. Rather, a diplomatic approach seems a logical alternative, and it holds out the possibility of greater leverage than is often recognized. But such leverage must meet the tests of timing, legitimacy, and appropriateness. We consider in subsequent sections when and what type of incentive should be used at the lowest cost to the intervener, keeping in mind a consideration for the uniqueness of the conflict. Our hope is that this overall focus will provide us with a framework in which to think about what we can anticipate from an incentives approach to managing intrastate conflicts and maintaining stable post–civil war situations.

Linking Mediation to Incentive Strategies

An active third-party diplomatic effort is often an essential aspect of ending civil wars and ensuring the continued protection of vulnerable peoples after the termination of conflict. Such diplomacy involves various strategic choices, including negotiation, conciliation, mediation, displacement, partition, protection, redistribution, reconstruction, and transformation. The selection of which strategy to apply in a particular case is dependent upon a third party's capacity, willingness to engage, and assessment of what will prove effective in advancing the objectives of peace and reconciliation at various stages of the conflict cycle. The choice is based on a statesman's perception of his or her country's interests and the ability of a strategic approach to achieve its desired purposes at a reasonable cost (Zartman 1995, 7).

An important option is mediation, which entails the intervention of an external third party or parties in the internal affairs of sovereign states. By intervening during and after conflict, the mediator exerts various levels of influence on state and substate (ethnoregional, religious, or other) elites in an attempt to get them to move toward a more cooperative relationship. Incentives represent a resource in the hands of mediators that increases their ability to influence the behavior of local actors in a desired direction. By interceding, the mediator invariably transforms the bargaining encounter from a dyadic to a triadic one, persuading or inducing the parties to alter their attitudes on the issues at hand.

A mediator's influence comes from her or his ability to facilitate an outcome that is minimally acceptable to both parties or that threatens a worse outcome by allying the third party with one of the local rivals. Diplomats have used their influence to perform various roles at one time or another. In a large number of African conflicts, such as those in Mozambique,

Burundi, and the Democratic Republic of Congo, third parties have used a variety of noncoercive means to keep open the channels of communication and provide information on the intentions of rival parties. At the next level, as in the Ethiopian-Eritrean War of 1998–2000 and Sudan and Liberia in 2003, mediators have been more proactive, persuading and criticizing, giving advice, encouraging the parties to reconsider their options, formulating proposals, and persuading them to stick to such agreements once peace has been achieved. Finally, as seen in the Angolan-Namibian negotiations, high-level public officials have intervened energetically and influenced the strategies of local actors through direct mediation and the manipulation of various pressures and incentives (Cortright 1997; Rothchild 1997; Haass and O'Sullivan 2000).

Mediation requires the calibration of the necessary means for assuring equitable outcomes among group interests or determining policies that will allay the fears of weaker parties. It may also involve facilitating effective governance, something that calls for considerable skill and judgment and extensive knowledge of local cultures. Effective great-power mediation of intrastate conflicts encounters resistance as well as domestic constraints of commitment and political will (Pruitt 2004, 78). It is a difficult task, and the possibility of failure and a return to civil war, as in Angola and Liberia in the 1990s, can never be discounted. This uncertainty can at times discourage potential mediators from taking on a diplomatic initiative, for it affects future ties between the mediator and the local parties—and even the reputation of the mediator himself or herself.

Ultimately, what pushes a great power such as the United States to intervene during conflicts and to stay on the scene to assist in the maintenance of peace, whether in a hard or a soft manner, is a perception that its own interests are at stake. In this respect, the encouragement of local actors to commit to a lasting stable peace is in line with broader US status quo objectives (Morgenthau 1960, 39).

Diplomacy and the Use of Incentive Strategies

Incentives wielded by a great power, alone or in combination with other countries or international organizations, demonstrate the determination of the intervener to promote change and to help sustain it once achieved. Incentives are a type of intervention, often but not always soft, that involve a trade-off between interference and the advancement of peace and protection (Nye 2002, 8). What intervening powers seek to do is to reduce uncertainty over the process leading to a peaceful resolution of conflict, helping to provide credibility for the negotiations to follow (Zartman 2001, 300). The effect, it is hoped, is to ease uncertainty about their future intergroup relations (North 1990).

Soft intervention consists of structural arrangements or distributive or symbolic rewards (incentives) or punishments (disincentives) used by third parties to encourage a target state or movement to shift its priorities in a desired direction and maintain them (Rothchild 1997, 19). Whether they are noncoercive or coercive, incentives attempt "to raise the opportunity cost of continuing on the previous course of action by changing the calculation of costs and benefits" (Cortright 1997, 273). If they are credible and sufficient to deal with the dispute at hand, they can help prevent the escalation of conflict and assist in keeping it abated once hostilities have ended. They make adversaries aware of the benefits of a negotiated outcome, while alerting them to the increasing costs of bargaining failure and to the possibility of a return to war. In real-world contexts, third parties sometimes apply packages of noncoercive and coercive incentives and disincentives, with coercive incentives becoming increasingly dominant as the costs of altering preferences and the intensity of conflict rises. Somewhat paradoxically, noncoercive incentives, when combined with a credible threat, are most likely to result in a durable peace, because rewards are viewed positively and they are less likely to cause resentment. Nevertheless, there may be no alternative at times to aid cutoffs, exclusion from international organizations, sanctions, or a threat or use of military force to deal with an immediate crisis. If coercive measures are applied, it is important to follow them up with "postconflict peacebuilding" incentives and activities (including generous programs of development aid and political reforms) in order to prevent a recurring cycle of conflict (Cousens 2001, 2). Incentives can involve rewards (purchase, security, recognition, development assistance) as well as disincentives or negative inducements—punishment, threats, or coercion. However, all in all, as Sudan's North-South negotiations or Liberia and Ethiopia and Eritrea show, the combination of positive and negative incentives has produced significant agreements leading to a peaceful outcome; the absence of such a combination, as in Darfur, can sometimes prove counterproductive.

Noncoercive Incentive Strategies

Third parties or internal actors, or both, can use three main types of *noncoercive incentives*—purchase, insurance, and legitimation—to facilitate the negotiation, implementation, and maintenance of peace agreements, while protecting the vulnerable (Rothchild 2009, 37–42). There are important differences between these incentive types: purchase and insurance are perceived in terms of benefits for the target as a whole or some of its constituent parts, while legitimation is perceived in terms of the credibility of the negotiating process and the eventual role of the third party (or third parties) in the postconflict phase. In addition, the list of noncoercive incentives could be expanded in certain cases: thus, even though diplomatic incentives have an important noncoercive dimension, we include them in the coercive category because of the extent of the pressures that are brought to bear on the target country or movement.

Purchase

During and after deeply conflictual encounters, purchase represents a relatively low-cost but sometimes quite effective means of facilitating cooperation both to help end hostilities and to maintain peace in the transition period immediately following the termination of the conflict. Third parties use purchase to reward actors, usually individuals but also groups, with personally targeted short-term fiscal or tangible rewards for acting positively to end conflict and to keep it from returning. By offering side-payments, the third party enlarges the pie in an effort to facilitate the possibility of reconciliation and peace after the conflict. It alters the payoff structure to transform a dispute from a constant-sum to a positive-sum game, thus enhancing the possibility of a compromise (Rubin 1981, 27; Touval 1982, 327). Third parties, particularly great powers that control substantial resources, have made extensive use of economic incentives during peace negotiations and after them once an agreement has been reached. Purchase is widely used, and despite its relatively low cost (in gaining RENAMO's agreement to a cease-fire in Mozambique, foreign donors contributed only $19 million in order to transform the insurgent organization into a political party), it can contribute significantly to furthering conflict management objectives (Rothchild 1997, 257). By themselves, such incentives are not likely to overcome the credible-commitment problem in intense conflict situations, but even here, their contribution is not to be dismissed lightly (Lake and Rothchild 1998, 13–17). Such efforts to extend side-payments, while most frequently deployed to persuade specific members of the various warring factions to commit to a peace agreement during negotiations, can also be envisioned as a tool to facilitate the implementation process. In this way, reluctant actors may be convinced by a purchase approach that they should maintain commitment to a peace process once it is already under way.

Insurance

External third parties or the state can attempt to transform an intrastate dispute by promising, during the negotiations or the transition period that follows, to provide cultural protections for minorities and for the participation of weaker parties in the political institutions of governance once the peace agreement is implemented. By making an effort to understand and empathize with the profound insecurities of vulnerable peoples about the survival of their culture or the protection of their persons and property during and after civil wars, actors offering such promises of political inclusion may go far in allaying these minority fears. Constitutional and legal protections have been written about frequently, and where they exist, as in Nigeria after the Biafran war, they provide a broad assurance for vulnerable minority peoples.

However, another potentially important incentive encouraging elites and leaders to negotiate on peace or on their safe exit from the zone of fighting is the offer of amnesty. In both Liberia in 2003 and northern Uganda more recently, amnesty incentives contributed significantly to promoting negotiations on ending the warfare and encouraging lasting peace. However, a problem exists as to the credibility of these amnesty incentives. The troublesome cases of Charles Taylor and Joseph Kony clearly illustrate this point. Amnesty incentives were important, but in light of the risks they entailed, their utility proved limited.

The problem of ensuring the representation of minority interests in the new institutions of state received considerable attention in Sudan's North-South and Darfur deliberations. Early on, former US senator John C. Danforth, President George W. Bush's special envoy for peace in Sudan, noted that any peace negotiations must explore ways of "*guaranteeing* religious freedom" if South Sudan people are to have confidence in the peace accord (Danforth 2002, 28). In the end, Sudan's 2005 Comprehensive Peace Agreement provided for a variety of institutional protections for non-Muslim interests, including the right of the South to self-determination, a referendum in the South on independence by the end of the sixth year, assurance that Sharia Law would not be implemented in the South during the transition, coexistence of the Sudanese Armed Forces and the Sudan People's Liberation Army during the transition period, international monitoring of the cease-fire, formulas for wealth and power sharing, and specified representation of the South on the committee to draft the interim constitution and in the National Assembly.

Encouraging as such promised guarantees are for minority security and well-being, there are nonetheless limits to their efficacy, for the majority party cannot credibly commit future leaders not to exploit smaller parties at a later date (Fearon 1998, 108). Moreover, third parties, under pressure from their domestic constituents to reduce overseas involvements, find it difficult in practice to honor fully the "guarantees" they give to uphold the agreement.

Incentives are sometimes difficult to arrive at through bargaining, because majorities are intent on centralized rule and minorities are determined to secure rigid constitutional constraints on this rule; even so, in some cases local bargaining parties can agree on incentives on their own (e.g., in Nigeria in 1979) or through mediation and bargaining after civil war (e.g., in Bosnia). In the best of circumstances, as in the Sudan, third parties and state leaders can reassure minority groups through promises of support for regular elections, political autonomy, inclusion of weaker interests on a proportional basis in the civil service and central government, the rule of law, judicial impartiality, rules on the proportional distribution of revenues, and protection of linguistic, religious, and ethnic rights.

Legitimation

Third parties can use legitimacy incentives to induce a target government or movement to cooperate in containing intense conflict and maintaining peace once it has been achieved. States and international organizations, in passing judgment on the validity or legitimacy of governments, can affect the reputation of ruling elites and their ability to enter into and to maintain beneficial relations with members of the international community. When used assertively to influence the behavior of local actors, as with apartheid South Africa on the Namibian question, legitimacy incentives can help to influence elite positions. However, when used weakly, without setting political conditions on acceptable standards of behavior toward new minorities in the successor states, as with the German recognition of Slovenia and Croatia, recognition can throw away the only influence that the international community can bring to bear on subsequent behavior.

US negotiators recognize the powerful attractiveness of legitimacy incentives in their call to governments to sign on to and abide by peace agreements. These incentives were a resource in the hands of US diplomats in the 1980s and 1990s as they sought to overcome South African resistance to Namibia's independence, and they were also a resource for the United States in attempting to extract concessions from the government in the bargaining over Sudan's Comprehensive Peace Agreement in 2005.

Coercive Incentive Strategies

Beyond these noncoercive incentives, it is important to note three partially or fully coercive incentives that third parties can employ to attempt to alter behavior in a desired direction. Despite their coercive features, we treat them as incentives for cooperation since external actors use coercive measures to change the calculations of costs and benefits of local parties and encourage them to alter policies accordingly and to maintain them. This inclusion of coercive incentives among the corpus of incentive strategies is different from the narrower approach adopted by some scholars, but it seems justified in terms of the purposes of the sending actor or actors.

Both noncoercive and coercive incentives are important instruments of leverage and are often used together, reinforcing one another. By acting in such a manner, the mediator creates pressures by placing conditions on political and economic relations to overcome stalemates and to sustain positive interactions. The mediator can also use her or his diplomatic prowess to threaten sanctions and the ending of relations, to cut off economic and military aid, or to offer positive inducements (Shattuck, Simo, and Durch 2003, 3). The mediator employs the resources at his or her disposal to enlarge private opportunity or state capacity and in this way make a shift toward peace, as well as the maintenance of peace once it has been achieved, more acceptable to a rival or rivals. In doing so, the third-party actor increases the value of certain alternatives in an effort to make them more politically acceptable to leaders who otherwise face a situation of limited choice.

Diplomatic Pressures and Incentives

Diplomacy, which incorporates both pressures and incentives, embraces a variety of policy approaches: political, economic, strategic, and military. Diplomats can raise awareness on all sides regarding the future costs of escalating conflict and of the reemergence of civil war once peace has been achieved. They may seek to alter the adversaries' perceptions and calculations and persuade them to make mutual accommodations in the present in order to avoid a costly conflict at a later date after peace has been achieved.

In order for a mediator to be in a position to exert pressure, provide incentives, or offer desirable alternatives, it is essential that he or she establish sufficient leverage (or influence) over the parties. When a mediator acts as a communicator or formulator, extensive leverage is not necessarily required for the intervention to be effective. During the negotiations leading up to the Oslo Accords, for example, the mediator helped to shape an agreement based on what I. William Zartman calls a "mutually enticing opportunity" (Zartman 1997, 197). It is when a conflict is intense and strong and third-party influence is needed that a mediator requires the capacity to raise the costs of proceeding on a given course of action (Cortright 1997, 273).

In the period between 2002 and 2004, the United States had leverage with both parties in the Sudanese negotiations, enabling it to play a constructive role in influencing the priorities of these rivals. The International Crisis Group deemed "sustained US pressure on the parties" to be "the single most important factor needed" in the Sudanese negotiations in August 2003 (International Crisis Group 2003, 1). In its relations with the Sudanese government, the United States held out the prospect of benefits in terms of trade and aid opportunities, while at the same time signaling that it had no intention of bombing Sudanese targets again or acting harmfully toward Sudan in the United Nations. In its relations with the Sudan People's Liberation Movement/Army (SPLM/A), which had close ties with members of the US Congress, the leverage of the United States came essentially from the damage that a lack of cooperation on the peace process would entail for the SPLM/A's reputation (i.e., the SPLM/A could not afford to be seen as opposed to negotiations on peace).[1]

The prospect of inclusion in or exclusion from an international organization is an additional diplomatic tool that may be wielded during both negotiations and the peace implementation phase. Weak states, and particularly those that have gained their sovereign independence only recently, crave recognition and acceptance in a world of states. The denial of this recognition or of acceptance by an international organization is a blow to the legitimacy of such states and may induce their cooperation to ward off an impending threat. In Africa, third parties made maximum use of leverage to isolate both the Ethiopian and the Eritrean governments during the 1998–2000 war, to some success. John Prendergast comments that "both governments, like most, wanted full integration in the global community, and wanted to participate in global decisions and issues; but Ethiopia and Eritrea were pigeonholed by the UN Security Council and most key governments as countries in conflict, which greatly limited their ability to participate normally in global affairs for the entire time of the conflict" (Prendergast 2001, 7).

In 2002, US diplomats threatened aid cutoffs to ensure that Uganda and Rwanda did not stoke the fires in the Democratic Republic of Congo. John Shattuck, Paul Simo, and William J. Durch comment, "Recent experiences show that when targeted conditionality is applied, Rwanda and Uganda are amenable to pressure." They continue: "A clear link has been drawn between Rwanda's agreeing to withdraw its troops from Congo and a US abstention from a vote at the IMF on an aid package to Rwanda in 2002." Reportedly, when Ugandan officials encountered similar threats, they also adopted a cooperative stance regarding the reduction of tensions in the Democratic Republic of Congo after negotiations had begun (Shattuck, Simo, and Durch 2003, 27). But cooperation does not follow automatically. The threat of an aid cutoff can lead to unintended consequences, as US leverage on a target state is reduced (for example, in Daniel arap Moi's Kenya) and the targeted actor is left free to pursue his repressive actions (Brown 2003, 84–85).

Sanctions

Others have dealt elsewhere with the role that economic, political, and strategic sanctions play in punishing those perceived as violating the norms of the international community. Here we concentrate on the value of such measures in inducing a targeted actor to change its behavior in a desired direction. If one views the impact of sanctions broadly, and includes the psychological and symbolic effects they have on the political environment in which bargaining takes place, it is clear they have the potential to reach beyond punishment and foster support for peace.[2]

The dual function of sanctions in punishing defections and providing incentives for more constructive behavior is exemplified by the role of incentives built into the US Comprehensive Anti-Apartheid Act of 1986. The act made manifest at its outset the link between US sanctions and a change of policies on apartheid in South Africa. US policies were "designed to bring about reforms in that system of government that will lead to the establishment of a nonracial democracy." The US government proposed working toward that goal by encouraging South African authorities to repeal the state of emergency, release Nelson Mandela and other political prisoners, permit members of all races to form political parties and to participate in the political process, establish a timetable to eliminate the apartheid laws, and negotiate with the representatives of all racial groups over the country's future political system. The act left open-ended the phases that would follow, stating that "the United States will adjust its actions toward the Government of South Africa to reflect the progress or lack of progress made by the Government of South Africa in meeting the goal set forth in [Section 101]."[3] Thus, the act made conscious use of various incentives and disincentives to advance both the rights of vulnerable people and the negotiating process.

The same was true in other high-profile US- and UN-sponsored interventions in Africa as well. The United Nations, seeking to prevent a widening war in Sierra Leone, imposed sanctions in 2001 affecting travel and the sale of conflict diamonds on the regime of President Charles Taylor in Liberia, which was providing support to the Revolutionary United Front (RUF) insurgents in neighboring Sierra Leone (Hirsch 2001, 25–28). Had Taylor remained in power for an extended period, his failure to take effective action against smuggling might well have led to further efforts to tighten these sanctions. Sanctions were also put into effect on the movement of money and timber exports and on suppliers doing business with the RUF in Sierra Leone. Such sanctions had an important symbolic dimension, signaling to the target movement the international community's displeasure with its brutal practices and threatening to take action to induce a change of conduct. In Zimbabwe, the United States put sanctions into effect against the ruling elite in February 2002, placing a ban on their travel in an effort to protest an election campaign that was marked, according to the Bush administration, by political violence and intimidation. On October 7, 2002, the US House of Representatives passed a resolution threatening sanctions unless the Sudanese government negotiated with the South in good faith. These actions indicate a cautiously positive view in US official circles of using sanctions to protect human rights and advance negotiations on the ending of civil wars.

But clearly the threat or imposition of sanctions must be credible if target states or movements are to take them seriously. International sanctions are likely to prove most meaningful when the demands for change are limited in scope and the sanctions are put in place by a strong state or coalition of states. Powerful states, as Saadia Touval notes, are in an advantageous position "to exert influence to persuade the disputants to change their stance and agree to terms they are reluctant to accept" (Touval 2002, 173). Their leverage gives them the ability to persuade the adversaries to adopt more cooperative positions on the issues that divide them. As a consequence, the United States was able to use the enormous global influence at its disposal to influence the preferences of negotiators in Angola, Liberia, and Sudan, but the weaker state of Norway proved much less capable of influencing Sri Lankan peace talks.

Moreover, in the African context, sanctions seem most likely to gain credibility and to alter the behavior of target governments when the state is closely linked to the global economy. Thus, the 1986 Comprehensive Anti-Apartheid Act, which had considerable support in principle from the international community, did raise economic and political costs on the status quo in relatively industrialized South Africa and appears to have contributed to the government's reevaluation of its priorities (Rothchild and Ravenhill 1992, 399). This experience was directly contrary to the warnings of Central Intelligence Agency director Richard M. Helms, who argued that South Africa, because of its reliance on gold production, was "one of the least vulnerable countries in the world to economic sanctions" (National Security Council 1966, 1053). Such predictions proved widely off the mark, failing to take account of possible restrictions on the importation of Krugerrands and other export products. As a basis for policy, such predictions contributed to US inaction at a critical juncture in history.

In addition to the actual use of sanctions, a credible third party, particularly a strong one such as the United States, can attempt to influence the priorities of the adversaries by threatening sanctions against a target state. In April 2004, the US State Department expressed frustration over the slow progress in the Sudanese North-South peace talks and warned of possible US sanctions under the 2002 Sudan Peace Act if the parties failed to reach an agreement soon (Gollust 2004). But the threat, while powerful, had limited impact. Sanctions have not proved to be relevant instruments against many authoritarian regimes or against weak states that have considerable autonomy from international influences. They can be difficult to apply where there is a lack of consensus on the part of the interveners. Sanctions, then, require careful application if they are to provide an incentive for sustainable change.

Military Enforcement

When noncoercive and minimally coercive incentives do not prove sufficient to prevent conflict from emerging or escalating, third parties may have little option but to raise the costs by making threats or using military means. In these circumstances, third parties intervene with military might to enforce the peace and protect the vulnerable. Provided the third parties' troops are sufficient in number to achieve their purposes and are well trained and armed, such military actions or the threat of military actions may be indispensable in strengthening a political initiative (Craig and George 1995, 258; Jentleson 2002, 274). When the United States refused to threaten or use force in a highly menacing situation such as Rwanda, the consequences proved disastrous. The main US representative to Rwanda at the time of the 1994 genocide, Deputy Assistant Secretary of State for African Affairs Prudence Bushnell, did contact Colonel Théoneste Bagasora and other high officials about stopping the genocide and holding people accountable for violations of international law. However, her efforts had little or no effect.[4] With the United States unprepared to commit its troops to halt the violence and pushing to withdraw UN troops on the scene, Bushnell's appeals lacked the quality of a credible deterrent needed in this situation. By contrast, the British used force effectively to protect a UN peacekeeping operation in Sierra Leone in 2000. Force may be a last resort, yet its threat or use may at times prove indispensable to further legitimate diplomatic objectives.

In buttressing peace agreements, military enforcement measures can play an important role in overcoming the credible-commitment and information problems that complicate the process of consolidating peace agreements (Lake and Rothchild 1998). By sharing knowledge about the intentions of rival actors and by monitoring the actions of adversaries to maintain the terms of a cease-fire and to disarm and demobilize their troops, a third party's use of military enforcement measures encourages the acceptance of new rules during the difficult transition period and imposes costs on any element who might attempt to break the terms of the bargain. The importance of involving a third party in the peace implementation process is underlined by Barbara Walter, who finds that the parties to an agreement are 20 percent more likely to follow through on the arrangement if a third party acts as a protector of the agreement (2002, 83). Thus, third parties are likely to play a critically important role in overcoming the uncertainties surrounding the political consolidation process, providing much-needed support to the state and raising costs for potential challengers (Hartzell, Hoddie, and Rothchild 2001, 203).

Military force can prove indispensable in protecting vulnerable peoples from illegitimate state and opposition leaders who attempt to seize, or succeed in seizing, state power. In principle, it can enforce a cold peace and provide the basis for "coercive diplomacy," enabling external diplomats to intercede and use their influence to "induce the opponent to revise his calculations and agree to a mutually acceptable termination of the conflict" (George 1971, 18). Hence, military enforcement can be coextensive with diplomatic pressures and incentives. When, in the Congo, the Adoula-Tshombe talks of 1962 and diplomatic and economic pressures failed to achieve a change of preferences regarding the reintegration of Katanga into the country, international actors used force to persuade Katangese leader Moise Tshombe to back down from his claim to sovereignty. The UN intervention threatened to bring increasing force to bear over time, and it succeeded, after several sharp clashes, in altering the target leader's preferences for a separatist course. US officials strongly backed the Congolese government during the Adoula-Tshombe negotiations, and the United

States exerted both political and economic pressures on Tshombe to act in a reconciliatory manner, including efforts to get the large mining company Union Minière du Haut Katanga to withhold income from Katanga.[5] US diplomats recommended various constitutional measures that would consolidate central control and specifically offered what they termed "inducements," such as an offer to assist in reequipping the armed forces as soon as an agreement was reached with Katanga.[6] With so much at stake, it is not surprising that diplomatic incentives were not sufficient to bring about Katanga's reintegration and that the critical factor in impelling change became the UN military initiative. In such circumstances military force may be viewed as "essential to rescue a challenged peace" (Doyle 2001, 546).

Military enforcement also provided US diplomats with a fleeting opportunity to use incentives to promote Somalia's reconciliation. Given the brutal circumstances that gripped Somalia in 1992, President George Bush decided on a humanitarian military intervention, with UN endorsement, to ensure a stable and safe environment for the delivery of relief supplies to the starving people of the country. US policymakers sought to provide an overwhelming military presence to ensure cooperation among Somali factional leaders on the ground. They therefore dispatched a twenty-five-thousand-person US military force to the country in December 1992 (Copson and Dagne 1993, 1). Operation Restore Hope had limited objectives, such as to enable the relief agencies and local authorities to distribute food and supplies, reopen the schools, reactivate the hospitals, and undertake economic rehabilitation. US authorities resisted appeals from the UN secretary-general to undertake the risky assignment of disarming the rival militias. Walter Clarke, the former deputy chief of mission at the US embassy in Mogadishu, Somalia, stressed that "to appreciate the special shape of the US intervention in Somalia, one must realize the extent to which the Somalia humanitarian enterprise was developed as a purely military operation" (1997, 9).

However, under circumstances in which a state has failed, it has proved nearly impossible to divorce a military undertaking from an effort to rebuild the state. This was the case in Somalia. The risks and cost of using military enforcement to rebuild the Somali state through a limited diplomatic initiative seemed lower than letting the opportunity go by default. Hence, US officials used the military-enforced peace to broach incentives that offered economic aid to rehabilitate the country in exchange for constitutional provisions furthering reconciliatory behavior. During a conference in 2000, US ambassador Robert B. Oakley commented on a December 1992 meeting during which he brought together Ali Mahdi and Aideed for the first time; he spoke about US pressure in Somalia to agree to a seven-point communiqué leading to a cease-fire in Mogadishu "and several other things that we, with a combination of persuasion and pressure, were actually able to get them to do in about 10 days" (Oakley 2000). On January 17, 1993, it was reported that Oakley met with factional leader Ali Mahdi at the US embassy, where they discussed negotiations on an agreement among warlords. At this meeting, Oakley, referring to the country's rehabilitation after civil war, offered support, saying that the United States would help Somalia stand on its feet (FBIS 1993c). Subsequently, Ali Mahdi urged the United States to play a more active role in the constitutional conference to ensure its success, and five days later, Ali Mahdi hosted a luncheon for Oakley where they discussed bilateral relations (FBIS 1993a). Oakley promised that during and after his stay in Somalia he would get actively involved in the rehabilitation effort (FBIS 1993b). The links here between promises of economic support and agreement on constitutional accommodation (i.e., insurance) and reconciliation are all too apparent.

Military force, then, creates some scope for coercive diplomacy, but only when favorable circumstances prevail and the threat is a credible one. It is often very hard for interveners to mobilize overwhelming force, raising doubts about the credibility of their threats. Wars appear to be changing in the twenty-first century, as militias replace armies and mix modern technology with guerrilla tactics to impose substantial costs on conventional armies (Hoffman 2006). In such situations, the notion of victory may be losing some of its meaning, because irregular forces will avoid surrender and melt into their communities until another opportunity presents itself. Moreover, external military force may prove counterproductive, bringing about a nationalist rally-round-the-flag effect where none existed previously. However, if the right conditions are present and a relatively benign third party uses its military capabilities to protect a peace agreement or to preserve the safety of vulnerable peoples, then military enforcement can play a constructive role and can provide pressures and incentives for intrastate political exchange (Jentleson and Whytock 2005–6, 52). But doing so inevitably involves a delicate task of facilitation. Should the third party be perceived as imposing the terms of agreement or favoring one of the parties, then the agreement is not likely to prove durable for the long term and may have to be renegotiated, possibly under less favorable circumstances.

The record described above shows a broad use of strategic incentives by US policymakers and others to facilitate negotiations on ending civil wars and to maintain peaceful relations after conflict, while achieving the objective of protecting vulnerable peoples. Drawing from experiences in Liberia, Sudan, South Africa, Somalia, Angola, Ethiopia and Eritrea, and elsewhere, we provide data indicating that while the United States has leverage in intrastate conflicts, it does not always make full use of it. This leverage is primarily diplomatic, not military, and it provides an advantageous basis for US soft intervention, especially when strategies of withdrawal and muscular intervention are inappropriate. The utility of a soft intervention strategy lies in its ability to enable US decision makers to exert a limited influence on political elites at a cost acceptable to American and world public opinion. These elites, as well as scholars, the general public, and policymakers generally prefer noncoercive to coercive incentives, because the sting of external imposition is less apparent and because the resulting bargain has a voluntary quality about it (Rothchild and Emmanuel, 2006). Whereas noncoercive incentives are less costly to apply and more likely to attract support from local citizens who seek acceptance from the international community, their coercive counterparts are more likely to produce stiff resistance, even a rally-round-the-flag effect (Nincic 2005). The problem is that noncoercive incentives may not raise the costs of noncompliance sufficiently. Hence, as the previous discussions of economic sanctions and military enforcement suggest, it is necessary at times to link diplomacy with the threat or use of force to achieve negotiating breakthroughs and to help sustain peace into the postwar period once it has been achieved.

But how might issues of legitimacy and appropriateness raise possible questions about the efficacy of an incentives strategy? Certainly, a great-power intervener can only be justified in intervening during and after an intrastate conflict if the third party meets the standards set out above on right intent, international sanctioning and monitoring, multinational action, proportionality, and the expectation of achieving the favored outcome (ICISS 2001, 32). To be effective in achieving their objectives, incentives have to be calibrated with the intensity of conflict in each context. In meeting the standard of legitimacy, we regard right intent to be the critical justification for external intervention, although other standards—such as international sanctioning, multinational action, and proportionality—can increase the likelihood that an intervener's right intent will gain international approval. Yet a caution here seems appropriate: even in the best of circumstances, foreign elites and publics may interpret incentives wielded by a great power to be bullying tactics, imposing liberal values in nonliberal contexts. The populations of states experiencing intrastate conflict do not always view the United States and its "benevolent hegemony" as being moral in its intentions (Fukuyama 2006, 66). Consequently, unless the use of incentives is justified by local support, the effect can be to build sympathy toward the target. Thus, despite the suspension of Robert Mugabe's government from full membership in the commonwealth in 2002 in an effort to push him toward more liberal policies, it is notable that some eleven months later, various African leaders, including the presidents of Nigeria and South Africa, urged its full reinstatement.

Some of the cases discussed above illustrate the presence of right intent on the part of US diplomats regarding the facilitation of peace processes and the protection of vulnerable peoples. Certainly, US policymakers have interests of their own, such as promoting regional stability, gaining access to valuable resources, and increasing bilateral trade and investment. Even so, these interests did not prevent them from acting at times in a progressive way. For example, in pressuring South African authorities to end apartheid practices and to negotiate with the African National Congress, in pushing negotiations in Sudan, and in providing incentives for regime change in Liberia (with strong local support), US diplomats were acting true to the guiding standards noted above. But the US involvement is not always so purposeful or well thought out. In the Democratic Republic of Congo, Angola, and Somalia, US incentives and pressures were in evidence, but the results envisaged—a frail power-sharing arrangement that valued the inclusion of potential spoilers or dissidents over a sustainable peace—raise questions about the soundness of the intentions at play (Rothchild 2005). Nevertheless, looking at the matter broadly, one can conclude that in cases where internal state pressures do not prove sufficient, an external intervener with the right motivations can seize the momentary opportunity and make a critical difference in a conflict situation through the use of diplomatic influences. As the positive cases examined here suggest, it seems important not to underestimate the benefits of appropriate intervention (Ferguson 2006, 71).

References

Bienen, Henry. 1995. "Ethnic Nationalisms and Implications for US Foreign Policy." In *Nationalism and Nationalities in the New Europe*, ed. Charles A. Kupchan. Ithaca, NY: Cornell University Press.

Brown, Stephen. 2003. "Quiet Diplomacy and Recurring 'Ethnic Clashes' in Kenya." In *From Promise to Practice: Strengthening UN Capacities for the Prevention of Violent Conflict*, ed. Chandra Lekha Sriram and Karin Wermester. Boulder, CO: Lynne Rienner.

Clarke, Walter. 1997. "Failed Visions and Uncertain Mandates in Somalia." In *Learning from Somalia: The Lessons of Armed Humanitarian Intervention*, ed. Walter Clarke and Jeffrey Herbst. Boulder, CO: Westview Press.

Copson, Raymond W., and Theodros S. Dagne. 1993. *Somalia: Operation Restore Hope*. Washington, DC: Congressional Research Service.

Cortright, David. 1997. "Incentives Strategies for Preventing Conflict." In *The Price of Peace: Incentives and International Conflict Prevention*, ed. David Cortright. Lanham, MD: Rowman and Littlefield.

Cousens, Elizabeth M. 2001. Introduction to *Peacebuilding as Politics: Cultivating Peace in Fragile Societies*, ed. Elizabeth M. Cousens and Chetan Kumar, with Karin Wermester. Boulder, CO: Lynne Rienner.

Craig, Gordon A., and Alexander L. George. 1995. *Force and Statecraft: Diplomatic Problems of Our Time*. 3rd ed. New York: Oxford University Press.

Danforth, John C. 2002. *Report to the President of the United States on the Outlook for Peace in Sudan*. April 26. Available at www.state.gov/p/af/ris/rpt/10150.htm. Retrieved May 15, 2006.

Doyle, Michael W. 2001. "War Making and Peace Making: The United Nations' Post–Cold War Record." In *Turbulent Peace: The Challenges of Managing International Conflict*, ed. Chester A. Crocker, Fen Osler Hampson, and Pamela Aall. Washington, DC: US Institute of Peace Press.

Fearon, James D. 1998. "Commitment Problems and the Spread of Ethnic Conflict." In Lake and Rothchild 1998.

Ferguson, Niall. 2006. "The Next War of the World." *Foreign Affairs* 85, 5: 61–74.

Foreign Broadcast Information Service (FBIS). 1993a. "Ali Mahdi Previews Reconciliation Conference." *Daily Report, Sub-Saharan Africa*, February 17.

———. 1993b. "Ali Mahdi, Ambassador Oakley on Operation Restore Hope." *Daily Report, Sub-Saharan Africa*, February 22.

———. 1993c. "President, US Envoy Discuss Peace Plans, Conference." *Daily Report, Sub-Saharan Africa*, January 21.

Fukuyama, Francis. 2006. "After Neoconservatism." *New York Times Magazine*, February 19, 62–67.

George, Alexander L. 1971. "The Development of Doctrine and Strategy." In *The Limits of Coercive Diplomacy*, ed. Alexander L. George, David K. Hall, and William R. Simons. Boston, MA: Little, Brown.

Gollust, David. 2004. "US Expresses Frustration over Impasse on Sudan Peace Talks." *VOA News*, April 12.

Grant, Ruth W. 2006. "Ethics and Incentives: A Political Approach." *American Political Science Review* 100, 1: 29–39.

Haass, Richard N., and Meghan L. O'Sullivan, eds. 2000. *Honey and Vinegar: Incentives, Sanctions, and Foreign Policy*. Washington, DC: Brookings Institution Press.

Hartzell, Caroline, Matthew Hoddie, and Donald Rothchild. 2001. "Stabilizing the Peace after Civil War: An Investigation of Some Key Variables." *International Organization* 55, 1: 183–208.

Hirsch, John L. 2001. *Sierra Leone: Diamonds and the Struggle for Democracy*. Boulder, CO: Lynne Rienner.

Hoffman, Frank. 2006. "Lessons from Lebanon: Hezbollah and Hybrid Wars." *Foreign Policy Research Institute*, August 24. Available at www.fpri.org/enotes/20060824.military.hoffman,hezbollahhybridwars.html. Retrieved August 29, 2006.

International Commission on Intervention and State Sovereignty (ICISS). 2001. *The Responsibility to Protect*. Ottawa, Ontario: ICISS.

International Crisis Group. 2003. *Five Minutes to Midnight in Sudan's Peace Process.* August 8. Available at www.crisisgroup.org/home/index.cfm?id=2210&l=1. Retrieved September 30, 2006.

Jentleson, Bruce W. 2002. "Use of Force Dilemmas: Policy and Politics." In *Eagle Rules: Foreign Policy and American Primacy in the Twenty-First Century,* ed. Robert J. Lieber. Upper Saddle River, NJ: Prentice Hall.

Jentleson, Bruce W., and Christopher A. Whytock. 2005–6. "Who 'Won' Libya? The Force-Diplomacy Debate and Its Implications for Theory and Policy." *International Security* 30, 3: 47–86.

Lake, David A., and Donald Rothchild, eds. 1998. *The International Spread of Ethnic Conflict: Fear, Diffusion, and Escalation.* Princeton, NJ: Princeton University Press.

Morgenthau, Hans J. 1960. *Politics among Nations.* 3rd ed. New York: Alfred A. Knopf.

National Security Council. 1966. "Summary Notes of the 561st Meeting of the National Security Council." National Security Council, Washington, DC, July 14. Available in *Foreign Relations of the United States, 1964–1968—Africa,* ed. Nina Davis Howland (Washington, DC: US Government Printing Office, 1999).

Nincic, Miroslav. 2005. *Renegade Regimes: Confronting Deviant Behavior in World Politics.* New York: Columbia University Press.

North, Douglass. 1990. *Institutions, Institutional Change, and Economic Performance.* New York: Cambridge University Press.

Nye, Joseph S., Jr. 2002. *The Paradox of American Power.* New York: Oxford University Press.

Oakley, Robert B. 2000. "The Urban Area during Support Missions, Case Study: Mogadishu- The Strategic Level." Briefing to MOUT Conference, RAND, Santa Monica, CA, March 22–23. Available at www.rand.org/pubs/conf_proceedings/CF162/CF162.appk.pdf. Retrieved May 20, 2006.

Prendergast, John. 2001. "U.S. Leadership in Resolving African Conflict: The Case of Ethiopia-Eritrea," September 7. Special Report, U.S. Institute of Peace, Washington, DC.

Pruitt, Dean G. 2004. *Social Conflict: Escalation, Stalemate, and Settlement.* 3rd ed. Boston, MA: McGraw-Hill.

Rothchild, Donald. 1997. *Managing Ethnic Conflict in Africa: Pressures and Incentives for Cooperation.* Washington, DC: Brookings Institution Press.

———. 2005. "Reassuring Weaker Parties after Civil Wars: The Benefits and Costs of Executive Power-Sharing Systems in Africa." *Ethnopolitics* 4, 3: 247–267.

———. 2009. "The U.S. Role in Promoting Peaceful African Relations." In *Africa in World Politics: Reforming Political Order,* ed. John W. Harbeson and Donald Rothchild. New York: Perseus Book Group.

Rothchild, Donald, and Nikolas Emmanuel. 2006. "U.S. Intervention in Africa's Ethnic Conflicts: The Scope for Action." In *Africa-U.S. Relations: Strategic Encounters,* ed. Edmond Keller and Donald Rothchild. Boulder, CO: Lynne Rienner.

Rothchild, Donald, and John Ravenhill, 1992. "Retreat from Globalism: U.S. Policy toward Africa in the 1990s." In *Eagle in a New World: American Grand Strategy in the Post–Cold War Era,* ed. Kenneth A. Oye, Robert J. Lieber, and Donald Rothchild. New York: HarperCollins.

Rubin, Jeffrey Z. 1981. Introduction to *Dynamics of Third Party Intervention: Kissinger in the Middle East,* ed. J. Z. Rubin. New York: Praeger.

Shattuck, John, Paul Simo, and William J. Durch. 2003. *Ending Congo's Nightmare.* Washington, DC: Human Rights Law Group.

Touval, Saadia. 1982. *The Peace Brokers: Mediators in the Arab-Israeli Conflict, 1948–1979.* Princeton, NJ: Princeton University Press.

———. 2002. *Mediation in the Yugoslav Wars: The Critical Years, 1990–95.* New York: Palgrave Macmillan.

Walter, Barbara F. 2002. *Committing to Peace: The Successful Settlement of Civil Wars.* Princeton, NJ: Princeton University Press.

Zartman, I. William. 1995. "Systems of World Order and Regional Conflict Reduction." In *Cooperative Security: Reducing Third World Wars*, ed. I. William Zartman and Victor A. Kremenyuk. New York: Syracuse University Press.

———. 1997. "Explaining Oslo." *International Negotiation* 2, 2: 195–215.

———. 2001. "Negotiating Internal Conflict." *International Negotiation* 6, 3: 297–302.

Notes

1. Francis M. Deng, interview by Donald Rothchild, November 17, 2003, Washington, DC.
2. For a dissenting view of the value of sanctions, see Bienen 1995.
3. Comprehensive Anti-Apartheid Act 1986, US Public Law 99-440, October 2, 1986, section 101.
4. Confidential interview, Foreign Service Institute, Virginia, October 15, 2003.
5. Edmund A. Gullion, ambassador, American Embassy, Leopoldville, telegram to secretary of state, May 5, 1962, National Security Files, Congo, Congo Cables, No. 2754, John F. Kennedy Library, Boston, MA.
6. Adlai Stevenson, ambassador, New York, telegram to secretary of state, May 28, 1962, National Security Files, Congo, Congo Cables, no. 3838, John F. Kennedy Library, Boston, MA.

SEVEN

Soft Intervention and the Transformation of Militias into Political Parties

TERRENCE LYONS

Creating sustainable peace after protracted civil wars is one of the most vexing challenges of our times. The recent growth of academic attention to civil war settlements reflects this imperative to understand how to negotiate an end to violent intrastate conflicts and how to implement such agreements (Stedman, Rothchild, and Cousens 2002; Walter 2002; Fortna 2004). The restoration or creation anew of peaceful society after conflict is a long-term undertaking, but it must begin during the interim period between the signing of the accord and the installation of the postwar government, generally sanctioned through elections. Elections usually are designated in peace accords as the culminating step to implement the agreement and bring to power postwar leaders and institutions.[1]

Such postconflict elections represent particular opportunities and risks as local leaders and communities assess the relative benefits of working to sustain peace and build democracy in societies still polarized and distorted by war and where demagogues and spoilers can capitalize on people's fears and insecurities. The first steps of the transition from war to peace and the first postconflict elections therefore are crucial because early precedents will shape which path key actors choose to follow. In particular, postconflict elections provide a critical context for processes to demilitarize politics.[2] The transformation of militarized actors (insurgents, military governments, paramilitaries) into nonmilitary actors such as political parties is a critical condition for sustainable peace-building. These processes of internal, institutional change are likely to be more important than external guarantees or formal agreements, which often lack sustainable impact. Third-party "soft

This chapter is dedicated to Donald Rothchild, a wonderful colleague and friend, full of ideas and generous with his time. He is much missed.

intervention," however, can support demilitarization of politics by using assistance to shift incentives and make strategies of electoral competition more attractive than a return to violence.

What processes encourage transitions that can move war-torn societies toward sustainable peace-building, and what roles can elections play in supporting or undermining peace? Patterns can be analyzed from cases of civil war settlement such as Angola (1992), Cambodia (1993), Mozambique (1994), El Salvador (1994), Bosnia and Herzegovina (1996), Liberia (1997), and Tajikistan (1999–2000), where elections formed a key, culminating event in the peace-implementation process. These cases suggest that elections sometimes have succeeded in providing a mechanism for selecting new political leadership and institutions capable of preserving the peace and initiating democratization. This was the result in El Salvador and Mozambique. In Cambodia, the outcome is less clear, but the 1993 election resulted in at least a partial opening for a period of time. However, postconflict elections can also trigger renewed conflict or result in entrenching undemocratic actors in power. In Angola, the move toward elections in 1992 precipitated renewed conflict. In other cases, such as Bosnia and Herzegovina, Liberia (for a time), and Tajikistan, elections served more as a mechanism of war termination, with only a secondary, limited, and perhaps damaging relationship to democratization. What explains these varied outcomes?

Protracted civil war and peaceful electoral competition require distinct sets of social institutions. Military-dominated regimes and insurgent forces, economies based on humanitarian relief, black market networks, predation, and social formations and identities shaped by insecurity and fear are all the result of and the necessary institutional basis for protracted civil war (Collier et al. 2003; Weinstein 2007). Civilian-oriented political parties, open economies and rule of law, civil society, and diverse, multifarious identities based on security and trust are created by and support sustainable peace and democratization. How can the institutions that sustained war become institutions capable of sustaining peace? In particular, can the transformation of militias into political parties reinforce the end of violence and the institutionalization of electoral competition? Are there opportunities for external parties to reinforce and promote such organizational conversions through soft intervention tactics, notably purchase and legitimation?

The Legacy of Fear and Voting for Peace

The demilitarization of politics is an essential component for postconflict elections to advance both peace and democratization. To demilitarize politics entails creating and reinforcing the incentives and opportunities for the institutions of wartime based on violence, insecurity, and fear to transform themselves into institutions of peacetime based on security and trust that can sustain peace and democracy. Demilitarization of politics therefore is a process of institutional transformation that may or may not take place in the transitional period. The powerful actors that developed and were sustained during a protracted civil war cannot be wished away. Neither can the enabling environment for peaceful political competition be proclaimed into existence through the signing of a peace agreement.

Fear, polarization, and power derived from violence and predation will shape the political context of postconflict elections unless politics is demilitarized during the transitional period prior to the election. The legacies of war strongly influence the path of postconflict transitions and the context for postconflict elections. Some scholars have advocated that postconflict elections should be held much later in the transitional process, that power-sharing pacts should be negotiated prior to elections to manage the uncertainty of the transition, or that electoral rules should be drafted to encourage inclusive regimes (Kumar and Ottaway 1998; Sisk and Reynolds 1998, 14). Others have argued that third-party "guarantees" backed by credible hard intervention such as robust peacekeeping missions are the critical variable in peace implementation (Walter 1997). Pacts, power sharing, and electoral rules, however, require a degree of confidence in the process that often is lacking in the hardest cases, and international guarantees are often not credible to parties emerging from protracted conflict. War-termination processes require rapid implementation to build on momentum and moments of ripeness; democratization often requires a much slower pace so that trust- and party-building may take place. Since ending the killing is imperative and a prerequisite to sustained democratization, quick elections are often necessary.

If politics has not been demilitarized, additional time, pacts, and electoral systems are unlikely to be sufficient to overcome the legacies of fear, and the powerful organizations of war are likely to dominate the campaign and win the election. The outcomes of postconflict transitions ending in elections are therefore shaped by the institutional legacies of war and whether or not these institutions are transformed through processes to demilitarize politics. Voters in postconflict elections often choose to use the limited power of their franchise either to appease the most powerful faction in the hope that doing so will prevent a return to war or to select the most nationalistic and chauvinistic candidate who can credibly pledge to protect the voter's community. Outside observers often regard these leaders as warlords or war criminals. To vulnerable voters, however, they are seen either as powerful protectors capable of defending the voter from rival military forces or as intimidators to be placated in order to preclude a return to the violence that they threaten to unleash if they lose. Civilian candidates and those who do not have a convincing answer to the issue of postelection security are unlikely to prevail.

Fear and the legacies of the institutions of war vary. Some peace-implementation processes took place in a context where the institutions of war remained powerful and entrenched. In such circumstances, unless politics was demilitarized during peace implementation, postconflict elections were held while the institutions and attitudes of war remained dominant. Candidates sometimes campaigned by making threats to return to war if they lost the election. In Liberia, these threats were successful: many voters cast their ballots to appease the most dangerous candidate, ex-factional leader Charles Taylor. Many Liberians believed—with good reason—that if Taylor lost the election, the country would return to war. Taylor's rivals pointed to his violent past during the campaign but could not propose credible actions to contain him if he refused to accept the results.[3] In the absence of plausible insurance from third parties, Liberian voters hoped that appeasement would pacify Taylor. In Angola, the insurgent UNITA similarly threatened a return to war if it did not win the election, but this strategy backfired, and the majority endorsed the incumbent MPLA government. Graffiti on the walls of several towns summed up the choice perceived by many Angolans: "MPLA steals but UNITA kills" (Vines 1993, 6). UNITA demonstrated that its threat was real and subsequently unleashed renewed conflict. In Cambodia, the Khmer Rouge also threatened to return to war but lacked the military strength to return the country to the full-scale conflict of the past.

In a second set of cases still distorted by the fears and structures of civil war, parties made appeals to protect their constituencies from other parties. In Bosnia and Herzegovina, parties campaigned in their ethnically defined constituencies by promising to defend the nationality's interests and by heightening the danger of supporting anyone other than a nationalist. In 1996 the Croatian Democratic Party (HDZ) issued warnings that the "survival of their nation" depended on the vote, while Republika Srpska television warned that a vote against the Serbian Democratic Party (SDS) would constitute a vote "against the Serb people" (International Crisis Group 1996). The main Bosnian Muslim party made the same sort of appeal: "A vote for the SDA [Party of Democratic Action] is a vote for the survival of the Muslim nation," went the slogan (cited in Woodward 1999, 96). Ethnic outbidding led to polarization, and moderate or multiethnic parties did poorly in the first postconflict election. Leaders who have the most violent pasts may make the most convincing claim that a vote for them is a vote for peace. In these cases, the best that postconflict elections may be able to do is to reduce the gap between de facto power derived from military strength and de jure power based on votes. Longer-term peace-building will be difficult in these circumstances.

In a third set of cases, processes to demilitarize politics during the transitional period created a new institutional context at the time of elections. In El Salvador, Mozambique, and (to a lesser extent) Cambodia, politics had been relatively demilitarized prior to elections and voters therefore had less fear that war would return. Both the ruling ARENA party and the insurgent FMLN in El Salvador transformed themselves into effective political parties before the elections and demonstrated a willingness to compete on the basis of electoral politics rather than through violence. In Mozambique, relatively effective demobilization, the creation of strong interim institutions based on consultation and joint decision-making, and the support given to RENAMO to encourage it to make the transition from a military to a political organization reduced the strength of the institutions of war relative to the institutions of democratic governance by election day. Cambodia is an ambiguous case, with some institutions such as the Funcinpec coalition making the transition from military to electoral politics more successfully than the ruling Cambodian People's Party or the Khmer Rouge. Interim administration was relatively strong but still insufficient to demilitarize the structures of the incumbent administration or the Khmer Rouge.

The outcomes of postconflict elections in Angola, Bosnia and Herzegovina, Liberia, and Tajikistan all reflect the powerful and enduring influence of the war on the voting process and the power retained by militarized institutions through the transition. The outcomes in Cambodia, El Salvador, and Mozambique, in contrast, point to the capacity of postconflict elections to promote sustainable peace-building if a process of demilitarization of politics has taken place. How did processes to demilitarize politics help some cases overcome the legacies and establish a new institutional framework for political competition prior to elections? How did soft intervention promote such institutional transformation?

Incentives, Opportunities, and the Demilitarization of Politics

To understand peace-implementation processes, it is useful to assume that the parties that enter into a peace process respond to incentives and rationally assess options with regard to which incentives and options best promise to assure their organizational survival. Successful demilitarization of politics entails both raising the costs of returning to war and simultaneously lowering the costs of working toward peace, thereby shaping whether key actors adopt military or electoral strategies. Nancy Bermeo makes this point with regard to leaders, but the same challenges face organizations: "Elites in emerging, post-war democracies face a double challenge. On the one hand, they must raise the costs of violent competition. On the other hand, they must lower the costs of electoral competition. The probability of stable democracy is a function of both these processes and the many variables that drive them" (2003, 163; see also Shugart 1992, 121). If perceptible progress on demilitarizing politics takes place during the transitional peace-implementation period leading to elections, then key decision-makers will alter their strategies and pursue electoral rather than military opportunities.

The manner by which interim institutions and new norms are established to manage the peace-implementation period will create precedents, expectations, and patterns of behavior that will shape how politics after the election functions. In some cases, institutions built around collaborative decision-making, transparency, and confidence-building managed the implementation process (Kelman 1999, 203). In Mozambique, for example, the two formerly warring sides engaged in joint decision-making processes on issues such as the electoral system and worked together to monitor the cease-fire and demobilization (Manning 2002a, 63–84; 2002b). Similar institutions operated in El Salvador and to a degree in Cambodia. In Angola, in contrast, the two parties rarely met during the interim and the transition was marked by suspicion and bad faith during the failed demobilization process. The interim administration during the implementation phase in Liberia similarly was stalemated because of the division of power among the warring factions. The manner by which interim institutions operate will influence whether postconflict elections move a war-torn state toward peace and democratization.

Demobilization and reform of the security sector similarly are at the heart of civil war settlements. Successful demobilization has positive effects on postconflict peace-building, including the reallocation of public expenditures from the military to civilian use (the "peace dividend"), reducing the threat of violence and increasing personal security, and providing individual and collective incentives that reinforce the transition from war to peace. Such processes also shape the political process of shifting power and authority away from armed groups and violence and toward civil institutions and electoral politics. As Berdal argues, there is "interplay, a subtle interaction, between the dynamics of a peace process and the manner in which the disarmament, demobilization and reintegration provisions associated with that process are organized, funded and implemented" (1996, 73). As demobilization proceeds apace and as the dividends of peace deepen, actors may become trapped in a politics of moderation whereby the attractiveness of maintaining the peace rises and the rewards for returning to war shrink, resulting in a higher probability of successful peace implementation. Financial support for well-designed demobilization programs is a valuable tactic of soft intervention. Demobilization encourages the demilitarization of politics both by decreasing the means and hence likelihood of a return to warfare and by increasing confidence in and hence the incentives to participate in a political process.

Transforming Militias into Political Parties

It is extremely difficult for insurgents, paramilitaries, military governments, and other militarized institutions that derived their power from conflict to play the role of competing political parties in a democratic system if they remain unreconstructed and organized as they were during the period of armed conflict. In the more successful cases of transition, particularly in El Salvador and Mozambique, processes to demilitarize politics encouraged military organizations to transform themselves into political parties able to operate effectively in an electoral context. In the less successful or failed cases, particularly Angola, Liberia, and Tajikistan, insurgents and military regimes retained the ability to operate as armed forces at the time of elections, thereby weakening the capacity of postconflict elections to mark a transition to civilian rule. These comparative cases suggest that if the powerful military organizations in place at the time of the cease-fire can be transformed into effective political parties by the time of postconflict elections, then the prospects for sustainable peace and democratization are greater. Transforming militarized parties into political parties therefore is a crucial component of successful processes to demilitarize politics; it makes sustainable peace and democratization more likely.

Successful Transformation of Militias into Political Parties

A key challenge to promoting postsettlement peace implementation and long-term sustainable peace-building, therefore, is to develop new incentives and opportunities so that the institutions of war can transform into the institutions of peace. The militarized parties that sign peace agreements are likely to remain the most powerful organizations in the immediate aftermath of civil war and will depend upon wartime mechanisms to provide the incentives to mobilize supporters. If the peace agreement holds, however, the general population will over time have less and less need to rally behind militant leaders whose main attraction is their promise to protect or their threat to do harm. In a secure context, individuals will gradually join and create new, more diverse social networks and institutions organized around the agendas of peacetime rather than the polarization and security agendas of wartime. The parties that dominated during the fighting will then have to transform themselves in order to be relevant and retain power during peacetime.

Institutions endure and thrive in part by their capacity to adjust to changing contexts. A change from violence to security will compel a transformation if the organization is to remain vital. Social movements, political parties, and other organizations seek self-preservation in the first instance through strategies to meet their maintenance needs. As Zald and McCarthy argue, "organizations exist in a changing environment to which they must adapt. Adaptation to the environment may itself require changes in goals and in the internal arrangement of the organization" (1987, 122). This adaptation will be particularly challenging when the context shifts dramatically from one set of incentives and opportunities, such as war, to another, such as electoral competition.

In Mozambique and El Salvador, postsettlement peace processes successfully generated institutional transformation of that most characteristic institution of civil war, the insurgency or military government, into that distinctive organization of electoral competition, the civilian political party. In these cases, the main insurgent movements succeeded in changing their character, organizational structure, and even, to a degree, leadership over the course of the transition. At the same time, particularly in El Salvador, the incumbent military government reformed itself to improve its chances of retaining political power through the ballot box, making participation in elections a less risky choice. In both cases, the institutions that competed in postconflict elections were significantly different from the organizations that engaged in the earlier armed struggle. These cases therefore suggest that the transformation of the militarized institutions of the war into political institutions capable of competing effectively in electoral processes is a key component of the process of demilitarizing politics and an important part of creating the conditions for sustainable peace and democratization.

Mozambique

A critical element in the successful Mozambique peace process was the extent to which RENAMO transformed itself, with external assistance, from an armed insurgency into a viable civilian political party able to play a constructive role in a multiparty democracy. In the process of negotiating the Rome Agreements, RENAMO's leadership concluded that resources and patronage would be necessary to operate in the new context of peace and electoral competition. During the negotiations, RENAMO tried (with some success) to extract material benefits from those interested in sponsoring the peace, most notably Italy but also private companies with interests in Mozambique such as Lonrho (Vines 1996, 143–145). UN Special Representative Aldo Ajello stated that "it was necessary to help RENAMO to achieve a minimum level that could allow the functioning of the whole mechanism" of the peace agreement (1995, 127; cited in Chachiua and Malan 1998, 22). RENAMO insisted that there could be "no democracy without money" and Ajello agreed: "Democracy has a cost and we must pay that cost" ("Mozambique" 1993, 4; Vines 1996, 146).

Dhlakama, the RENAMO leader, emphasized the need for resources to transform his military organization into a political party: "This transition is a hard task, because the means we need have changed. During the war, we could attack an enemy position and capture enough material. In this work of transition things have changed; we need offices, fax machines, financing. And the means we have are not sufficient. The only problem we have in transforming ourselves is this one, of resources" (*Mozambique Peace Process Bulletin* 1993). After initial concerns from donors reluctant to fund a party with a particularly brutal reputation, a $19 million fund was established to help RENAMO transform itself into a political party. These resources allowed RENAMO to provide severance packages to some of the high-level military officers most worried about their future in a peaceful Mozambique and to recruit new party officials (often recently returned exiles). Some of the delay in implementing the peace agreement was due to RENAMO's desire to have more time to complete its transformation into a political party prior to voting (Manning 2002a, 2002b).

The willingness of key international donors to provide resources to underwrite RENAMO's transformation from insurgent group to political party was critical, perhaps essential, for the implementation of the Rome agreement. This intervention was reinforced through relatively well funded and managed demobilization programs that reduced RENAMO's ability to return to the bush. Policies of purchase represented a successful form of soft intervention; they help explain the demilitarization of politics in Mozambique.

The ruling FRELIMO party went through its own transformation. The party began as a national liberation movement, then transformed itself into a Marxist-Leninist vanguard party, then in 1989 changed again into a broad "democratic socialist" organization that endorsed a multiparty constitution in 1990 (Simpson 1993). FRELIMO's reforms may have been motivated by a desire to undercut RENAMO's claims. The transformation gathered momentum, however, as those within the party who benefited from the changes rose to more powerful positions. It was this new political organization, rather than the Marxist-Leninist party, which had fought the civil war earlier in the 1980s, that made peace with RENAMO and engaged in the postconflict elections.

In Mozambique, therefore, processes to transform both RENAMO and FRELIMO from wartime organizations into political parties able to compete in multiparty elections were critical to the peace-implementation process. The institutions that developed during the war were not the same as the organizations that participated in the 1994 elections. The demilitarization of politics that supported short-term peace implementation also was critical for sustainable peace and democratization.

El Salvador

Similarly in El Salvador, one of the keys to the success of the peace process was the insurgent FMLN's ability to successfully convert itself into a legal political party capable of winning significant votes. The United Nations noted that the FMLN's "transformation into a political party and the full reintegration of its members . . . into the civil, political, and institutional life of the country, are at the very core of the Peace Accords."[4] During the period leading up to the 1994 elections, the ruling ARENA party also reformed itself from an organization engaging in violent repression to protect the privileges of landowners into a political party able to mobilize new constituencies through peaceful means.

The FMLN's conversion to an organization seeking electoral strategies to pursue its political goals began before the conclusion of the peace talks. During the late 1980s, the coalition explored opportunities to engage in electoral politics, and some perceived new possibilities with the electoral successes of Rubén Zamora and the leftist Convergencia Democrática party. The insurgents began to create autonomous "poder de doble cara" (two-faced power) structures to organize the countryside in a semiclandestine, semilegal manner. By 1989 the FMLN was systematically building up its political capacity and had formed links with labor and other urban mass organizations. Top FMLN organizers explained that they were exploring alternatives for wide participation and popular democracy for after the war (Miles and Ostertag 1991, 231; Byrne 1996, 132–136).

As the negotiations progressed, and as an all-out offense to capture San Salvador failed, FMLN leadership became increasingly convinced that political processes could advance their agenda more than military campaigns. As the election neared and as confidence in the peace process grew, the FMLN concentrated its resources on creating a national network of party activists and building alliances with other parties on the left. In response to changing opportunities and incentives, the FMLN made the "shift from the armed left to the democratic left" (Munck and Boniface 2000, 46).

As the FMLN was moving away from its origins as a Marxist guerrilla movement, the incumbent ARENA party also shifted its base of support and its strategy to retain power. Initially founded by individuals closely associated with the repression of the Left to protect large landowners, it evolved in the late 1980s into a political party that represented a broad range of landowners, bankers, merchants, and industrialists. Leadership of ARENA shifted from Roberto D'Aubuisson, who had ties to right-wing death squads, to the more moderate, probusiness, Alfredo Cristiani. As one analyst argues, "with the creation of ARENA, and its evolution into a successful electoral competitor, the upper classes and their political allies no longer needed the military to act as a political guarantor and interlocutor" (Stanley 1996, 220, 254–255; see also Miles and Ostertag 1989; Wood 2000, 75). ARENA's ability to win votes in elections convinced the economic elite that it could break its links to death squads without risking the loss of its economic position.

Postconflict elections in Mozambique and El Salvador therefore provided the opportunity for both insurgents and incumbents involved in the civil war to make the transformation from warring factions into political organizations able to compete effectively in elections. To the extent that powerful military leaders and their followers perceive that they have the option to operate as a political party rather than as an insurgency or military government, the chances of a successful transition are increased. Thus, demilitarizing politics through the transformation of military organizations into political parties promotes both war termination and democratization.

Unreconstructed Parties and Postconflict Elections

In other cases insurgents or the incumbent regime remain unreconstructed and retain their institutional structure throughout the transition. Such failure to demilitarize politics makes it likely that the transition will end in an election that reaffirms the power and enhances the authority of those groups and leaders that developed during the war. Such an outcome may lead to war termination in the short run but may make a transition to long-term sustainable peace difficult. The peace-implementation process in such circumstances is unlikely to build the incentives or create the opportunities to entice militarized organizations to transform themselves into political-electoral organizations capable of sustaining peace and democratization.

In some cases, unreformed militarized organizations have tried to derail a peace process or refused to accept the transition to electoral competition. UNITA in Angola acted as a spoiler that used violence to disrupt the peace process. Some observers expected UNITA to make the transition from insurgency to political party. UNITA's "sophisticated, versatile organization with proven resilience and discipline" would make the transition from insurgency and de facto governing authority over large parts of Angola into an effective political party relatively easily, according to some. An early preelection assessment stated that "given standard indicators for organizational effectiveness—chain of command, responsiveness of policy decisions to local as well as national demands, resilience and regeneration in the face of disruptions, etc.—UNITA ranked favorably against established political parties in Central and South America, the Caribbean, Central Europe, and the Balkans" (Henderson and Stewart 1991, 9). But in the end UNITA did not transform itself and participated in the elections as a military organization.

In Liberia, Bosnia and Herzegovina, and Tajikistan, militarized organizations competed in and won postconflict elections. In a context where politics had not been demilitarized and where insecurity and fear remained pervasive, militarized organizations had the capacity to mobilize significant constituencies, win elections, and form the ensuing postconflict government. It remains uncertain whether any would have acted as spoilers like UNITA if they had lost. In the case of Bosnia and Herzegovina, it further remains uncertain how a potential spoiler might have acted if the hard intervention of international peacekeeping had been less powerful.

Charles Taylor's National Patriotic Party (NPP) was a direct descendant (or a fresh incarnation) of his insurgent National Patriotic Front for Liberia (NPFL). The NPP essentially provided a civilian platform to compete for votes in 1997, but the organization remained fundamentally unreconstructed and continued to derive power through military might, the manipulation of fear, and patronage derived from illegal trade. As an institution capable of mobilizing large numbers of people, the NPP demonstrated enormous capacity. But the unreconstructed institutions of war could not sustain the peace, and civil war returned in 1999. Later, in 2001, the United Nations imposed sanctions and banned diamond exports after Liberia failed to cut its ties to the Revolutionary United Front in Sierra Leone. These sanctions (along with Taylor's indictment by the Special Court in Sierra Leone) contributed to undermining Taylor's access to sufficient patronage to maintain his clientelistic network. This soft intervention, along with the very hard intervention of Nigerian-led Economic Community of West African States Cease-Fire Monitoring Group forces, eventually drove Taylor from power.

In Cambodia, the Cambodian People's Party (CPP) behaved during the transition not as a political party in a multiparty context but as the "governing apparatus of Cambodia," complete with village cells and a highly organized nationwide network of cadres. As one report concluded, "the CPP clearly prefers to stick to the age-old strategy of patronage and intimidation, rather than real reform, to ensure popular support" (International Crisis Group 2000, 6–7). The CPP retained key advantages of incumbency throughout the transition, including control over a vast array of state institutions, from the army and state media through to low-level civil and political organizations in the distant communes. All the major political parties emerged from militarized organizations and shared what one Cambodian leader called the "violent and undemocratic tradition of the past" (cited in Frieson 1996, 183). While Cambodia has not returned to civil war, processes of democratization have been marked by violence.

Other unreconstructed military parties participated in elections but lost the poll and consequently became less relevant in the postconflict state. The United Tajik Opposition won few seats and became a less important player in Tajikistan after the elections. In Liberia, other military factions failed to make the transition to political party that the NPFL made. Some, such as the Liberian Peace Council (a militia) or the United Liberation Movement of Liberia for Democracy (ULIMO), tried but failed, demonstrating that their constituencies were limited in peacetime. One fraction of ULIMO brought in some exiled politicians to lead the political campaign of its newly created All Liberian Coalition Party, but these new leaders never gained sufficient power to transform the militia into a party or to mobilize significant numbers outside of its small ethnic base among the Mandingo of Lofa County (Lyons 1999). In Cambodia, the failed efforts by the Khmer Rouge to derail the peace process left them out of the electoral competition and hence a less important political player in postelection bargaining. Postconflict elections therefore may promote new institutional alignments by marginalizing organizations that fail to demonstrate the ability to mobilize constituencies in the context of electoral competition.

The demilitarization-of-politics perspective focuses attention on how post-settlement policies may support institutional transformation that can sustain peace and promote democratization. At the time of the initial cease-fire, organizations made powerful by the war will dominate the political landscape. During the transitional period leading up to postconflict elections, a new framework can shift the incentives and opportunities organizations face and thereby encourage the transformation of institutions whose origins lay in violent conflict into institutions whose future lies in democratic competition. In this way, postconflict elections are both the context for demilitarization of politics to take place and the event that will demonstrate the extent to which that transformation has taken place.

Postconflict elections have become a ubiquitous component of civil war settlements supported by the international community since the end of the cold war. Postconflict elections often are criticized for failing to advance democratization. This criticism is often true, but it misses the potential for such elections to promote important war termination goals even if they fail to promote democratization. Policymakers seeking to address the challenges of postconflict reconstruction cannot afford to make democratization their one and only goal and must accept that in many of the difficult cases, war termination is the only available short-term option that provides at least the potential for long-term stability and eventual transition to democracy.[5] In this way, moving forward with elections even in a context where politics remains militarized may be the "least bad" option.

Peace implementation should focus on what kinds of institutional transformations may take place in the period between the signing of the peace accord and the postconflict election. In the most difficult cases, such as Angola, El Salvador, Cambodia, Mozambique, Bosnia and Herzegovina, Liberia, and Tajikistan—as well as Iraq, Afghanistan, and the Democratic Republic of Congo—there will be few opportunities to promote peacebuilding and democratization through power-sharing pacts, electoral system engineering, or delaying the elections until security is firmly established. Even these difficult cases, however, often have openings to advance the demilitarization of politics by encouraging the transformation of the institutions of war into political institutions that can support peace, as was seen in Mozambique and El Salvador.

For the international community, the peace-implementation process following civil war presents numerous opportunities to deploy soft intervention. Greater emphasis should be placed on the processes that shape how the parties to the conflict relate to each other during the transition rather than to elements in the peace agreement itself or to the hard-intervention options of international peacekeeping policy. Emphasizing the internal dynamics among parties and institutions during the interim phase, rather than power-sharing arrangements or international guarantees, shifts the issue of what policies support successful implementation. Rather than trying to negotiate a power-sharing pact (a difficult challenge given the imperatives to negotiate a cease-fire) or promising an international security "guarantee" (a guarantee that is rarely credible), it is more useful to ask how the implementation process can strengthen interparty patterns of cooperation and trust and overcome insecurity. The peace agreement becomes the starting point for another series of negotiations, bargaining, and institution-building rather than a blueprint to be enacted. The outcome of this period of continued bargaining and maneuvering for advantage provides the context for postconflict elections more than the initial agreement or the international community.

To the extent that a process to demilitarize politics can be initiated, the precedents and institutional basis for sustainable peace and democratization can be supported. Forms of soft intervention and donor support for strong and effective interim administrations, particularly those based on consultation and collaborative problem-solving, can help create a new institutional context that converts the structures of war into structures that can sustain peace and democracy. In particular, donors and international organizations should examine electoral commissions and recognize them not only as opportunities to administer good elections but also as openings for confidence-building and potential models for new forms of cooperation and peaceful competition (Lyons 2004). The transformation of militarized institutions into political parties has enormous potential to bolster both the war-termination and the democratization agendas of postconflict elections. The process of implementing peace and promoting democracy following civil war is difficult. Recent experience suggests that processes to demilitarize politics can—and must—begin during the transitional period and that strategies of soft intervention can support the transformation of the institutions of war into the institutions of peace.

References

Ajello, Aldo. 1995. "O Papel da ONUMOZ no Processo de Democratização." In *Moçambique: Eleições, Democracia e Desenvolvimento*, ed. B. Mazula. Maputo, Mozambique: Inter-Africa Group.

Berdal, Mats R. 1996. *Disarmament and Demobilisation after Civil Wars*. Adelphi Paper No. 303. London: International Institute for Strategic Studies.

Berkeley, Bill. 2001. *The Graves Are Not Yet Full: Race, Tribe, and Power in the Heart of Africa*. New York: Basic Books.

Bermeo, Nancy. 2003. "What the Democratization Literature Says—or Doesn't Say—about Postwar Democratization." *Global Governance* 9, 2: 159–177.

Byrne, Hugh. 1996. *El Salvador's Civil War: A Study of Revolution*. Boulder, CO: Lynne Rienner.

Chachiua, Martinho, and Mark Malan. 1998. "Anomalies and Acquiescence: The Mozambican Peace Process Revisited." *African Security Review* 7, 4. www.iss.co.za/PUBS/ASR/7no4/Anomalies.html.

Collier, Paul, V. L. Elliott, Havard Hegre, Anke Hoeffler, Marta Reynal-Querol, and Nicholas Sambanis. 2003. *Breaking the Conflict Trap: Civil War and Development Policy*. Washington, DC: World Bank.

de Zeeuw, Jeroen (ed.). 2008. *From Soldiers to Politicians: Transforming Rebel Movements after Civil War*. Boulder, CO: Lynne Rienner.

Fortna, Virginia Page. 2004. *Peace Time: Cease-Fire Agreements and the Durability of Peace*. Princeton, NJ: Princeton University Press.

Frieson, Kate. 1996. "The Politics of Getting the Vote in Cambodia." In *Propaganda, Politics, and Violence in Cambodia: Democratic Transition under United Nations Peacekeeping*, ed. Steve Heder and Judy Ledgerwood. Armonk, NY: M. E. Sharpe.

Henderson, Robert E., and Edward B. Stewart. 1997. *Unita after the Cease-Fire: The Emergence of a Party*. Washington, DC: National Republican Institute for International Affairs.

International Crisis Group. 1996. *Elections in Bosnia and Herzegovina*. ICG Europe Report No. 16. September 22. www.crisisgroup.org.

———. 2000. *Cambodia: The Elusive Peace Dividend*. ICG Asia Report no. 8. August 11. www.crisisgroup.org.

Jarstad, Anna, and Timothy Sisk (eds.). 2008. *From War to Democracy: Dilemmas of Peacebuilding*. Cambridge: Cambridge University Press.

Kelman, Herbert C. 1999. "Transforming the Relationship between Former Enemies: A Social-Psychological Analysis." In *After the Peace: Resistance and Reconciliation*, ed. Robert L. Rothstein. Boulder, CO: Lynne Rienner.

Kumar, Krishna, and Marina Ottaway. 1998. "General Conclusions and Priorities for Policy Research." In *Postconflict Elections, Democratization, and International Assistance*, ed. Krishna Kumar. Boulder, CO: Lynne Rienner.

Lyons, Terrence. 1999. *Voting for Peace: Postconflict Elections in Liberia*. Washington, DC: Brookings Institution Press.

———. 2002. "The Role of Postsettlement Elections." In Stedman, Rothchild, and Cousens 2002.

———. 2004. "Postconflict Elections and the Process of Demilitarizing Politics: The Role of Electoral Administration." *Democratization* 11, 3: 1–27.

———. 2005. *Demilitarizing Politics: Elections on the Uncertain Road to Peace*. Boulder, CO: Lynne Rienner.

Manning, Carrie. 2002a. "Conflict Management and Elite Habituation in Postwar Democracy: The Case of Mozambique." *Comparative Politics* 35, 1: 63–84.

———. 2002b. *The Politics of Peace in Mozambique: Post-Conflict Democratization, 1992–2000*. Westport, CT: Praeger.

———. 2008. *The Making of Democrats: Elections and Party Development in Postwar Bosnia, El Salvador, and Mozambique*. New York: Palgrave Macmillan.

Miles, Sara, and Bob Ostertag. 1989. "D'Aubuisson's New ARENA." *NACLA Report on the Americas* 23:14–38.

———. 1991. "The FMLN: New Thinking." In *A Decade of War: El Salvador Confronts the Future*, ed. Anjali Sundaram and George Gelber. New York: Monthly Review Press.

"Mozambique: Funding for Peace." 1993. *Africa Confidential*, May 14, 4.

Mozambique Peace Process Bulletin. 1993. September.

Munck, Geraldo L., and Dexter Boniface. 2000. "Political Processes and Identity Formation in El Salvador: From Armed Left to Democratic Left. " In *Postmodern Insurgencies: Political Violence, Identity Formation, and Peacemaking in Comparative Perspective*, ed. Ronaldo Munck and Purnaka L. de Silva. New York: St. Martin's Press.

Shugart, Matthew Soberg. 1992. "Guerrillas and Elections: An Institutionalist Perspective on the Costs of Conflict and Cooperation." *International Studies Quarterly* 36, 2: 121–152.

Simpson, Mark. 1993. "Foreign and Domestic Factors in the Transformation of Frelimo." *Journal of Modern African Studies* 31, 2: 309–337.

Sisk, Timothy D., and Andrew Reynolds. 1998. "Democratization, Elections, and Conflict Management in Africa." In *Elections and Conflict Management in Africa*, ed. Timothy D. Sisk and Andrew Reynolds. Washington, DC: United States Institute of Peace Press.

Söderberg-Kovacs, Mimi. 2007. "From Rebellion to Politics: The Transformation of Rebel Groups to Political Parties in Civil War Peace Processes." Ph.D. diss., Uppsala University.

Stanley, William. 1996. *The Protection Racket State: Elite Politics, Military Extortion, and Civil War in El Salvador*. Philadelphia: Temple University Press.

Stedman, Stephen John, Donald Rothchild, and Elizabeth M. Cousens (eds.). 2002. *Ending Civil Wars: The Implementation of Peace Agreements*. Boulder, CO: Lynne Rienner.

Vines, Alex. 1993. *One Hand Tied: Angola and the UN*. London: Catholic Institute of International Relations.

———. 1996. *Renamo: From Terrorism to Democracy in Mozambique*? London: James Currey.

Walter, Barbara F. 1997. "The Critical Barrier to Civil War Settlement." *International Organization* 51, 3: 335–364.

———. 2002. *Committing to Peace: The Successful Settlement of Civil Wars*. Princeton, NJ: Princeton University Press.

Weinstein, Jeremy M. 2007. *Inside Rebellion: The Politics of Insurgent Violence*. Cambridge: Cambridge University Press.

Wood, Elisabeth Jean. 2000. *Forging Democracy from Below: Insurgent Transitions in South Africa and El Salvador*. Cambridge: Cambridge University Press.

Woodward, Susan L. 1999. "Bosnia and Herzegovina: How Not to End Civil War." In *Civil Wars, Insecurity, and Intervention*, ed. Barbara F. Walter and Jack Snyder. New York: Columbia University Press.

Zald, Mayer N., and John D. McCarthy (eds.). 1987. *Social Movements in an Organizational Society*. New Brunswick, NJ: Transaction.

Notes

1. There has been a surge in research on this issue. See de Zeeuw 2008; Soderberg-Kovacs 2007; Jarstad and Sisk 2008; Manning 2008.
2. Lyons 2005 elaborates this concept.
3. For example, anti-Taylor posters with pictures of the brutalities of the war and the caption "Chuck [Charles Taylor] Did It" served to increase the levels of fear and raise anew concerns that the civilian candidates would not be able to prevent him from doing it again. "Chuck Did It" was a slogan that appeared on NPFL T-shirts during the war. See Berkeley 2001, 52.
4. Further report of the secretary general on the United Nations Observer Mission in El Salvador (ONUSAL), S/26005, June 29, 1993, para. 11.
5. For more on the multiple roles of postconflict elections, see Lyons 2002.

EIGHT

Cautionary Tales: Soft Intervention and Civil Society

MICHAEL W. FOLEY

No intervention, hard or soft, will succeed in bringing peace in civil conflicts without the cooperation of key domestic actors. This is the lesson of Iraq and Afghanistan under the American occupation, Sudan, and Congo today. It is also the lesson of Somalia, where civil conflict persists not despite but because of foreign interventions, both hard and soft. The notion that civil conflicts bespeak "failed states" and thus require more forceful and thoroughgoing international commitments has gained renewed currency lately; but it flies in the face of these experiences (see Paris 2004; Doyle and Sambanis 2006; Lake, chapter 2 of this volume). It also ignores the facts that, however incapable many of these states are of extinguishing insurgencies, they are quite capable of resisting international pressures where their interests are most affected and that, unlike their opponents, even states in temporary abeyance, such as the Cambodian government of Hun Sen at the time of the peace accords, generally maintain the upper hand in the course of peace implementation.

International efforts to bring peace must take into account the positions and capabilities of domestic actors. But which ones? Clearly, governments and their armed antagonists are key figures in winning the peace. What of the larger society? A growing sentiment suggests that civil society must play an important role in postconflict peacemaking and that where civil society is weak, unable or unwilling to play this role, the peace is not likely to last. Are such claims plausible? To the degree that they are correct, what precisely can civil society do to promote lasting peace, and what sorts of civil actors are best suited to this task? How can international actors use soft intervention to strengthen the hand of civil society in peacemaking?

This chapter examines three cases in which some scholarly attention has been paid to the role of civil society in peacemaking and enforcement. The situation facing civil society in each case differed from the situations in the others. In two of these, Northern Ireland and Bosnia, civil conflict revolved around communal identities; in El Salvador the conflict claimed the form of an elite-popular struggle. Bosnia stands out as coming closest to the sort of international "protectorate" favored by some. In El Salvador the peace was relatively "self-enforcing," as both the government and the rebel Farabundo Martí National Liberation Front (FMLN) retained some power to enforce implementation in the early stages of the process. In the importance of the main protagonists to achieving and preserving peace, Northern Ireland resembled El Salvador more than it did Bosnia, but the United Kingdom's ability to resume direct rule in the province provided conditions more reminiscent of a protectorate than of a sovereign entity and its opponents working out peace on their own terms.

A close examination of these varying cases suggests the difficulties that civil society faces in contributing to peace implementation and the limits of such a role even in the most favorable instances. It also raises some cautions about where and how the international community might effectively intervene to support that role.

First, a word of clarification. By *civil society* I mean that portion of society, outside those groups and individuals contesting directly for political power, that exercises some voice in public debate on issues of broad concern (Alagappa 2004). Civil society thus includes neither political parties nor armed contenders for power, though it may be linked to both in a variety of ways. Individuals as well as groups participate in civil society, and both individuals and groups may come and go as circumstances change and public space expands or contracts. Moreover, there is nothing inherently virtuous about civil society. All actors have their own peculiar views of "the public good," some of them closely tied to those of antagonists in the field (and at times more supportive of conflict than of reconciliation), some of them purely "selfish" in motivation, others "public spirited." Thus, despite the use of a collective noun, we cannot presume that civil society is united. Just to name a handful of possible civil-society actors—unions, religious groups, independent educational and cultural institutions, charitable organizations, professional and trade associations, women's groups, neighborhood associations, and NGOs[1]—is to underline their diversity and suggest the difficulties of bringing them together in a broad-based movement.

Civil Society and Peacemaking in Practice and Theory

The literature on peace-building has paid scant attention to the role of civil society. Scholarly attention to the role of civil society in peace processes, in fact, has tracked a growing theoretical presumption among both scholars and practitioners in favor of an important role for civil society. International funding for civil-society "strengthening" or "promotion" in postwar settings has grown substantially since the early 1990s. Rationales for expending money on civil society run a rich gamut of expectations: monitoring and controlling state power; encouraging the socialization of citizens in democratic practices and values; and creating channels for the articulation of societal interests outside the political parties (Sejfija 2006).[2] As we shall see, these goals are rarely realized in practice. Moreover, international efforts to bring to fruition these high expectations have been fumbling at best.

In cases of ethnic conflict, another rationale generally stands out, namely the importance of civil society for the "reconciliation" of society, without which a lasting peace is said to be impossible. The notion of reconciliation is rarely, if ever, defined in the literature, nor is any empirical evidence for the far-reaching claims made on its behalf generally offered. Yet its importance is assumed to be so self-evident as to be unassailable.[3] Nevertheless, a case can be made that reconciliation is less important, even in ethnically divided societies, than a decision by elites on both sides that peace provides a far less costly setting in which to dispute their differences and pursue their interests than continuing war (Zartman 1995).[4] Donald Rothchild was preoccupied throughout his career with the ways in which ethnic differences are successfully negotiated at the elite level (see especially Rothchild 1997). The importance assigned to reconciliation at the societal level assumes that violence between ethnic, religious, or even sharply defined political communities is inevitable so long as "polarization" persists. But this idea—reflected in works like Robert Kaplan's unfortunate *Balkan Ghosts*—stems from the sociologically naive assumption that violence must sooner or later emerge from the mere fact of difference (Kaplan 1993). The subtle accommodations by which the former Yugoslavia recognized ethnic difference and the actual dynamics that destroyed that polity are equally invisible under such assumptions (Woodward 1995).

Based on such notions, Western governments and NGOs have assumed that the goal of reconciliation can best be advanced through the promotion of a "multi-ethnic civil society." This assumption has its roots in some of the oldest commonplaces of American political science.[5] Recently the work of Ashutosh Varshney on communal violence in India has been taken to support such a strategy (2001, 2003). Varshney himself has argued that "interethnic and intraethnic networks of civic engagement play very different roles in ethnic conflict. Because they build bridges and manage tensions, interethnic networks are agents of peace, but if communities are organized only along intraethnic lines and the interconnections with other communities are very weak or even nonexistent, then ethnic violence is quite likely" (2001, 363). Unfortunately, Varshney's own research does not support these broad-ranging conclusions (Chandra 2001). Both the traditional argument and Varshney's contemporary version of it abstract from the political and motivational context in which violence and nonviolence must inevitably play out, a context clearly laid out in Varshney's empirical studies.

Social divisions must be put into play by interested parties before they can be mobilized politically and militarily (Tilly 2003). Once leaders have been brought to the table and convinced of the necessity of forging a peace agreement, violence between communities will disappear or be easily isolated and subdued. This being the case, civil society's primary role—however important its work in attempting to heal the wounds of war—is to keep elites to their promises and ensure their continued commitment to the peace. As we shall see, civil society may act through monitoring and pressure on the parties, by sharing in implementation of key provisions of the peace accords, and, more indirectly, through the support it provides to those former antagonists who seek a peaceful path to resolving conflict. In the brief case studies that follow, we look at the record of civil-society involvement in peace implementation and international actors' efforts to pursue a soft "civil-society strategy" to enforce the peace.

El Salvador: Forging a Civil-Society Role

Few accounts have taken seriously the role of civil society in the Salvadoran peace process. Most focus on the principal sides, the rebel FMLN and the government, on one hand, and on international actors, particularly the United Nations, on the other. Unremarked in most accounts, a combative civil society mobilized late in the war into the National Debate for Peace, which pressed both sides to negotiate. Nevertheless, FMLN and government negotiators subsequently hammered out a peace agreement with little reference to civil society; and the government expended considerable effort to exclude civil-society organizations from the reconstruction process, fearing that the FMLN would reap the political benefits of reconstruction carried out by these organizations (Ramos Gonzalez 1993; Whitfield 1994, 317–321; Byrne 1996). Throughout the implementation process, from the signing of the peace accords in January 1992 to 1995, the parties to the accords, sustained and prodded by a forceful UN implementing mission, remained the key actors. Nevertheless, civil society played a significant role in monitoring progress, implementing the accords, and supporting the commitment of the principal actors to the peace process. International support was often crucial to civil society's protagonism.

As the process of forging an accord came near to success, the government, with technical assistance from the UN Development Programme (UNDP) and the advice of the US embassy, began formulating plans for postwar reconstruction. UNDP, which was to take prime responsibility for coordinating international participation in implementation and reconstruction, pushed to bring representatives of civil society to the table, in accord with provisions of the peace agreement. The government, backed by the United States, resisted. When the government insisted on channeling reconstruction funds through its own agency—reconstituted from its chief counterinsurgency office—European donors responded with a partial embargo of government implementing agencies, choosing instead to finance projects through Salvadoran NGOs and community groups, many of which they had supported during the war as a counterweight to US policy (Lawrence 1992; Sollis 1993; Foley 1996). This combination of incentives and disincentives from the disparate sponsors of postconflict reconstruction provided space for both government and opposition civil-society organizations to plot their own course over the next four years.

Since 1983 the United States had pursued a policy of building a series of civil-society institutions dominated by El Salvador's business elite; meanwhile European states had provided funds through European NGOs for the beleaguered "popular sector," including many organizations created by the FMLN. Elements of the latter were prolific institution-builders, so that by the time of the signing of the peace accords, a dense network of NGOs, community organizations, unions, cooperative associations, and peasant organizations were tied in one way or another to the rebel forces. Other organizations, decidedly a minority and mostly NGOs, had carved out a middle path largely dedicated to serving the communities marginalized by the government's counterinsurgency campaign.

Both the United States and the Europeans took up the task of funding elements of the peace agreements that the government pleaded unable, or proved unwilling, to finance, thus purchasing acquiescence to aspects of the accords that ruling party supporters opposed. These included resettlement and reintegration of ex-combatants, the new civilian police force, judicial reform, and the new office of Human Rights Ombudsman. But while the United States often turned for implementation to the private-sector-dominated organizations it had helped create during the war, European donors preferred to work through UNDP and the NGOs.

Patterns of funding thus followed the political purposes, commitments, and habits of the donors (Rosa and Foley 2000). Besides the private-sector-affiliated organizations, for example, the United States also turned to a small number of mostly large, invariably US-based, international NGOs to channel funding for the peace process. All of these exacted large overhead payments, ensuring that US aid returned to the United States in proportions consonant with congressional requirements. European states and the European Union continued funding popular-sector organizations while demanding greater accountability. The Europeans thus combined the reward of legitimation with the power of purchase to shape postwar civil society.

Very little of the aid aimed at civil society in the immediate postwar period was directly involved in "peace implementation," if by that we mean achieving compliance with the explicit provisions of a negotiated settlement. Most was devoted to reconstruction: housing assistance in the cities and the countryside, medical care and public health projects for the underserved, microenterprise programs, and agricultural development. Some aid, however, was directly tied to implementation of the accords. The FMLN's January 26 Association received European funding to survey and organize communities eligible for land under the reinsertion clauses of the accords. The US Agency for International Development, through the Southwest Voter's Research Institute, funded a number of smaller Salvadoran organizations to organize voter registration, carry out civic education campaigns, and monitor the official Supreme Electoral Tribunal in the run-up to the historic 1994 elections. Most of the funding going to civil-society organizations, however, had only indirect implications for peace implementation. And much of the US funding went to "capacity building" for Salvadoran NGOs.

It is important that we stop to consider just what is meant by *"capacity building"* since the term is widely used to describe the contribution of the international community to civil-society strengthening. Most such efforts are astoundingly narrow and bureaucratic in character. Early in the peace process, for example, USAID, feeling the sting of accusations that the United States was refusing to work with popular-sector organizations, engaged an American aid agency, Private Agencies Collaborating Together (PACT), to carry out capacity building with a broad range of local NGOs.

PACT, which repatriated half its contract to the United States as overhead, gave a series of courses on such matters as how to write a mission statement, how to use a spreadsheet, and how to write a grant application.[6] Aid, in effect, was being used principally to learn how to get more aid.[7] Capacity building is a persistent feature of international spending on strengthening civil society, but it rarely goes beyond such training. There is little regard, in these efforts, for helping organizations root themselves in their communities, adopt practices that will make them accountable to the larger society, or manage the difficult waters of political advocacy—largely because these concerns are foreign to the international NGOs and agencies that are doing the capacity building (Smith 1990).

In the Salvadoran case, however, the renewal of civil society that postwar funding supported had some positive indirect effects for the peace process that are worth noting. Organizations that had been associated with the FMLN provided employment for many of the higher-level cadres of that party, particularly those who would soon become involved in the political process. Indeed, as the historic election of 1994 approached, many NGOs were drained of staff as militants joined the political campaign on behalf of the FMLN and other parties of the opposition. The indirect impact on the peace process was important. Civil society provided necessary employment for ex-combatants and militants of the rebel organizations and a launching pad for the redirection of their struggle in the forums of "normal politics." At the same time, both NGOs and community organizations were beginning to assert their independence from the FMLN, sometimes in response to the new accountability demanded by funders, sometimes in resentment at the party's political manipulations. Civil-society and political actors were becoming increasingly differentiated, and civil-society actors were assuming increasingly critical stances, on the Right as well as the Left.

International actors contributed to these developments, legitimating the return to civil society of the rebels and providing resources to underwrite this process. Resources were not just incentives or rewards for favored behavior, though these effects were important in demands for financial accountability. More significant was the use of foreign resources to enable actors to do *what they had already decided to do*. By and large, the commitment of FMLN militants to the peace was not in question. What was needed and provided by foreign aid were the resources necessary to make possible reintegration and facilitate the commitment of the FMLN to the political process.[8] The elite business community whose new organizations the United States had nurtured was likewise committed to peace, if often sympathetic with government foot-dragging on specific items of implementation. US aid gave its civil-society organizations a greater stake in the process. Finally, if only on a limited basis, foreign aid strengthened the ability of civil society to hold both sides accountable in the implementation of the peace accords.

Bosnia: Pathologies of NGOization

When Bosnia's civil war ended with the 1995 signing of the Dayton Accords, the international community focused initially on deploying peacekeeping troops and setting the stage for elections. But when elections overwhelmingly returned ethnic nationalist politicians to office, both governments and private international aid agencies turned increasingly to civil-society promotion. By this time the strengthening of civil society was widely seen as a core component of promoting both reconciliation and democracy. USAID spending on civil-society initiatives had grown globally to $165 million in 1995, from just $56 million in 1991 (Carothers 1999, 50). The European Community launched a $393 million Peace Fund for Northern Ireland when the IRA declared a cease-fire in 1994. The World Bank began to provide a portion of its development assistance worldwide through civil-society organizations. Civil-society aid thus became an important component of the international community's commitment to implementing the peace in Bosnia.

The Dayton Accords called for the creation of a tripartite state, the Muslim-Croat Federation of Bosnia and Herzegovina, controlling 51 percent of national territory, and the Republika Srpska, the Serb Republic, occupying 49 percent. Some sixty thousand NATO peacekeepers were initially deployed to enforce the peace, and Bosniac (Muslim), Croat, and Serb military forces were downsized (but not abolished). The federal government, with a presidency rotating among the three ethnoreligious groups, was tasked with international relations, managing the national currency, control of a new all-entity police force, and oversight of Brčko, a multiethnic city that straddles the divide between eastern and western portions of the Republika Srpska. In practice, the federal government has struggled to function in the face of the intransigence of entrenched nationalists. The Office of the High Representative, given "semi-protectorate" authority by the major powers who make up the Peace Implementation Council, has intervened repeatedly in both subentity and federal affairs, removing elected officials and pushing through laws where Bosnians themselves refused to act or failed to act in accord with the High Representative's expectations.[9]

Not surprisingly, the NGO sector was small in Bosnia at the close of the war. Roughly a hundred organizations were working on reconstruction, infrastructure development, human rights, and women's issues (Smillie 2001). These depended on funding and support from the roughly 150 international NGOs present in the country, intergovernmental organizations, and donor governments. The UN High Commission for Refugees and the World Bank were soon funding Bosnian NGOs, and the Organization for Security and Cooperation in Europe took on the tasks of hosting, training, and providing logistic support to Bosnian groups.

Donor governments and international NGOs alike stressed the importance of developing a strong civil society to achieve reconciliation, prevent human rights abuses, promote a democratic society, and protect the peace. As the Peace Implementation Council (PIC) put it in 1998, a strong civil society in Bosnia was "'essential to a democratic society' and vital to 'promote the healing of the wounds of war, to protect the peace.' The PIC situates civil society as 'a balance to government structures' and encourages its representatives to 'play an active role in advocacy and to hold public officials accountable for their actions'" (Belloni 2001, 167). Yet, just as in El Salvador a few years before, the vast majority of funds going to civil society were for reconstruction and social service projects. According to Ian Smillie, "Donors (and many international NGOs) characterize their interest in supporting local NGOs as an investment in a strong, pluralist, socially integrated civil society. And yet what was happening in Bosnia [in the mid-1990s] was entirely different: in funding NGOs, donors essentially sought—and found—cheap service delivery" (2001, 33).

By most accounts international efforts to build civil society have been insufficient at best, counterproductive at worst. One reason is the near-exclusive focus on NGOs. While professionalized local service providers may be ideal vehicles for "cheap social service delivery," they are widely acknowledged to be far less apt at holding governments accountable or promoting more widespread citizen participation, let alone reconciling former enemies. The Salvadoran NGOs founded by members of the FMLN were unique in being grounded, thanks to their party ties, in the communities they served. The situation was (and is) far bleaker in Bosnia, where few NGOs spring from organized communities and few community-level organizations, aside from the nationalist parties, persist from the prewar period. Moreover, donor strategy generally ignores those organizations with roots in society. As Sejfija notes, local grassroots organizations are rarely funded (2006, 134). In funding NGOs, rather than helping to strengthen community organizations of all sorts, the international community has failed to build the sort of civil society it claims to want, choosing instead the comfortable path of re-creating familiar forms of organization on foreign turf.[10]

Support for civil society through capacity building underlines the point. As in the case of El Salvador, the focus was on creating organizations capable of writing proposals and rendering reports to funders. As a rule donors refused to provide operational expenses, confining themselves to clearly defined projects, often of the donor's own making. Projects changed with donor tastes, and there was little long-term or strategic funding for promising initiatives. A few large NGOs whose staff had mastered the art of proposal writing quickly came to enjoy favored status, but even these could be remarkably weak, once donor attention waned (Smillie 2001; Evans-Kent and Bleiker 2003; Fagan 2005). Adam Fagan notes that of the roughly seventy-three hundred domestic NGOs registered in 2003, "only a handful" were active, "of which the majority are service-provider organizations with little or no political aspiration" (2005, 410). Monica Llamazares and David Crosier ask: "How is it possible to 'construct civil society' unless responsibility is given to local communities to build their own futures? Yet, international reconstruction aid for the development of civil society often does not allow such responsibility to develop. Instead, grassroots community organizations either turn themselves into efficiently organized operations that are capable of responding to the agenda defined by the international donors, or they die out. Instead of serving the needs of the community, they begin to serve the needs of their donors" (1999, 555). These were by now widely recognized pathologies of "NGOization,"[11] but they appear to have been repeated in Bosnia with a vengeance (see Edwards and Hulme 1996; Hulme and Edwards 1997; Carothers 1999). Even Ismet Sejfija's more positive recent appraisal records the same litany of problems with donor-NGO relations (2006). The most important improvement in the situation since the 1990s, according to Fagan, is the willingness of some local government authorities to work with NGOs (2005, 410).

Fagan's observation underlines a key issue: civil society's impact will inevitably be limited in the face of a hostile government. Bosnia's governments, especially at the subentity level but even at the municipal and cantonal levels, have been largely hostile or indifferent to the organizations supported by the international community (Belloni 2001). By the early part of the new century, this situation had changed somewhat. Ismet Sejfija notes that by 2005 "the number of NGOs exclusively concerned with monitoring and critically scrutinizing the authorities and their work [had] increased substantially in BiH [Bosnia and Herzegovina]" (2006, 127). Donor pressures on local governments, in some cases withholding funding as punishment for excluding civil-society organizations, had some effect. Besides the increasing openness among municipal and cantonal authorities, Sejfija cites the new law establishing citizens' rights to an initiative and referendum process. A changing legal and political environment, much more than donor sponsorship, seems to have made the difference in these cases. However important a vibrant civil society may be to ensuring democratic accountability, democratic accountability is equally important to promoting a strong civil society, the "paradox of the civil society argument" of which Michael Walzer speaks (1992, 102–103; Foley and Edwards 1996).

A strong argument can be made that international intervention has actually weakened the development of civil society. In addition to the problematic constitution bequeathed to the country at Dayton, the increasing power of the High Representative has undermined indigenous activism, according to Belloni and others. For example, the Office of High Representative took over initiatives originating in local NGOs to formulate a legal framework for nonprofit organizations. The OHR gathered comments from the Council of Europe and the International Centre for Not-for-Profit Law, finalizing the draft legislation and overseeing its adoption by the Bosnian legislature—"thus making a mockery of civil society's advocacy role" (Belloni 2001, 171). Similarly, James Lyon—who is far more sympathetic to the OHR—records a process of developing and passing legislation on police reform that betrays little room for input from Bosnian civil society (2006).

The results of international intervention on behalf of reconciliation have received similarly mixed reviews. Sejfija presents the more optimistic portrayal, but even he prefers the term *civil sector* to *civil society*, because of its small scale, and he goes on to note that the political system is "still based on ethnic principles" (2006, 137). Indeed, these are built into the constitution outlined at Dayton, a fact that has made most observers pessimistic about the prospects for interethnic cooperation outside a few privileged enclaves. Patrice McMahon, after noting the successes of reconciliation efforts in recent years, goes on to recount just how thin the layer of interethnic organizations is. Even in Brčko, highly regarded as a case in which Muslims and Serbs work together in municipal government, she found that each ethnic group has its own NGOs, which rarely work together (2005). In reality, as I argue in the conclusion, this is to be expected, and international efforts should be focused on supporting civil society's commitment to the peace rather than interethnic organization per se. The Northern Ireland case that follows underlines this point.

Northern Ireland: Part of the Problem, Part of the Solution?

By all the usual criteria, Northern Ireland has a rich and vibrant civil society, yet most observers agree that it has had little role to play in the peace process. In contrast to most of the literature on other cases of civil war settlement, we find a wealth of studies, some of them systematic, of Northern Ireland's civil society in the peace process. Two major reasons for the lack of civil-society impact on the process have been adduced. First, civil society is manifestly part of the problem, because it is largely organized along communal (or sectarian) lines. Second, the major actors in the conflict have perforce attended more to one another than to civil society, relying on secure bases of support in the larger population to bolster elite-made decisions. Thus, despite significant expenditures by the European Union and Great Britain to encourage civil-society support for the peace process, results have been indirect at best.

Today, ten years after the signing of the Good Friday Accords, and in the wake of apparently final steps in their implementation, Northern Ireland remains a divided society. As Adam Guelke notes, "civil society in general has failed to have a significant impact on attitudes in Northern Ireland society at large" (2003, 68). The parties responsible for the breakthrough in January 2008 and which share government today, the Democratic Unionist Party of Ian Paisley and Sinn Fein, represent the poles of Northern Irish politics, not its uncertain center.

Communal divisions between the Protestant majority and the Catholic minority fueled the conflict, but these same communities also gave birth to what one sociologist characterizes as "perhaps the most comprehensive 'peacemaking industry' of all world conflicts" (Brewer 2003, 69). Brewer lists some two dozen different sorts of efforts: from ecumenical activities of all sorts to mediation and conflict-resolution groups to efforts to deal with the effects of the violence on victims, ex-combatants, and prisoners (2003, 75).

The international community contributed significantly to this proliferation of organizations. In 1995, the European Union responded to the paramilitary cease-fire of autumn 1994 with a $393 million Peace Fund. The program was designed "to reinforce progress towards a peaceful and stable society and to promote reconciliation by increasing economic development and employment, promoting urban and rural regeneration, developing cross-border cooperation and extending social inclusion" (quoted in Byrne, Matic, and Fissuh 2007, 92). What has since been labeled "Peace I" (the program was reorganized and refunded with the signing of the Good Friday Agreement in 1998) established a series of intermediate funding bodies in Northern Ireland and border counties of the Republic of Ireland to provide small grants to community groups that had previously not received support. In this respect, it differs markedly from donor behavior in Bosnia a couple of years later; but the continuation program, Peace II, focused much more on local governments and larger organizations. Peace I itself was criticized for complicated application procedures, a problem that became worse under Peace II, and for privileging Catholic areas, where local structures created by the Nationalist community could more easily tap into funds than the less well-organized Protestant areas (Harvey 2003).

Despite the initial efforts to fund local community groups, both programs suffered from many of the pathologies we have already encountered. Bureaucratic requirements overwhelmed many community organizations. Donor preferences shaped awards of grants and thus the activities of funded organizations. A high proportion of funding went to agencies administering the grants. Mandated coordination with local officials faced obstacles where officials felt threatened by community initiatives. And, perhaps most telling, macroeconomic measures and cuts in government expenditures meant that joblessness was rising and government services becoming scarcer at the same time that the project tried to leverage economic development on behalf of peace (Byrne, Matic, and Fissuh 2007). It is little wonder that researchers and practitioners alike are hard pressed to find a payoff in the peace process for the one billion ECU expended by the end of 2004.

And the divisions these efforts were meant to heal persist. The work of countless community groups notwithstanding, discrimination, distrust, and occasional incidents of violence continue to characterize relations between the communities. Timothy D. Sisk and Christoph Stefes summarize this judgment bluntly: Despite considerable funding by the United Kingdom and the European Union for initiatives to promote a more tolerant and integrated community life, "the process of encouraging an integrated civil society in Northern Ireland has foundered" (2005, 312). Moreover, most associations, even among those considered part of Brewer's "peacemaking industry," remain divided along sectarian lines, led by, representing, and serving exclusively Protestants or Catholics. As Feargal Cochrane concludes, "the motivations behind the establishment of human rights organisations, reconciliation groups, church-based peace groups and community development organisations were similar to those behind the main paramilitary factions in Northern Ireland. The sense of *community values* and the desire to defend, protect or augment that community's position have led to a strong (though dichotomous) community cohesiveness in Northern Ireland" (2006, 265). The persistence of communal divisions, even among those dedicated to forging the peace, makes clear that Ashutosh Varshney's formula for intercommunal peace—crosscutting associational life—is harder to achieve than imagined, even in the best of circumstances (2003).

On the positive side, Feargal Cochrane and Seamus Dunn find a process of renovation at the grassroots level, with eventual implications for the peace process and, above all, for the ultimate decision to stand behind the 1998 Good Friday Agreement. They underline the possibility that grassroots initiatives led to a slow, incremental process of renovation among political elites, contributing to the ultimate peace agreement (2002, 162). Most critically, "at least four of the political parties involved in negotiating the Good Friday Agreement have been substantially influenced by community sector politics, and many of these people have been elected to the Northern Ireland Assembly to implement the Agreement" (179). As Benjamin Gidron, Stanley Katz, and Yeheskel Hasenfeld read the evidence, peace and conflict-resolution organizations laid "the groundwork for the emergence of important locality-based political institutions that could influence the peace process, . . . producing new leaders and activists within the local communities who, over a period of time, had a significant effect on the political process" (2002, 210–211). As in El Salvador, the most effective civil-society actors were those who organized within their own partisan communities to urge peace upon communal leaders.

The impact of these changes was felt most strongly in the immediate wake of the Good Friday Agreement, with the campaign in support of a "Yes" vote in the referendum on the agreement. The "Yes" campaign was the first step in implementation of the Good Friday Agreement, which depended on massive public support for its survival. More or less imposed upon the parties by the British and Irish governments when mediator George Mitchell seemed unable to forge an agreement between the Ulster Unionist Party (UUP, then the majority Protestant party) and its Catholic counterparts, the agreement needed convincing support from the general public, including the Protestant community. As it happened, the "Yes" received 71 percent of the vote, with estimates of approval rates among Nationalists (Catholics) ranging between 91 and 96 percent and among

Unionists between 51 and 57 percent. The latter was particularly important, because without its community's support, the UUP was unlikely to stick to the agreement. In large part, the successful outcome can be attributed to the civil-society-run "Yes" campaign, which targeted precisely undecided Unionist voters (Couto 2001).

Although Northern Ireland's political parties all publicly supported the agreement, the major pro-Agreement effort was organized by civil society, in particular by actors drawn from the traditional nonprofit sector. Quintin Oliver, who became director of the campaign, was a former director of the Northern Ireland Council for Voluntary Action, representing nonprofits such as hospitals and social service agencies across the communal spectrum. Paul Nolan, who took the initial steps and became chair of the campaign, was well known in community organization circles and headed a group called New Agenda, which had attempted to facilitate dialogue among political parties. Along these lines, the framers of the campaign had hoped to act as a sort of nonprofit clearinghouse for the pro-Agreement parties. The parties, particularly on the Unionist side, wanted nothing to do with it, for reasons that are worth considering. As Richard Couto describes the situation, David Trimble, head of the UUP, "had stretched his political tether to the limit in signing the Belfast Agreement. Party members were divided over the wisdom of that move. Some feared the party's grassroots might rebel if the leadership pushed the Agreement too hard. The most important demographic of the referendum—moderate Unionists—were at the core of the UUP. Their support would be imperiled by a joint campaign, so the UUP refused to join such an effort" (2001, 227–228). Other parties respected this decision and likewise declined to work in a joint campaign. It is likely, in fact, that Sinn Fein may have feared a similar split in its ranks. The result was that the political impact of the civil-society initiative was stymied from the start by the logic of party politics. The campaign would have to proceed on its own.

Similar discord accompanied the organizers' attempts to enlist other elements of civil society. Churches, the business community, and many leaders of the nonprofit sector declined to participate. As Couto notes, "Although they had skills, experience, and, in some cases, a keen interest in politics, getting involved in a political campaign was anathema to the leaders of the third sector. They cherished political impartiality. Taking a political stand would inevitably mean offending some constituents, members, or clients" (2001, 234). If civil society is to play the roles commonly ascribed to it in peace processes (and democracies), *it has to be politicized,* as the leaders of the "Yes" campaign rightly saw; but politicizing it requires overcoming powerful inhibitions on the part of most leaders of organizations generally thought to stand at the center of civil society.

The leaders of the "Yes" campaign were disappointed, too, in their hopes of stimulating a grassroots movement on behalf of the Agreement. As it turned out, the leaders and organizations at the forefront of the campaign, like the NGOs of Bosnia, had only shallow roots in local communities. Without the support of the majority of the churches or community service organizations, the campaign lacked a broad constituency. "Yes" organizers and staff could draw upon the networks they had in the nonprofit community to stimulate local activity, but this effort was limited by the apolitical stance of many in those same networks. In the end, organizers were left to rely on a massive publicity campaign.

Despite these shortcomings, the "Yes" campaign seems certain to have had an impact on the vote. And behind the campaign and the vote may well lie the sort of long-term change in attitudes and renovation of political elites at the grassroots that civil-society initiatives were intended to provoke. Such is clearly the view of Cochrane and Dunn, otherwise highly skeptical of claims for the political efficacy of civil society in Northern Ireland, who argue that "it would be fair to conclude [from the success of the "Yes" campaign] that 'civil society' in Northern Ireland is relatively healthy. . . . Individuals, P/CROs [peace and conflict resolution organizations] and other networks such as the churches, trade unions, business groups and the media, have largely bought into the philosophical ethos promoted by peace/conflict resolution organizations over the last thirty years" (2002, 181). However, the vote for the Agreement may also be interpreted as an expression of war-weariness and of the fact that ordinary people, as Nancy Bermeo has shown, may be far less polarized than elites suppose them to be (2003).

In fact, civil society's performance in the implementation crises that followed ratification of the Agreement has been dismal. Adam Guelke notes that "the elements of civil society that had supported the Agreement in the referendum have tended to be marginalized in the series of crises that have threatened the peace process since May 22, 1998" (2003, 74). On the one hand, Guelke attributes this performance to the centrality of struggles between pro-Agreement and anti-Agreement factions within the UUP (there were similar struggles within Sinn Fein). On the other, he argues that continued uneasiness over participation in "political" struggles hamstrung civil-society actors, including those who had participated in the "Yes" campaign. Moreover, given the responsibility put upon the parties in the consociational settlement that the Agreement represented, civil society evidently felt paralyzed to act to break the various impasses that followed ratification. As Gidron, Katz, and Hasenfeld argue, "The British government's direct rule preempted local political institutions and greatly diminished the role of conventional political parties," discouraging citizen activism in the process (2002, 214). The costs of a protectorate evidently include the suppression of local initiatives (see Zahar 2005).

There is no doubt that in many respects Northern Ireland represents the best of circumstances for civil-society action on behalf of peace. As Brewer notes, the low level of violence in Northern Ireland allowed civil society to survive, whereas it has been overwhelmed in other parts of the world (2003). Individuals committed to peace and grassroots organizations and initiatives had the benefit of a relatively strong civil society to fund and support their efforts. Northern Ireland's first-world status also meant an outpouring of financial aid to civil-society peace efforts and continued international attention, despite the relatively low intensity of the conflict. The Northern Ireland case thus warns us against attributing too much power to civil society.

Civil Society and Civil Peacemaking: Potential and Limitations of Soft Intervention

Civil society's role in peace implementation, even in the best of circumstances, is likely to be limited. There is some potential that international actors can promote it through judicious action, but their record is scarcely more encouraging than it is for hard intervention strategies. Not only is international leverage limited, but international actors are often divided among themselves; they face elites with the ability to stall, distort, and destroy peace agreements; their understanding of and access to civil society is uncertain; and their standard operating procedures may do more to distort civil-society development than promote the peace. Where peace has been achieved, it has depended more than anything else on the motives and actions of domestic actors, with foreign intervention playing at best a subsidiary role. That role has nevertheless been an important one in many cases, and there is no prospect that foreign interventions in civil conflicts will soon cease, however wary we should be of encouraging precipitate action. It is important, accordingly, to draw some lessons from recent experiences.

1. *Soft-intervention strategies in support of civil society cannot be confined to providing "incentives" and "disincentives."* Equally important is the provision of resources to *enable actors to do what they already intend to do*. The readiest avenue for supporting civil-society initiatives on behalf of a peace agree-

ment is through citizens already committed to the peace. These individuals need resources to build organizations, spread their networks, and recruit the uncommitted to the peace process. In some cases, civil-society organizations can serve as implementers of provisions of peace agreements, particularly in helping to reintegrate ex-combatants, resettle refugees, aid marginalized populations, and rebuild infrastructure. International organizations and foreign governments can help by providing resources, legitimacy, and what Donald Rothchild and Nikolas Emmanuel call insurance—efforts to protect citizens and organizations in the exercise of their rights, through publicity, pressure, and direct action (chapter 6, this volume; also see Keck and Sikkink 1998). At the same time, international sponsorship can sometimes threaten to delegitimate such actors in the eyes of politicians and the general public. The concrete circumstances must be taken into account in formulating any plan of action in support of civil-society actors.

2. *The ability of civil-society actors to play an advocacy role on behalf of peace agreements is limited by the political structures they must operate under and by the political openness of key actors.* Strong or weak, in all of our cases civil society enjoyed little opportunity to directly influence the parties. As peace agreements were reached in each of these cases, prospects for civil-society influence became dimmer, rather than brighter, as a process already under way and overseen by major actors took much of the urgency out of civil-society mobilization and much of the reason out of continued unity. A weak and divided political system may offer few opportunities for pro-peace civil-society influence, as in the case of Bosnia. A system that privileges ethnic division, as in Bosnia, or places major responsibility for implementation on power sharing between former enemies, as in Northern Ireland, will discourage citizen action outside those frameworks.[12] And where outside actors exercise significant power over domestic decisions, as in the case of the Office of the High Representative in Bosnia or the British government in Northern Ireland, it is understandable that civil society's efforts will be limited. But explicit provisions for citizen involvement in policymaking can stimulate the development of civic capacity, even if they make peace implementation more cumbersome in the short term. International actors can play a role in encouraging parties to agreements to broaden the ownership of peace agreements through referendums, citizens' committees and commissions, and decentralized decision-making.

The character of the conflict, moreover, has a major impact on the relevance of civil society to the major actors. In both Northern Ireland and Bosnia, what are commonly referred to as ethnic conflicts were in reality constitutional struggles. In Northern Ireland the Anglo-Irish Agreement of

1985 launched a series of negotiations over the constitutional questions of Northern Ireland's relationships with Britain and the Republic of Ireland in which Sinn Fein came to see a political solution as the only way out of the impasse affecting all sides (Arthur 2002). But the compliance of militias and Northern Ireland's fragmented parties was necessary for that solution to come to pass. Civil society was largely irrelevant except insofar as it could influence the individual parties. That influence was minor precisely because all of the parties, but the most militant among them in particular, were much more beholden to their own constituencies than to the larger citizenry.[13] We have seen similar dynamics in Bosnia, where a much weaker civil society was expected to confront entrenched nationalist elites.

3. *Civil society is not confined to NGOs nor particularly well represented by such organizations or by the traditional nonprofit sector.* Although professionalized service and advocacy organizations meet many of the funding characteristics demanded by international agencies—or can be trained to do so—and although they can carry out some of the functions of monitoring and service provision that may be crucial to peace implementation, they typically lack deep roots in their own societies. Thus they are unlikely to be able to build constituencies in support of implementation or put meaningful pressure on the parties to uphold their agreements.

4. *Support to civil society should not be confined to multiethnic or otherwise "nonpartisan" organizations. Indeed, the most important groups to reach in most postconflict settings are those that best represent their communities and that have the potential to serve as advocates for the peace.* It is time to give up the assimilationist prejudices of the American civil religion and recognize that ethnic and religious differences are a semipermanent part of any polity. Communal (ethnic, religious) groups have a critical role to play in bringing about and sustaining peace between communities, as the Northern Ireland case clearly shows.[14] While building bridges across communities may be a worthy long-term goal, the objective of foreign civil-society strategies in the immediate aftermath of a peace agreement should be to strengthen support for the agreement on all sides of a conflict, particularly among those most representative of their respective groups. The important task is to sustain communities in the decision to give up violence and forge a common polity and buy support for such a decision where that is weak.

From a theoretical perspective, we must abandon the notion that difference per se provokes generalized violence. Difference has to be sharpened and mobilized for even localized spontaneous violence to result in civil conflict. These steps are the work of political entrepreneurs, backed by political or politicized organizations and, usually, by governments, as

Varshney's cases actually demonstrate (Tilly 2003). Preventing future violence depends upon ensuring that political elites abandon violence as a tactic. The reconciliation of communities will occur in due course, once that crucial decision is in place. Intercommunal organization at the level of civil society may well be important to stem localized violence; it may also encourage politicians to renounce recourse to intercommunal violence. But the first task of peace implementation is to ensure the adherence of the parties to their agreements; and their own communities are likely to be the best source of influence upon them.

5. *The pathologies of international funding for postconflict peacemaking and reconstruction are deeply rooted in the structural realities of international politics and will be difficult to overcome.* This is perhaps the hardest lesson of our cases but one of the most important to bear in mind for those who assume that the international community has the ability to intervene for the good wherever it deems itself needed. In reality intervention obeys the political interests of governments, and the more governments involved, the more disparate the goals and strategies likely to be at work. The same is true of intergovernmental organizations, agencies, and NGOs. As Llamazares and Crosier put it, harshly but accurately, the so-called international community is in reality "shorthand for a motley collection of usually uncoordinated international governmental and non-governmental organizations, the intervention techniques of which in troubled countries often reveal more about their own internal functioning than they do of their understanding and modes of response to real societal needs" (1999, 553).

The "internal functioning" of such actors starts with their responsibility to their own funders—taxpayers, in the case of government agencies; government, church, and private donors, in the case of INGOs. Government agencies impose enormous bureaucratic trammels on grantees in the name of protecting the taxpayers' interests. INGOs set their priorities according to those of their donors, moving from one troubled corner of the world to another, prioritizing a changing array of goals in each spot. Both governments and INGOs are accountable to outsiders, not to the society they ostensibly serve. These are structural conditions, and they shape most of the pathologies to which foreign funding is subject. Some governments, IGOs, and INGOs have striven mightily to correct some of the problems uncovered in the cases examined here, but with only limited success to date (Hulme and Edwards 1997).

6. *Civil society is by no means a unitary entity.* Civil society may be full of organized actors, but it is rarely organized. This fact has several implications: First, some elements of civil society will be pro-peace and pro-

agreement; others will oppose an agreement, for whatever reason. Still others, significantly, will choose to stand on the sidelines, often, as we saw in the case of Northern Ireland, out of a reluctance to be involved in "politics." Our cases should make clear that *only actors willing to be politicized are likely to make a positive contribution to the peace process*, turning on its head the concern of the American political science of the 1950s and 1960s about the dangers of a "politicized" society (Huntington 1968). Precisely for that reason we must avoid the temptation to single out categories of society that are insufficiently "civil" or tolerant or "civic minded" and deny them part in (unqualified) "civil society" (Chambers and Kopstein 2001; Paris 2004). As Kristian Berg Harpviken and Kjell Erling Kjellman wisely note, "accommodating civil society actors with an 'uncivil' record may prove particularly important in the long term" (2004, 2).

Second, as we have seen, organizations capable of having an impact on peace implementation must be sufficiently rooted in society. Pro–peace accord groups may represent the broader aspirations of society without being able to translate those aspirations into effective political pressure because their mobilizable base remains small. International actors can help by providing the resources and advice needed to broaden that base.

Third, civil society is difficult to mobilize in the first place, and its unity around a desire for peace is equally difficult to sustain. The momentum in peace processes is generally in the hands of "the guys with the guns"—actors who lay claim to a legitimate monopoly of force (government, military, police) and those who challenge that claim (militias and insurgents). These are the actors who enjoy effective veto power over steps toward a lasting peace. Once space for crafting a lasting peace is carved out, civil society may have some influence, but that is likely to wane as normal political processes resume, given the rules of the democratic game in the contemporary world. Those rules accord political elites relative autonomy with respect to society, subject only to electoral outcomes. In the new world of political contention following a peace accord, civil-society actors will find it increasingly difficult to enforce a peace that the politicians—or powerful behind-the-scenes actors—do not want.

Given these realities, the trick for pro-peace activists and their international supporters alike is winning and securing widespread agreement around an acceptable settlement of differences. In that process the key question becomes that of capacity. One clear conclusion emerges from this research: The capacity of civil society to enforce a hard-won peace is highly contingent. It depends much less on the "vigor" or "strength" of civil society measured in numbers or visibility of organizations (and even less on their ability to generate external funding) than on the degree to which pro-peace leaders can draw on broad bases of support within their communities. Most important, it depends on the vulnerability of more central actors to public pressure and their willingness to take some direction from the larger society, a willingness rare enough under normal circumstances and difficult to come by indeed in the wake of violent societal conflict. The international community has limited ability to ensure that either condition is met, but it can work on both fronts, strengthening the most representative civil-society organizations while pressing the parties to peace agreements, and particularly governments, to recognize and respect civil society's voice.

References

Alagappa, Muthiah. 2004. "Civil Society and Political Change: An Analytical Framework." In Civil *Society and Political Change in Asia: Expanding and Contracting Democratic Space*, ed. Muthiah Alagappa, 25–60. Stanford, CA: Stanford University Press.

Almond, Gabriel A., and Sidney Verba. 1965. *The Civic Culture: An Analytic Study of Political Attitudes and Democracy in Five Nations*. Boston: Little, Brown.

Arthur, Paul. 2002. *Special Relationships: Britain, Ireland, and the Northern Ireland Problem*. Belfast: Blackstaff Press.

Belloni, Roberto. 2001. "Civil Society and Peacebuilding in Bosnia and Herzegovina." *Journal of Peace Research* 38, 2: 163–180.

Bermeo, Nancy. 2003. *Ordinary People in Extraordinary Times: The Citizenry and the Breakdown of Democracy*. Princeton, NJ: Princeton University Press.

Brewer, John D. 2003. "Northern Ireland: Peacemaking among Protestants and Catholics." In *Artisans of Peace: Grassroots Peacemaking among Christian Communities*, ed. Mary Ann Cejka and Thomas Bamat, 67–95. Maryknoll, NY: Orbis Press.

Byrne, Hugh. 1996. *El Salvador's Civil War: A Study of Revolution*. Boulder, CO: Lynne Rienner.

Byrne, Sean, Mislav Matic, and Eyob Fissuh. 2007. "The European Union Peace and Reconciliation Fund Impact on Northern Ireland." *International Journal on World Peace* 24, 2: 85–109.

Carothers, Thomas. 1999. *Aiding Democracy Abroad: The Learning Curve*. Washington, DC: Carnegie Endowment for International Peace.

Chambers, Simone, and Jeffrey Kopstein. 2001. "Bad Civil Society." *Political Theory* 29, 6: 59–91.

Chandler, David. 2005. "From Dayton to Europe." *International Peacekeeping* 12, 3: 336–349.

Chandra, Kanchan. 2001. "Civic Life or Economic Interdependence?" *Commonwealth and Comparative Politics* 39, 1: 110–118.

Cochrane, Feargal. 2006. "Two Cheers for the NGOs: Building Peace from Below in Northern Ireland." In *A Farewell to Arms? Beyond the Good Friday Agreement*, ed. Michael Cox, Adrian Guelke, and Fiona Stephen. 2nd ed. Manchester, UK: Manchester University Press.

Cochrane, Feargal, and Seamus Dunn. 2002. *People Power? The Role of the Voluntary and*

Community Sector in the Northern Ireland Conflict. Cork, Ireland: Cork University Press.

Couto, Richard A. 2001. "The Third Sector and Civil Society: The Case of the 'Yes' Campaign in Northern Ireland." *Voluntas* 12, 3: 221–238.

Di Palma, Giuseppe. 1990. *To Craft Democracies: An Essay on Democratic Transitions.* Berkeley: University of California Press.

Doyle, Michael W., and Nicholas Sambanis. 2006. *Making War and Building Peace: United Nations Peace Operations.* Princeton, NJ: Princeton University Press.

Edwards, Michael, and David Hulme. 1996. *Beyond the Magic Bullet: NGO Performance and Accountability in the Post–Cold War World.* Boston: Kumarian Press.

Evans-Kent, Bronwyn, and Roland Bleiker. 2003. "Peace beyond the State? NGOs in Bosnia and Herzegovina." In *Mitigating Conflict: The Role of NGOs,* ed. Henry F. Carey and Oliver P. Richmond, 103–119. London: Frank Cass.

Fagan, Adam. 2005. "Civil Society in Bosnia Ten Years after Dayton." *International Peacekeeping* 12, 3: 406–419.

Foley, Michael W. 1996. "Laying the Groundwork: The Struggle for Civil Society in El Salvador." *Journal of Interamerican Studies and World Affairs* 38, 1: 67–104.

Foley, Michael W., and Bob Edwards. 1996. "The Paradox of Civil Society." *Journal of Democracy* 7, 3: 38–52.

Gidron, Benjamin, Stanley Katz, and Yeheskel Hasenfeld. 2002. "The Efficacy of the Peace and Conflict-Resolution Organizations: A Comparative Perspective." In *Mobilizing for Peace: Conflict Resolution in Northern Ireland, Israel/Palestine, and South Africa,* ed. Benjamin Gidron, Stanley Katz, and Yeheskel Hasenfeld, 202–224. New York: Oxford University Press.

Guelke, Adam. 2003. "Civil Society and the Northern Irish Peace Process." *Voluntas* 14, 1: 61–78.

Harpviken, Kristian Berg, and Kjell Erling Kjellman. 2004. "Beyond Blueprints: Civil Society and Peacebuilding." Concept Paper commissioned by the Norwegian Agency for Development Cooperation, International Peace Research Institute, Oslo.

Harvey, Brian. 2003. "Review of the Peace II Program." Report for the Joseph Rowntree Charitable Trust, York, UK.

Hulme, David, and Michael Edwards. 1997. *NGOs, States, and Donors: Too Close for Comfort?* New York: St. Martin's Press.

Huntington, Samuel P. 1968. *Political Order and Changing Societies.* New Haven, CT: Yale University Press.

Jonas, Susanne. 2000. *Of Centaurs and Doves: Guatemala's Peace Process.* Boulder, CO: Westview Press.

Kaplan, Robert D. 1993. *Balkan Ghosts: A Journey through History.* New York: St. Martin's Press.

Keck, Margaret E., and Kathryn Sikkink. 1998. *Activists beyond Borders: Advocacy Networks in International Politics.* Ithaca, NY: Cornell University Press.

Lawrence, Stewart. 1992. "Postwar El Salvador: Funding for Peace?" Unpublished GAO report made available by Lawrence.

Lederach, John Paul. 1997. *Building Peace: Sustainable Reconciliation in Divided Societies.* Washington, DC: U.S. Institute of Peace Press.

Lipset, Seymour Martin. 1963. *Political Man: The Social Bases of Politics.* New York: Anchor Books.

Llamazares, Monica, and David Crosier. 1999. "The Myth of Civil Society: Approaches to Societal Reconstruction in Southeastern Europe." *Higher Education in Europe* 24, 4: 553–560.

Lyon, James. 2006. "Overcoming Ethnic Politics in Bosnia? Achievements and Obstacles to European Integration." In *Peacebuilding and Civil Society in Bosnia-Herzegovina: Ten Years after Dayton*, ed. Martina Fischer, 49–68. Münster: Lit-Verlag.

McMahon, Patrice C. 2005. "Moving Reconciliation along in Bosnia? An Institutionalist Analysis of Civil Society Development." Paper prepared for presentation at the annual meeting of the International Studies Association, Honolulu, Hawaii, March 1–5.

Paris, Roland. 2004. *At War's End: Building Peace after Civil Conflict*. New York: Cambridge University Press.

Pearce, Jenny. 2004. "Assessing Civil Society Participation: War and Post War Contexts." CFP Evaluation Series 2003–2006, No. 4, Learning by Design, Randwijk, Netherlands. Available at www.partos.nl/uploaded_files/12-CSP-Pearce-paper.pdf.

Porter, Norman. 2003. *The Elusive Quest: Reconciliation in Northern Ireland*. Belfast: Blackstaff Press.

Putnam, Robert D., with Robert Leonardi and Raffaelli Y Nanetti. 1994. *Making Democracy Work: Civic Traditions in Modern Italy*. Princeton, NJ: Princeton University Press.

Ramos Gonzalez, C. G. 1993. "Solución Político-Negociada y Fuerzas Sociales Mayoritarias en El Salvador (1984–1990)." Master's thesis, University of Costa Rica.

Rosa, Herman, and Michael Foley. 2000. "El Salvador." In *Good Intentions: Pledges of Aid for Postconflict Recovery*, ed. Shepard Forman and Stewart Patrick, 113–158. Boulder, CO: Lynne Rienner.

Rothchild, Donald. 1997. *Managing Ethnic Conflict in Africa: Pressures and Incentives for Cooperation*. Washington, DC: Brookings Institution Press.

Sejfija, Ismet. 2006. "From the 'Civil Sector' to Civil Society?" In *Peacebuilding and Civil Society in Bosnia-Herzegovina: Ten Years after Dayton*, ed. Martina Fischer, 125–140. Münster: Lit-Verlag.

Sisk, Timothy D., and Christoph Stefes. 2005. "Power Sharing as an Interim Step in Peace Building: Lessons from South Africa." In *Sustainable Peace: Power and Democracy after Civil Wars*, ed. Philip G. Roeder and Donald Rothchild, 293–318. Ithaca, NY: Cornell University Press.

Smillie, Ian, and Goran Todorovic. 2001. "Reconstructing Bosnia, Constructing Civil Society: Disjuncture and Dilemma." In *Patronage or Partnership: Local Capacity Building in Humanitarian Crises*, ed. Ian Smillie, 25–50. Boston: Kumarian Press.

Smith, Brian H. 1990. *More than Altruism: The Politics of Private Foreign Aid*. Princeton, NJ: Princeton University Press.

Sollis, Peter. 1993. "Reluctant Reforms: The Cristiani Government and the International Community in the Process of Salvadoran Post-War Reconstruction." Washington Office on Latin America, Washington, DC.

Tilly, Charles. 2003. *The Politics of Collective Violence*. New York: Cambridge University Press.

Varshney, Ashutosh. 2001. "Ethnic Conflict and Civil Society: India and Beyond." *World Politics* 53, 3: 362–398.

———. 2003. *Ethnic Conflict and Civic Life: Hindus and Muslims in India*. New Haven, CT: Yale University Press.

Walzer, Michael. 1992. "The Civil Society Argument." In *Dimensions of Radical Democracy: Pluralism, Citizenship, Community*, ed. Chantal Mouffe, 89–107. London: Verso.

Warren, Mark E. 2001. *Democracy and Association*. Princeton, NJ: Princeton University Press.

Whitfield, Teresa. 1994. *Paying the Price: Ignacio Ellacuría and the Murdered Jesuits of El Salvador*. Philadelphia: Temple University Press.

Woodward, Susan L. 1995. *Balkan Tragedy: Chaos and Dissolution after the Cold War*. Washington, DC: Brookings Institution.

Zahar, Marie-Joëlle. 2005. "Power Sharing in Lebanon: Foreign Protectors, Domestic Peace, and Democratic Failure." In *Sustainable Peace: Power and Democracy after Civil Wars*, ed. Philip G. Roeder and Donald Rothchild, 219–240. Ithaca, NY: Cornell University Press.

Zartman, I. William. 1995. "Dynamics and Constraints in Negotiations in Internal Conflicts." In *Elusive Peace: Negotiating an End to Civil Wars*, ed. I. William Zartman, 13–30. Washington, DC: Brookings Institution.

Notes

1. It is important to distinguish NGOs (nongovernmental organizations) from other manifestations of civil society. NGOs are small, professionalized service and advocacy organizations. They are distinguished from the traditional nonprofit sector in that the latter are generally large, locally funded organizations. Nonprofits run hospitals and schools and promote the arts; NGOs promote public health and carry out adult education. Obviously, the distinction is not airtight. NGOs, like larger nonprofits, are generally not membership organizations. Whereas community organizations, civic associations, unions, and churches are (to varying extents) run by their members (even where they have one or two paid staff), NGOs are run by their staff, overseen in most cases by a board of directors. In postconflict settings, international relief agencies often create domestic counterparts to carry on the work they initiate; like their parent organization, these generally take the form of NGOs.
2. These functions reflect recitals of the virtues of civil society common in recent democratization literature, starting with Robert Putnam's *Making Democracy Work* (1994). For a critique of such litanies and a careful examination of the democratic potential of civil society, see Warren 2001.
3. John Paul Lederach 1997 is the reference of choice for proponents of this argument, but Lederach's work is largely prescriptive and offers only anecdotes as evidence of the importance of reconciliation for lasting peace. For a careful, skeptical examination of the notion of reconciliation in the Northern Ireland context, see Porter 2003.
4. Giuseppe di Palma (1990) makes a similar argument with regard to democratization.
5. Among these is the notion that individuals with multiple loyalties will be less likely to take impassioned stances on behalf of their own group (Lipset 1963; Almond and Verba 1965; Huntington 1968). The emphasis in this work was on cooling political passions and suppressing (or correctly "channeling" [Huntington]) citizen participation in the interests of "stability," a key goal of post–World War II American foreign policy. Social organizations that bridge societal divides were thought to be important to "crosscut" dominant societal cleavages and render them less salient. Not just American foreign policy concerns, but the American (and European)

bias for erasing group differences through assimilation arguably lay behind these assumptions.

6. To its credit, PACT attempted to help the many organizations that had experienced obstacles getting legal registration, but it was ill equipped to make much headway.
7. Interviews by author, January 1994.
8. Rational-choice language tends to leave out of account this second component of action. Actors must not only be motivated to do this or that. They must also be persuaded that their actions have some chance of achieving their goals. The latter requires resources.
9. For a critical overview of the evolving extension of the powers of the Office of the High Representative, see Chandler 2005. For a more favorable view of the OHR's intervention in the issue of police reform, see Lyon 2006.
10. In one effort to strengthen civil society on its own terms that was notable for its flexibility, CARE International found that self-help groups (membership groups, cooperatives, trade unions) were as likely to sustain long-term commitments to their communities as NGOs were—perhaps more likely, in fact—and that relatively small financial investments could have long-term payoffs (Smillie 2001). But this sort of thinking remains rare among international donors.
11. This awkward term is borrowed from Pearce 2004.
12. Roeder, chapter 3, this volume, develops an ambitious agenda for more propitious institution-building.
13. The IRA, according to one Sinn Fein official, was constrained in its ability to comply with requirements in the Good Friday Agreement to decommission arms, despite widespread public pressure, because these were a prized symbolic resource within their community, and decommissioning was seen as an admission of defeat (confidential interview, Londonderry, March 1999).
14. The strengthening of the Mayan community as a result of the peace process in Guatemala is also a case in point. See Jonas 2000.

NINE

Soft Intervention and the Puzzling Neglect of Economic Actors

SUSAN L. WOODWARD

Could external actors who intervene to help countries end a civil war increase their leverage if they added economic incentives and actors to the current preoccupation with warring parties, peacekeeping forces, and demobilization? Even the most casual understanding of the evolution of peacemaking and peace-building practice since 1990–91 would consider this a foolish question. Although current international strategy does emphasize cooperation among armed groups and security guarantees, and by the mid-1990s, pressure had mounted to use military instruments for compliance—coercive diplomacy, "robust" (military) implementation of international norms and mandates, and peace "enforcement"—there has also been an increasing emphasis on economic instruments. Indeed, far from seeing economic considerations as alternatives, the current era of international activism in peacemaking and peace-building treats coercive and noncoercive instruments as complementary in the drive to expand in every way possible the resources, tools, and leverage at its disposal.[1] The more resources, in brief, the more likely efforts at peace are to be effective.[2]

That the composition of a resource package might be internally contradictory or that coercive strategies might have negative consequences appears of little significance in the hunt for resources. Of the resources employed, the most common are economic incentives—from credits and loans to the offer of trade agreements and access to export markets, or the threat of isolation from such economic goods and from legitimation. The assumption is that these resources will induce cooperation with external interveners and in implementing a peace agreement.[3] Is this assumption correct? The evidence is surprisingly thin. Moreover, the literature is extremely vague on the target of such incentives. To the extent that actors are discussed at all, the focus is on the army of external economic actors—the international financial institutions (IFIs), aid donors, multilateral development banks and agencies, foreign investors, and civil-military reconstruction teams—who seek to provide a "peace dividend" (a form of purchase) through physical repairs and promises of aid for economic recovery. When local recipients are identified, they are primarily political actors: the general population as voters, militia leaders and ex-combatants, or politicians.

To assess the conditions under which a noncoercive strategy for peace implementation might succeed, this chapter turns attention directly onto local economic actors. It argues that local economic actors are critical to the creation and sustainability of the peace, but that the current economic-incentives approach fundamentally misunderstands their role and its causes. Further, to understand that role and the room for third-party leverage, one needs a political-economic understanding of civil war and of peace agreements. The essence of a peace agreement after civil war is the reform or reconstitution of a state, and all states are characterized by the interests they represent. However, international actors also have economic interests in the kind of state that a particular peace agreement aims to establish. The current approach to incentives from third parties to local actors presumes that outsiders are autonomous vis-à-vis the political calculations of local actors, whereas, in fact, outsiders' economic and political interests are endogenous to the trajectory and outcome of a peace process.

The chapter begins by laying out the assumptions that underlie the current approach of international economic intervention. It then turns to the conditions under which local economic actors can be expected to be peace-promoting, in two ways—first in terms of the political settlement and second in terms of economic policies that business prefers. The chapter ends by questioning the puzzle of current policy and practice, the silence on, neglect of, and often even disincentives to domestic entrepreneurs and economic activity. This puzzling behavior is particularly surprising given that economic actors are so prominent in the literature of greatest influence on international policy as a (perhaps the) cause of civil war and its prolongation and also that the newest vogue in peace-building policy circles, as this volume goes to press, is "private-sector development," already known by its acronym, PSD.

Economic Causes of and Solutions to Civil War

Current international policies to end civil wars include a wide and complex range of economic incentives, policies, and projects that third parties offer to consolidate a peace agreement and its implementation. To the extent that there is a theoretical basis to these policies, that is, that they are grounded in expectations about the association (preferably causal) between these policies and peace, they are now primarily shaped by a literature on the economic causes of and related solutions to civil war by researchers at the World Bank that became extremely influential in policy circles during the latter 1990s. These causes are basically two: motivations (in later versions, sometimes called opportunities instead) that lead individuals to choose violence and organize a rebellion, and structural conditions, called "risk factors," that are said to make a country vulnerable to civil war. Of the two, only the first focuses on economic actors.

Civil wars are caused, according to this first motivations explanation, by opportunities to make a profit through war from "lootable natural resources" (e.g., diamonds, gold, timber, coffee, coltan), under the cover of violence and rebellion. War profiteers, greedy rebels, and looting, terms based on an analogy with organized crime but now commonly called the "greed hypothesis," promote and prolong war.[4] Although the literature on such individual motivations is vast and highly contested, the policy world appears to find the "greed" version compelling. Thus, to get those who control armed groups to the negotiating table, external policies aim to increase the economic costs of the war (primarily for those identified as rebels), by means of such strategies as economic sanctions, both targeted and generalized; trade embargoes; and international prohibitions on conflict-financing commodities, such as the Kimberly Process on diamonds. Once an agreement is negotiated and signed, what follows is an offer to remove prior sanctions and provide economic benefits to those who fulfill their signed agreements and to retain or increase economic sanctions and isolation on those who do not. Funds may also be offered to reward specific peace tasks (although their meager amounts may not be much of an incentive), for example, to party-signatories to transform their armies into political parties and to former combatants to hand over their weapons and return home.

There is, thus, a fundamental contradiction between the characterization of actors' economic interests at the start of or during war and the assumption that positive economic incentives will produce behavior that promotes peace once an agreement is signed, as if those interests became transformed overnight. In fact, interveners ignore this contradiction by thinking of those actors as political, not economic, at this crucial moment of a cease-fire and peace. This understanding is explicit in the concept of "peace conditionality," promoted by analysts who argue for more explicit calculation of external aid as a reward to political leaders for specific implementation of the provisions of the peace agreement or as a punishment for delays or obstruction, but the concept is not popular with the World Bank and most donors because of the economic costs to the structural solution of economic growth (see below) that would come from starting and stopping projects in relation to political actions (Boyce 2002, 2008). The one exception was the World Bank agreement with US-led sanctions on any aid to Bosnian Serbs in the first two years of implementation of the December 1995 Dayton Peace Accords until their leaders complied with specified political demands, although the policy was never portrayed as peace conditionality.

The economic incentives offered regularly to the general population are conceived as a "peace dividend," not as a selective reward or punishment but as an extension of the humanitarian impulse of wartime relief and as a way to buy support from local communities for the peacekeeping troops as one element of a "hearts and minds" campaign. These quick-impact projects, pioneered by the UN high commissioner for refugees and the International Organization for Migration in Guatemala and Cambodia but now standard, aimed to reintegrate internally displaced persons and refugees into their original communities with early recovery projects that were then supposed to be continued by other UN agencies or INGOs. Those used to win support for military peacekeeping troops, pioneered by British troops in the NATO-led Implementation Force in Bosnia and Herzegovina in 1996–97, are small, local projects of repair and recovery that can be undertaken with small amounts of money immediately—such as the reconstruction and repair of schools, local roads, and water wells—and identified by civil-military officers with local authorities (Woodward et. al 1999).[5]

Targeting of economic incentives to political leaders, particularly signatories to peace agreements and former leaders of militias, also tends to succumb to the more common assumption among donors that economic assistance in general is a strong incentive to peace and the task of implementation is a matter of available financial resources and local "absorptive capacity," not incentives. Thus, there has been a growth since 1999 of trust funds for general budgetary support of new governments or monies for police training or ex-combatant disarmament and reintegration. However, the range of restrictions on these funds, such as that they be separately managed by the United Nations or the World Bank, owing to the lack of trust among donors in the financial probity and accountability of postwar governments and politicians, would appear more likely to serve as disincentives to peace commitments. Donors also insist that project implementation be done by nongovernmental organizations (NGOs), almost always international ones (INGOs), while the World Bank gives prominent place early in its economic assistance to an anticorruption program. Case studies of aid routinely show that almost half of all aid to a country emerging from war is spent on foreign consultants and contracts reserved for companies from the donor country.[6] Forms of ever more intrusive international oversight on economic governance and public financial management in the first years of implementing a peace agreement, such as the Governance and Economic Management Assistance Programme (GEMAP) required of Liberia by the International Monetary Fund (IMF), the World Bank, the European Commission, the US Treasury, and USAID, appear to be an increasing trend.[7]

By far the more substantial use of economic tools in peace implementation strategies is that aimed at the "risk" or structural factors associated with war and peace, on the theory that the best guarantee for a sustained peace is economic growth. Such economic assistance is universally based on neoliberal growth strategy, sometimes called the Washington consensus, plus its institutional preconditions, the political reforms called "good governance" to produce a government willing and able to adopt these economic policies.[8] Based on economic and political theories that the more globally open an economy, the faster it will grow and the more likely it is to be politically stable, these policies comprise a long-term, transformative agenda, not a short-term policy of incentives, even though their adoption is given early priority—rapid and complete liberalization of monetary and trade policies, privatization of productive assets and effective enforcement of those property rights (sometimes called "the rule of law"), and immediate priority for monetary stability through orthodox macroeconomic policy.[9] The target of such policies is the private investor, above all foreign investors whose capital and expertise are considered necessary but who need a substantial incentive to invest where physical security and security of contract are not easily guaranteed. These policy prescriptions do also aim at the assumed motivations for war, to force the informal and illicit elements of the war economy into the formal, legal sector of the economy, but their inflexibility across different economic and political conditions suggests that they are viewed more as axioms than as policy instruments. Their occasion, moreover, is negotiations between the war-torn country and the IMF over its debt arrears so as to gain or renew membership in the IMF, without which a country cannot access loans or credits from the World Bank and regional development banks and capital markets—unrelated, in other words, to incentives for or interests in peace.

Alongside these macroeconomic policies, it is now common after a peace agreement is signed to require a national reconstruction strategy, usually designed by the World Bank with supplementary projects designed and funded by bilateral development donors and regional banks, based on a joint needs assessment mission by the IFIs and UN agencies and leading to a donors' conference. Under the rules for Heavily Indebted Poor Countries, and also as a precondition for access to IMF and World Bank loans or credits in general, governments are also required to formulate a national Poverty Reduction Strategy Paper (PRSP) through participatory processes, starting first with an Interim PRSP. In line with neoliberal growth theory, these strategies emphasize reconstruction of wartime damage, especially to infrastructure (roads, bridges, dams), and liberal economic reforms, as preconditions of both foreign and domestic investment and export revenues. Domestic entrepreneurs fall in the policy category of small and medium enterprises (SMEs), whose access to credit is foreseen as the outcome of a banking sector reform on private, commercial bases, but within the IMF macroeconomic framework of an independent central bank and currency regulations that are highly restrictive on the price of credit and the scope of governmental policy.

Local Economic Actors and the Class Basis of a Stable Peace

With the possible exception of banking reform aimed at SMEs, current policies thus include few or no positive incentives to local entrepreneurs as economic actors. Such incentives do figure in the burgeoning PSD agenda, but as a source of additional finances for peace-building tasks to complement official development assistance. These tasks are what International Alert calls "peace entrepreneurship": the local private sector should focus its profit-making activities on the *political* objectives of a peace agreement, providing employment for demobilized soldiers, youth, women, returning refugees, and persons internally displaced; ending the decades or even centuries of socioeconomic exclusion; and generally contributing to reconciliation, security, and peace advocacy (International Alert 2006). What the economic incentive is to invest in such political tasks, an externally designed list that does not originate in local conditions and its profitable opportunities, is not clear.

Nevertheless, local economic actors *are* critical to the creation and sustainability of peace. Their role is even more fundamentally political in the extent to which the postwar state that the peace agreement establishes conforms to their class interests. To understand how third parties can design noncoercive strategies for implementing a peace agreement that successfully engage local economic actors, we need to think in terms of their interests as a class and as collective actors. Equally, we need to view the third parties in class terms and interests. The current economic-incentives approach of selective rewards and punishments misunderstands the behavioral motivations of both domestic and foreign economic actors.

I propose that success in implementation will depend on the extent to which the state created by the peace agreement conforms to the class interests of both domestic capital and the relevant external power(s). The less the domestic business sector is defined as a class or the more its class interests or those of domestic business and foreign powers are divided, the more fragile the peace and its sustainability will be. This section explores this relationship and variation with selected case studies.

A particularly useful start is the explanation given by Mark Peceny and William Stanley for the success of third-party strategies in achieving and implementing peace in Central America in the early 1990s, because the success was based, they argue, on a noncoercive strategy (Peceny and Stanley 2001). No forceful security guarantees were provided or necessary; indeed, at one point when the United States, as a major intervening power, chose a security-based policy, it backfired. The security approach, they argue, was only able to obtain cooperation instrumentally, not to transform the parties' interests and values into cooperation that was self-interested and, therefore, would last. Instead, the third parties (primarily the United Nations and the United States in these three cases) succeeded because they gained the commitment of the "dominant groups"—the former ruling coalition of conservative politicians and business elite—to "liberal norms and practices" that sent signals addressing "the fears of vulnerable combatants to such an extent that the demobilization of combatants [became] unproblematic." This "liberalizing domestic coalition" emerged in three phases: "in the first [purely instrumental] phase local actors adopt liberal practices as part of tactical efforts to legitimate themselves to the international community" (Peceny and Stanley 2001, 151). Business elites were prominent in this phase, motivated by fear of regionwide trade sanctions and their desire for access to US markets in a regional trade pact, both aimed by the United States as incentives to negotiate credibly for peace and abandon repression. In the next two phases, a transformation in the interests and corresponding practices of this political and economic elite supplanted international legitimation and economic benefits because, Peceny and Stanley argue, "virtually every international actor, including those with significant material influence and those with the greatest moral legitimacy, spread the same message and cooperated in socializing Central American political actors according to liberal principles" (150).

One must, however, add to this strategy the critical ingredient of economic interdependence between the two sides (government and rebels). The more the rebels could credibly threaten economic disruption, the greater the incentive for business elites to find a peaceful resolution. The outsiders' insistence on liberal economic policies acted to reinforce that necessary condition of economic interdependence, while the regional trade pact embedded that domestic interdependence in regional economic interdependence. Nonetheless, the details of the actions, monitoring, and consistency described by Peceny and Stanley and required for the strategy to be effective suggest that outsiders' actions were significant but also no simple task. The parallels with the US strategy for peace-building after World War II in Europe also make clear the crucial role as well of outsiders' interests.[10] These two ingredients, the extent of economic interdependence that motivates the class interests of local political and economic elites and the class interests of the dominant third party, also help explain the variation among the three Central American countries in the strategy's effectiveness—greatest in El Salvador, middling in Guatemala, and least in Nicaragua. That is, the economic incentives of interdependence, trade, and liberal economic policies supported a peace settlement based on liberal *political* principles and peace to the extent that such a postwar state was in the economic (class) interests of the business elite or, if not necessary to their economic activity, at least not in direct conflict with it. Similarly, the liberal economic strategy was in the economic interest of the main intervening power and was not in conflict with the interests of other donors and international actors on the scene.

The difference among the three cases also demonstrates, however, that business support for liberal principles was a result of a transformation in local class interests, as Elisabeth Wood shows beautifully for the case of El Salvador, that resulted from the war itself, not from the strategy of third parties. The civil war waged by the FMLN was, Wood argues, a war against the oppressive labor system in the Salvadoran countryside, a system based on a political-economic alliance between the landed oligarchy and a repressive state apparatus that landlords needed to ensure a cheap supply of peasant labor tied to agrarian production (2000). The war ended not because of military defeat—it was a stalemate—but because the economic interests of the landowning class had changed. Responding to the ever-rising costs (and in some areas, the impossibility) of agricultural production as a result of the war in the countryside, landowners sought alternative opportunities for profit in the cities, shifting investments to export-oriented manufacturing and commercial firms in the towns and ports. They thus no longer needed an authoritarian state to repress labor; indeed, such a state was a growing hindrance to their commercial interests, which included an expansion of trade with the United States and the region. The business elite could abandon its former class allies in the state apparatus and agree in negotiations to establish a democratic state, a compromise in the original FMLN goals but one they were willing to accept. No change occurred in the class basis of the state—the FMLN were in no military position to demand more—and thus the peace agreement could be successfully implemented. As one of the leading UN negotiators explained, their success in securing an agreement that could be implemented was precisely because the new government (ARENA) still represented the upper class in a society that remained highly stratified and was able to deliver the army, which had initially refused to sign the negotiated settlement.[11] Moreover, the design of the key FMLN demand for agrarian reform, the land-for-peace program, was the one proposed by the conservative government to be acceptable to the business class, which easily explains its many weaknesses, including the poor quality of land given to the ex-combatants and the refusal by business to provide the financing necessary to make it work.[12] The failure of the peace to improve the lives of the majority of the population, the frustrations of the demobilized FMLN soldiers, and the high levels of postwar violence analyzed by Charles Call and William Stanley (2002) led many to expect a collapse of the peace. Its continuing success (by the currently dominant definition of successful peace implementation)[13] can be explained by the crucial balance of class power that the peace agreement represented: a congruence of economic and political interests of the dominant economic class and of the primary regional economic power (the United States) with the terms of the political settlement.

The noncoercive intervention strategy analyzed by Peceny and Stanley was not uniformly successful in Central America, one can argue, because of variation in the economic interests of the elite and the intervening powers in relation to the peace agreements being implemented and the balance of class power locally. In Guatemala, although US interests were the same as in El Salvador, the wartime transformation of the economic elite and their class interests was less complete (Stanley 2007, 132–133). The war did alter the structure of the economy toward a greater role for services and industry, and thus it created a constituency for less repressive, more liberal policies, but the changes were "not as dramatic" as in El Salvador, and divisions remained within the business sector over businesspeople's preferred economic policies and especially the kind of state they could accept (Peceny and Stanley 2001, 171). These differences on the political right did not prevent capital, in general, from getting a peace agreement it could support, however, because the URNG (Guatemalan National Revolutionary Unity [in Spanish, Unidad Revolucionaria Nacional Guatemalteca]) rebels were much weaker politically and militarily than the FMLN. The political and economic elite conceded to the rebels' demand for liberal democratic reforms, write Peceny and Stanley, "to legitimize themselves to the international community" (2001, 170). Indeed, the business community even reacted strongly when President Jorge Serrano attempted to overthrow Congress and the courts and assume dictatorial powers. However, commitments in the peace agreement for socioeconomic reform were very vague, and "little of what was agreed to was actually implemented" (Stanley 2007, 134). In particular, the government insisted on a subsequent referendum on the reforms outlined in the peace agreement, and it was roundly defeated in May 1999 in large part as a result of a well-financed publicity campaign by sectors of business against it. Even strong pressure from the UN mission and the international financial institutions (acting surprisingly against type in this case) to include a commitment in the peace agreement to raise taxes and government expenditures was not sufficient to protect against its rejection in the referendum.

In Nicaragua the strategy was least effective, because the class interests of the United States were opposed to the political outcome of the anti-Somoza revolution of 1979. The United States waged a long and brutal war against the Sandinista government, which conceded in 1990 to the regional mediators' Esquipulas accord to hold internationally supervised elections in hopes of defeating the US-supported Contras. When the Sandinistas did not win the election, their leadership was persuaded to agree further to a power-sharing pact with the new president, Violeta Chamorro, but the war continued as the parties of business used the elections as an opening to push for a total reversal of the Sandinistas' revolutionary changes in property as well as the power-sharing agreement that kept those changes alive. The IFIs and donors also weighed in on the side of this right-wing business agenda and conditioned their assistance on a severe austerity package for macroeconomic stabilization and structural adjustment that prevented implementation of any of the socioeconomic commitments made in the peace settlement, including even those made to the Contras, and which completed the reversal of most of the socialist legislation.

This pattern of variation in the crucial role of business interests (local and foreign) in a political settlement that they can support and thus will be implemented can be seen elsewhere even without the international strategy that Peceny and Stanley argue was critical in Central America. The cases of

South Africa in 1990–94 and, even more so, Haiti since 1994 have striking similarities to what happened in El Salvador, whereas the cases of Haiti in 2004 and Mozambique appear to parallel the Nicaraguan case. After winning its national war of liberation against Portugal, the socialist regime of FRELIMO was forced to fight a second war against neighboring Rhodesia and South Africa in the form of a civil war with RENAMO and an economic blockade from the United States, the United Kingdom, and others. That war also ended as a result of changed class interests both internationally (with the end of the racist regimes in Rhodesia and South Africa and a change in Soviet foreign policy) and domestically, within FRELIMO, when party members in the countryside had grown wealthy during the war and military officers were increasingly engaged in economic activities. This new economic elite pushed for and won an internal party battle to allow private property and entrepreneurship in 1982–83. Already in 1985, the socialist government began discussions with the IMF and the World Bank for support, in part because financial aid from the USSR and Cuba collapsed but also because of the economic interests of this winning party faction. Although Italian support for peace negotiations surely helped, the interests of this emerging business class among the FRELIMO party cadre in access to rents and foreign aid through state power and peace combined with the interests of the new, large foreign-owned firms responding to the government policies required by the IMF program to encourage foreign direct investment. This resulted in opportunities for oligopolistic markets in beer, sugar, cement, and the massive energy complex on the border with South Africa and encouraged support for the resulting peace agreement and its implementation. As in El Salvador, the failure of postwar economic developments to make even meager change in the lives of the majority of the population did not prevent the world from calling the Mozambican peace process a success or donors (including the IFIs) from seeking to keep this "success" from reversal with extreme levels of Mozambican aid dependence more than a decade later (Cramer 2006, 259–272; Castel-Branco 2007). Implementation of the peace agreement can thus be attributed to an alliance of economic interests that included domestic landowners, domestic traders of raw materials (especially cashews), foreign investors (especially in sugar, the MOZAL energy complex on the border with South Africa, and other megaprojects) (Ryan 2004), and aid donors. As with South Africa and Haiti, however, one can question the long-term stability of a peace based on democratic principles that concede so little economically to the majority.

For all the economic power of private business, however, business class interests cannot influence political outcomes without acting collectively, that is, as a class, and such collective action is not always easy, especially given the competition of a market economy (Ben-Porat 2005). If business is too internally fragmented to mobilize as a politically unified force, it may concede to a negotiated agreement but not support its implementation, as the Guatemalan case suggests. Even more difficult are those countries where domestic entrepreneurs are too small in numbers or too weak economically to form a class and to articulate their class interests in the nature of the state. The high robust association between poverty and civil war may even reflect this situation.

According to Roland Marchal, for example, Somali businesses want peace and have been willing to finance militias and especially, by the late 1990s, the Islamic courts to give them security, but they continue to focus on their short-term commercial interests and are both internally divided and ambiguous about the kind of state they want. "Overly dependent on the State for major contracts and opportunities" between 1969 and 1991, the business class has grown ever more diversified and autonomous as a result of war since then, but it "still has a long way to go before it can acquire an autonomous consciousness of its social function" (Marchal 2000, 23, 21). Because the Somalia civil war is a "modern war, a war about the concept of the State," the resulting inability to conclude debates about representation, including the weak level of organized representation and related collective consciousness of business, precludes a stable peace settlement (2002, 16). In Alex de Waal's analysis, the war is competition among businesses over the economic interests the state will represent, specifically "riverine agricultural land, pastureland, remittances from overseas workers and the resources that can be captured and dispensed by a sovereign state, including foreign aid and currency," and the expectations that any "future government will be able to bestow the same benefits on its favoured capitalists" as it did in the 1980s—and thus also the fear of being excluded from these benefits. Peace in Somaliland, by contrast, can be explained by the presence of a regionally dominant class that can "stabilise the state": the Berbera-based livestock traders "who were terrified by the commercially disastrous implications of the fighting in Berbera in mid-1992" but who, in the crucial "absence of major property disputes . . . arising from former state patronage" that persist in Mogadishu and the Jubba and Shebelle valleys, were also able to create "hegemonic control over regional resources" (de Waal 2002).

These two analyses suggest the conditions under which an international strategy of economic incentives may not succeed in ending civil wars. By focusing on the profit motive of "warlords" in prolonging the war and thus sanctions or incentives to shift the economic interests of warring parties toward peace, such a strategy is likely to fail if it does not first analyze the productive base and class interests of those parties. They may well bargain to protect their own capital assets but not have an articulated class interest in the kind of state, and thus implementable political settlement, that they seek to protect those interests. The current diplomatic emphasis on power sharing makes the same mistake. As de Waal concludes for Somalia, those economic and ownership conflicts must be settled prior to the formation of a government; a power-sharing strategy, by contrast, legitimates all interests as a political incentive to come to a negotiating table and then only stimulates political competition over the rent-seeking possibilities of access to state power and thus perpetuates the conflict and the war (de Waal 2002). It is as if third-party mediators viewed the state as a collection of state portfolios to be portioned out like capital assets as an economic incentive to agree to cease fighting forever. A federal, power-sharing political settlement may well work to get signatures on a piece of paper where warring parties have bases of economic wealth and capital that are territorially specific, as in those often labeled "resource wars"—between the North and South of Sudan, between the mining interests of Kabila and forest interests of Bemba in the 2002 Sun City agreement for the Democratic Republic of Congo, in the autonomy concessions to Aceh and to Papua by the Indonesian government in Jakarta, or in the oil agreement and related political institutions that were hashed out in 2007–8 in Iraq. But territorial autonomy over capital assets is not the same as common agreement on the economic role of the state and its regulatory and coercive powers; an agreement on the distribution of revenues from natural resources, similarly, is not sufficient to define the interests and property rights that a new state will represent and protect. Therefore, one can hypothesize, power sharing alone will not be stable. The crisis in Sudan in 2008 over the position in the North-South agreement of Abyei Province, not to speak of the ongoing conflict over Darfur and eastern Sudan, which were not included in the peace accord although territorially part of the country; the collapse of the Sun City agreement in the Democratic Republic of Congo (DRC); and the continuing conflict over the status of Kurdish Iraq all illustrate this point. Indeed, by introducing incentives, third parties may make matters worse by misunderstanding the state and the role of their own interests. While the US government pressured both sides to agree in Iraq, American oil companies (encouraged by the White House and the State Department) signed contracts with the Kurdish regional government and thus worked against a resolution by altering the economic balance of power before a common agreement on the Iraqi state was complete (Rubin and Kramer 2007; Glanz and Oppel 2008).

Peace agreements based on a power-sharing solution, because it is centered on a distributive understanding of state protection and not a class concept of the state, are even more difficult to implement because they are vulnerable to exogenous changes in the relative balance of economic power and interest among the parties and thus also to the refusal by at least some of the parties to be locked in. In Lebanon, the Ta'ef agreement of 1990 was a consociational strategy based on an economic balance among Lebanon's confessional groups that was, in fact, already out-of-date at the time of signing, making the agreement extremely vulnerable to disruption, as soon became clear.

Business Self-Interest in Peace and Its Limits

The idea that third parties can design a noncoercive strategy for peace implementation based on economic incentives to local economic actors is based, it would appear, on the "greed hypothesis" of Paul Collier and his associates in the literature on the causes of civil war and on the war-economies literature of David Keen, Karen Ballentine, and others. That is, rebels and "warlords" must be given material incentives to abandon their gains from the looting, criminal trafficking, and resource predation that war allows. This premise encounters two problems. First is its very narrow concept of civil war, excluding all cases of social revolution (such as in Nicaragua, Nepal, El Salvador, and aspirationally in Haiti), nation building (in Palestine and Sri Lanka), and secession (in all of the former Yugoslav wars and those in the Caucasus), and thus the types of political settlement one might expect. It also conflicts with most empirical studies of wartime economic activity. Case evidence is strong, in fact, that not only the vast majority of the population who are trying simply to survive, but also most business people, would always choose peace over war.[14] The business elite are often those most actively pressing for peace. As Guy Ben-Porat writes, "peace dividends [which he equates with "economic incentives"] are the result not only of decisions made by major states, but also of the investment strategies of private business. . . . the business community is sensitive to the costs of the conflict and, due to its global linkages, aware of the potential benefits of its resolution" (2005, 331n30). In those instances in which business interests favor the current international preference for liberal intervention (Peceny and Stanley) or liberal internationalism (Paris), third parties have natural allies in business without any need to design incentives.

Case studies also suggest, however, that business pressure for a liberal peace is not sufficient for successful implementation of a peace agreement; the economic and political consequences of such a peace and associated economic policies also matter. Analyses by Ben-Porat of Israel and Northern Ireland and by Sunil Bastian of Sri Lanka provide support for this argument. The economic crisis of the 1980s in Israel, Ben-Porat writes, led the government to undertake in 1985 a liberalizing economic reform, reducing among other things the protected relationship of business to government and emphasizing an export-oriented strategy and global expansion beyond regional markets and investment, especially for a growing high-tech sector. As occurred in El Salvador as a consequence of war, changes in the source of profit and composition of the dominant sectors of the business class produced a change in their views of the conflict with Palestinians. Now the economic costs of the conflict and the occupation (particularly with the start of the first Intifada in 1987) became constraints on their new "global ambitions" and on the general success of this economic reform. The business community strongly supported the electoral victory of Labor in 1992 and Shimon Peres's concept of a "New Middle East" in which Israel would become the logistic and marketing center of the region and, in turn, become a global player; business thus embraced the Oslo principles in 1993 as a necessary component. Ben-Porat records how the Israeli stock market soared in response to the Oslo agreement while major newspapers drew the conclusion of "investors betting on peace" (2005, 339) and associated the peace accords with a coming economic boom. And indeed, new markets opened up beyond the Middle East with the end of the Arab boycott, and foreign investment flowed into Israel (increasing ten-fold within a few years).

The political consequences, however, were not as Labor and the business community expected because the benefits of this growth were not widely shared. The Palestinian economy, as a result of the accords, went "from bad to worse" (Ben-Porat 2005, 342). Arab states began to fear an Israeli economic takeover because of the distinct differences in their competitiveness regionally. Rapid liberalization brought growing inequalities within Israel, revealing the upper class and Ashkenazi bias of the business community because other social strata and non-Ashkenazi were negatively affected, and business itself "invested few if any resources to incorporate alienated sectors" (343). In the elections of 1998, Likud won, according to Ben-Porat, because Labor had become identified as the party of big business and because of growing popular alienation at the economic consequences within both Israel and the Palestinian territories.

Ben-Porat concludes, however, that the Israeli business community made a tactical error in becoming too much associated politically with the peace process and the Labor Party. Had it retained autonomy, the peace agreement could have been sustained. He supports this argument by turning to Northern Ireland, where the business community also began to view regional and global economic opportunities as the source for new growth, in part out of the demonstration effect of growth in the Irish Republic and in part out of concern that British subventions would not last forever at a time when the Ulster economy had been declining sharply for almost twenty years. As in Israel, they perceived the limit to such economic profits to be the civil war. Business (including a majority of Protestant businesses) began to call for greater cross-border economic interaction and a "single island economy," North and South, and despite alarms raised from Protestant politicians, the Northern Ireland Confederation of British Industry (CBI) even published a paper in 1994 supporting the 1993 joint Social Democratic and Labour Party (the principal nationalist Catholic party) and Sinn Fein statement and the Downing Street Declaration on the grounds of the economic implications. Almost immediately the Irish Republican Army (IRA) announced a cease-fire and six weeks later came the Loyalist declaration. The economic results, as in Israel, were striking: tourism soared, unemployment fell, and aid and investment flowed in from the European Union, the British government, the United States, Canada, and Australia. Manufacturers and larger businesses were particularly optimistic.

Nonetheless, by 1996, negotiations over demobilization ("decommissioning") were at a stalemate, and the cease-fire broke down. Divisions within the business community began to emerge over economic policy, such as between the expansionist goals of big business and less competitive, smaller, local businesses and between big business and the trade unions, and the chambers of commerce representing small and medium enterprises withdrew from the big-business-dominated CBI. Realizing that business was also divided over the referendum in 1998, the CBI then chose to distance itself from any explicit political support and also "declared its commitment to 'social responsibility,' understanding that its desire for market economics could not be fully realized" (Ben-Porat 2005, 344). The Good Friday Agreement was accepted in 1998, although full implementation took almost a decade in the face of continuing divisions within both business and political communities.

Bastian's analysis of the Sri Lankan case adds the crucial role of elections, in this story of the consequences of pressure for peace from the business community (both domestic and international), for liberal economic, globalizing reform. He begins with a seminal article by Newton Gunasinghe on the role of the liberalizing market reforms in the late 1970s in provoking the 1983 anti-Tamil violence because of "the loss of state patronage in the case of small businesses and undermined welfare benefits received by the urban poor" (Bastian 2008, 1). The new United National Front (UNF) government elected in December 2001 entered into peace negotiations with the Tamil Tigers (LTTE) and obtained a cease-fire that lasted until 2007, but its goal, too, was to respond to an economic crisis in 2001 with a new round of market reforms. The platform of the UNF election campaign, representing its primary social base, the interests of capital (Bastian 2008, 7), was that peace negotiations were "necessary to revive the economy" and get it "back on track" (6). The starkness of this economic motive is revealed in the government's apparent disregard for the political consequences of the macroeconomic policies of orthodox stabilization and structural adjustment policies; that is, implementation of those macroeconomic policies also required a radical political reform of the central state, supported by the business elite, a reform directly counter to the political compromise on state reform that would be necessary for peace with the LTTE. As in other cases as well, the UNF government devised no program to address the potential social costs of this policy, so convinced was it, apparently, of the trickle-down benefits of liberalization.

International donors and multilateral banks rushed in with large doses of economic assistance to the Colombo government (including agreements with the IMF and the World Bank) in support of both economic reform and the 2003 cease-fire agreement, but this aid advantaged one party to the conflict only (the Sinhala government). All projects for the Tamil North or East remained hostage to the delays in the peace process, and donors never calibrated aid to reward or punish progress or setbacks related to the cease-fire agreement. Indeed, the IFIs and the donors focused their support entirely on the economic agenda and took the cease-fire for granted. The result was a total electoral defeat of the UNF in April 2004 by the government's own constituency, the Sinhala population harmed by the reforms. There had been growing regional inequalities, rising poverty and unemployment, drastic cuts in state employment, an end to most employment protections, and total removal of the protections since independence for the small-scale peasant farmers growing paddy, the largest component of the electorate. That the reforms were perceived to benefit "only big business" reinforced the alienation their outcomes caused. The electoral reaction brought to Colombo a new government committed to a military strategy against the LTTE, a breakdown in the cease-fire by early 2007, and by 2008 9, open war aimed at total defeat of the LTTE.

Strictly speaking, the Israeli and Sri Lankan cases represent the failure of a cease-fire agreement to consolidate into a sustainable peace agreement, though it would have been supported by business, not its failed implementation. The case of Lebanon suggests that this distinction among stages in ending civil wars may be too artificial. The same relation among the economic interest of business (and the government it supports) in peace and the influence on its sustainability of the consequences of those economic interests (as in a liberal economic policy) can also derail the first, fragile years after a formal peace agreement (e.g., Ta'ef in October 1990).

Of all the cases yet discussed, Lebanon has the most developed business class, but it is divided along sectarian lines—Christian (Maronite), Sunni, and Shiite—and the political settlement of its civil war in 1990 enshrined the distribution of wealth and economic power among them at the time in a power-sharing design for the state (as opposed to the alternative that many argue is necessary to a sustainable peace in Lebanon, a secular democratic system). However, while segments of the business community did not agree to Ta'ef because the war had changed their economic interests, as in El Salvador, the war and exogenous forces together did unleash changes in the demographic and wealth balance among them. As Ghassan Dibeh explains, "an influx of capital from the Gulf mainly through Sunni channels was already shifting the sectarian distribution of commercial bank ownership in the 1980s," there was an "incursion of Muslims into traditionally held wealth spaces" of Christians in the commercial and service sector, and a fight erupted in 2002 over the law on exclusive dealerships in 2002 (the "hallmark of Lebanese capitalism") between "Christian merchants who dominated the commanding heights of the import sector" and the Sunni-dominated Hariri group that had come to control the influential Council of Development and Reconstruction (CDR) (2005, 20).

While the economic outcomes of government policies after the Ta'ef accords are a complex story, local analysts emphasize two that were particularly damaging to the peace. First, the government chose a finance-based approach to economic growth, strongly supported by the IFIs and the donors, which, in the context of a peace agreement that required distributive justice, could only lead to a fiscal crisis (Dibeh 2005). When peace after civil war requires a reknitting of national identities, loyalties, and goals, this economic policy approach also prevents the kind of state policies necessary to a national development plan and inclusive, countrywide policies.

Instead, the CDR planned and donors supported a collection of specific projects based on sectional rent-seeking, as usual.

Second is the role of Rafik Hariri in designing the program for postwar development as a private entrepreneur through his private development company, Solidere, before and during his multiple terms as prime minister. The Hariri policies represented the balance of economic power in Lebanese capital and their focus on the central (and wealthy, elite) areas of Beirut to the exclusion of the suburbs and the rest of the country, a massive transfer of property rights from homeowners to his company, and the assumption of "trickle-down development" and focus on private profit for an "internationally connected elite" rather than public goods (such as transport and social housing).[15] The effect was not only widespread protests within Beirut from intellectuals, homeowners, and squatters, but also the creation of a constituency for Hezbollah in Lebanese politics among those excluded outside Beirut and in its suburbs and, in 2006, the social basis on which to challenge the state itself. As Kathrin Höckel wrote in 2007, Hariri's reconstruction policies for private benefit not only contributed to further instability in Lebanon but also created "new conflicts over assets, influence and identity, problems with which the country continues to struggle" (2007, 2). Both Dibeh and Höckel emphasize that the vertical inequalities created by Hariri's economic policies compounded the horizontal (sectarian) clientelism of the Ta'ef agreement and its rigidity as a sustainable political compact.

The role that outside actors can play in gaining the support of private economic actors—the business community—in implementing a peace agreement is usually focused on the first years after war, although their role in the kind of agreement negotiated is crucial to its implementation also. Whereas a local business community, or factions, will support an agreement that they perceive to be in their immediate and long-term interests, and if they achieve that, no additional incentives will be needed, the logic of the economic consequences and their political implications of a particular peace agreement that big business can accept or even may promote may also play out over a much longer period. Awareness of this relationship by third-party negotiators, who should have more room for choice, and by those such as the IFIs and the donors who provide initial financial support (often as incentives), could go a long way toward avoiding choices that build in long-term trouble, as in the very clear case of the compromises in the 1979 Lancaster House Agreement for Zimbabwe, particularly on land ownership. Similarly, commitments made in peace agreements, such as racial redress in the South African accords of 1990–94 or the "peace dividend" so common in the rhetoric of external interveners in general, require a state with sufficient public control over economic resources to fulfill them, not the immediate and extreme liberalization (and its beneficiaries) of the current conventional wisdom coming from outsiders.

International Strategy and Entrepreneurs

The most puzzling aspect of current intervention approaches to ending civil wars is their ambivalence about local entrepreneurs. If economic incentives are meant to promote support for peace, if a peace dividend is conceived in terms of economic benefits, and if the private business sector is the essential economic actor in current strategies, why are there so few incentives and so many disincentives to the encouragement of a domestic entrepreneurial class? One explanation may be the parallel ambivalence in the literature on causes and solutions: do entrepreneurs profit through war or peace? An alternative explanation is more specific to peace-building interventions and the fundamental distinction for most external actors between the short term and the long term.

The striking metaphor posed in 1994 by Alvaro de Soto and Graciana del Castillo in their analysis of the El Salvador peace process of a patient on the operating table with two surgeons, a curtain drawn along the center of the body and each working on only one half, with a different diagnosis and oblivious to the other—the political mandate for peace of the United Nations mission and the economic mandate of the IFIs—had a salutary effect in provoking better cooperation on the long-term goal of peace.[16] If that patient were the local entrepreneur, whether small or large, the metaphor of partition would still hold, transposed to roles seen as necessary to peace in the short run and those focused on the long run.

In the short run, the aim of external economic assistance and incentives is defined politically—the specific tasks that international actors define as peace implementation: disarmament, demobilization, and reintegration (DDR); reconciliation and transitional justice; human rights; rule of law; democratic elections; and refugee return. To achieve these tasks, there is growing attention to private-sector development (PSD) by the UN Peacebuilding Commission, the UNDP and the International Labor Organization, major development agencies such as the British Department for International Development (DFID) and the German Gesellschaft für Technische Zusammenarbeit (GTZ), the World Bank, and major NGOs working on conflict, such as the London-based International Alert. Their focus, however, is motivated by the ceaseless search for more resources that, they hope, the private sector can provide in the absence of public-sector resources internationally or in the postwar country.[17] The targets of PSD, however, are foreign investors (and the economic policies needed to attract their investment) and the country's diaspora (whose patriotism is evoked to gain money for the homeland) on the assumption, apparently, that there is no private sector to tap within the country.

The economic consequences of the international strategy for this short-term phase of peace-building, moreover, appear to act more as disincentives to peace. The case literature on postconflict countries is replete with evidence from public opinion surveys and ethnographic narratives that people resent the economic framing of a peace dividend, insisting that they cannot be "bought" and seeing such assistance as a "bribe" inappropriate to the nature of their wartime sacrifices and the political and moral issues at stake (Griffiths and Barnes 2008, 3–4).[18] When asked what their priorities are in the first years, they uniformly, regardless of context, emphasize economic survival. As one Sierra Leonean researcher was told repeatedly, "Now we have the vote and we can say freely what we think, but we have no job."[19] Civil wars occur in local communities, and they disrupt most the economic and social networks necessary for the survival of small traders, farmers, and craftspeople (Mwanasali 2000; Kalyvas 2006; Wood 2008).[20] Quick-impact projects and microprojects do not even intend to be developmental or employment-generating, and evidence is overwhelming that they are rarely economically viable even in the short run ("Evaluation of the Western Bosnia Rehabilitation Programme" 1999; Woodward 2004, 5). They do not produce the needed income or "jobs." Initial development projects in peace-building operations are currently based on what USAID, the World Bank, and other donors call "community development." However, these projects are confined to participatory mechanisms for choosing a local project for donor financial support, not on building the many links among communities, from transportation and communication to national regulations, that are necessary for economic activity. Among these links are those that enable farmers to market their produce, enable traders to function, and connect suppliers and producers in such a fashion as to make an economy function and make capital accumulation possible.

The intended disincentives to wartime commanders to go into business after the war, either because of policies aimed at punishing them as "warlords" and "war profiteers" or at transforming them into peacetime politicians, is particularly curious when their wartime tasks clearly required highly sophisticated entrepreneurial and managerial skills. If rebels are, indeed, motivated by stifled opportunities for profit in the legal economy, as the "greed" school in the World Bank research group argues, then policies to provide such opportunities and incentives for entrepreneurs would seem to make more sense. A glance at the later career paths of wartime leaders in cases where a leadership dispute or electoral defeat provokes their departure from politics reveals a notable parachute into business.[21] Even the examples that pepper much of the literature on postwar corruption focus on the business activities of those who remain in politics.[22]

Civil wars may not produce political revolutions, especially if third-party negotiations aim at a political compromise among parties, but they almost always entail social revolution, because they remove normal constraints, whether generational or social-status constraints, on upward mobility.[23] They also reward risk-takers who can maneuver in informal and highly globalized economic conditions, promoting new entrants and businesses where some protection against violence can be found. Yet the economic conditions in the immediate postwar period are currently defined by the IMF, the terms of its agreement on debt arrears and its priority on monetary stability through orthodox macroeconomic policy, which has been shown to create such tight credit markets that most local producers cannot compete with foreign investors. The IFI demand of immediate trade liberalization is devastating to vulnerable domestic producers when cheap imports rush in. Even the innovative World Bank project in Bosnia and Herzegovina in the first postagreement year to promote investment by providing a strategic insurance facility against investor risks was aimed at foreign investors, not domestic entrepreneurs.

The failure of the usually massive presence of international actors, both military and civilian, to provide incentives and opportunities to local business in the first years after war is even starker. Although their presence does inject an immediate stimulus to the real estate market and services such as restaurants, mainly in the capital city, a systematic study by Michael Carnahan, William Durch, and Scott Gilmore in eight active UN field missions (Kosovo, Timor-Leste, Sierra Leone, DR Congo, Haiti, Côte d'Ivoire, Liberia, and Burundi) found that less than 10 percent of all spending by the international mission went directly into the local economy, that "77–95 percent of the mission's economic impact was concentrated in or near the capital city" and "in those industries and sectors directly supporting the mission," such as construction and contracting, not on businesses that could survive the departure of the international presence. "Of the goods and services that missions bought for themselves, about 80 percent" was spent on "imported goods or as profits to foreign firms who were awarded contracts."[24] Donors notoriously insist on tied aid, requiring their country's products and consultants, and there is a "pervasive bias against local suppliers" among donors and international organizations in postconflict settings, even though studies show that the foreign prejudices about corruption and low quality of local businesses that are said to deter local procurement have no basis in any factual difference between local and offshore procurement (Boyce 2008, 32, 34). Huge portions of aid budgets go, in fact, to consultants who are also outsiders.[25] As has long been well documented, local labor markets are also seriously distorted by international wage and salary scales, with which the local private sector (and the civil service as well) cannot compete. While raising labor costs for local businesses, they also drain skilled talent away to international agencies but not into positions that utilize their local skills, thus seriously depressing local human capital in the long run.

The failure of third parties to structure incentives for local entrepreneurs and entrepreneurial talent and the vast disincentives to economic activity in the first years after an agreement, however unintended, do not logically follow from neoliberal economic strategy and liberal political strategy, with their rhetorical emphasis on the private sector, markets, commercial profit, and the "rule of law" (emphasizing private property rights), unless the economic agenda is focused on the long term. Certainly the PSD agenda in countries both vulnerable to violent collapse and emerging from war is to *develop* a private sector, not to identify and utilize an existing one.[26] The economic policies of the multilateral banks and development donors, their donors' conferences, and national reconstruction plans and PRSPs, similarly, aim at long-term, structural transformation. In the short run, it is said, absorption capacity is low (but by this statement, what is meant is the government), while the incentives to domestic investment will only emerge in the long run after a framework of laws and regulations is in place. But this strategy takes a long time to show results, and unless there is already a robust domestic business class, the beneficiaries tend to be foreign investors and INGOs, not domestic actors.

Given the prominence of attention to the role of economic interests and profit in the causes and prolongation of civil wars and the place of economic incentives in the war-termination and peace-implementation policies of third parties since about 1994–95, the pervasive silence in such international strategies and actions about local economic *actors*—the business class, local entrepreneurs—is puzzling. This chapter has argued that domestic entrepreneurs are crucial to the successful implementation of a peace agreement in four ways that provide substantial leverage for third parties who would seek to use it. The first precedes a peace agreement: the costs of war may well change the political interests of the business class in such a way that its members are willing to abandon the regime and support negotiations over a new kind of state. They may even bring the greatest pressure to bear on a government for peace. International policies aimed at that cost calculus, such as economic sanctions, trade embargoes, or promises of aid and trade pacts, if they change the economic activities and class interests of business, can contribute to that transformation in political interests, but those policies can also make the postwar peace-building process more difficult if they—as currently—are not tailored to the specific nature of class power and economic activity in the particular country. Sanctions, for example, always strengthen political hardliners, making a negotiation less likely, and the effects of all economic incentives and disincentives on the population do not end with the signing of a peace agreement.

Second, the extent of business support for a peace agreement depends on the extent to which businesspeople perceive the new state as representing, or at least protecting, their economic interests. The incentives are intrinsic to the agreement. Third parties, however, also have interests, and when these converge with the domestic elite's interests, the third parties will communicate their support in a range of rewards and reinforcement. When these interests oppose the likely political outcome of the civil war, it will not end, however much the local economic actors wish to have it end—and vice versa.[27] The idea that third parties can use incentives to obtain local business support for the peace wrongly assumes autonomy between the economic and political interests of both local business and third parties and the content of the peace agreement. Strategic choices and outcomes are endogenous to the power constellation in the negotiating period and to the equally or more fluid and contested period of its implementation. If third parties wish to influence the implementation positively, they are likely to be more successful if they are more attentive to the political consequences of their economic aid and policies.

Thus, third, if the goal of peace for the business class is a set of economic policies that have the consequence of increasing unemployment, both vertical and horizontal inequality in postwar society, and the antagonism of key political groups, then the peace process will remain fragile and at a stalemate. The question is how flexible third parties currently are with regard to their own economic, philosophical, or geopolitical interests in specific economic policies and models of the proper state. The evidence for local policy space and choice over state forms and economic policies in the immediate postwar period, particularly in ways that could consolidate the peace, is meager.

The greatest room for third-party leverage on the role of economic actors in supporting the peace would seem, instead, fourth, to be direct economic support for local businesses—the middle-class social basis for liberal democracy—and the domestic entrepreneurs who will create employment. Such a policy would entail no change in outsiders' convictions that economic recovery and growth are the strongest peace dividend and foundation of a sustainable peace. It would require radical change in their practices and their prejudices. A national bourgeoisie will not guarantee peace, but until one emerges in both economic and political (class) terms, the political bases of a sustainable peace will be absent.

References

"Afonso Dhlakama Goes into Business in Mozambique." 2007. *Indian Ocean Newsletter*, December 1.

Ballentine, Karen, and Heiko Nitzsche (eds.). 2005. *Profiting from Peace: Managing the Resource Dimensions of Civil War*. Boulder, CO: Lynne Rienner.

Bastian, Sunil. 2008. "Politics of Market Reforms and the UNF-Led Negotiations." Unpublished manuscript, in Woodward's collection.

Ben-Porat, Guy. 2005. "Between Power and Hegemony; Business Communities in Peace Processes." *Review of International Studies* 31, 2: 325–348.

Berdal, Mats, and David M. Malone (eds.). 2000. *Greed and Grievance: Economic Agendas in Civil Wars*. Boulder, CO: Lynne Rienner.

Boutros-Ghali, Boutros. 1992. *An Agenda for Peace: Preventive Diplomacy, Peacemaking, and Peace-Keeping*. New York: United Nations.

Boyce, James K. 2002. *Investing in Peace: Aid and Conditionality after Civil Wars*. Adelphi Paper No. 351. Oxford: Oxford University Press.

———. 2008. "Post-Conflict Recovery: Resource Mobilization and Peacebuilding." Working Paper Series No. 159, February, Political Economy Research Institute (PERI), University of Massachusetts, Amherst.

Brahimi Panel. 2000. *Report of the Panel on United Nations Peace Operations*, August 21. Available at www.un.org/peace/reports/peace_operations/. Retrieved November 11, 2008.

Call, Charles T. 2002. "Assessing El Salvador's Transition from Civil War to Peace." In *Ending Civil Wars: The Implementation of Peace Agreements*, ed. Stephen John Stedman, Donald Rothchild, and Elizabeth M. Cousens, 383–420. Boulder, CO: Lynne Rienner.

Call, Charles T., and William Stanley. 2002. "Civilian Security." In *Ending Civil Wars: The Implementation of Peace Agreements*, ed. Stephen John Stedman, Donald Rothchild, and Elizabeth M. Cousens, 303–326. Boulder, CO: Lynne Rienner.

Carnahan, Michael, William Durch, and Scott Gilmore. 2006. "Economic Impact of Peacekeeping: Final Report," March, United Nations Department of Peacekeeping Operations and Peace Dividend Trust. Available at www.stimson.org/pub.cfm?id=277. Retrieved November 11, 2008.

Castel-Branco, Carlos Nuno. 2007. "Aid Dependency and Development: A Question of Ownership? A Critical View." Available at www.iese.ac.mz. Retrieved May 19, 2008.

Collier, Paul. 2007. "Economic Causes of Civil War and their Implications for Policy." In *Leashing the Dogs of War: Conflict Management in a Divided World*, ed. Chester A. Crocker, Fen Osler Hampson, and Pamela R. Aall, 197–218. Washington, DC: U.S. Institute of Peace.

Collier, Paul, and Anke Hoeffler. 1998. "On Economic Causes of Civil War." *Oxford Economic Papers* 50, 4: 563–573.

Cortright, David (ed.). 1997. *The Price of Peace: Incentives and International Conflict Prevention*. Lanham, MD: Rowman and Littlefield.

Cramer, Christopher. 2006. *Civil War Is Not a Stupid Thing: Accounting for Violence in Developing Countries*. London: Hurst.

De Soto, Alvaro, and Graciana del Castillo. 1994. "Obstacles to Peacebuilding." *Foreign Policy* 94 (Spring): 69–83.

De Waal, Alex. 2002. "Class and Power in a Stateless Somalia." Discussion paper posted on Somalia Watch, www.somaliawatch.org/archivejun02/021015201.htm, on October 15. Retrieved May 19, 2007.

Dibeh, Ghassan. 2005. "The Political Economy of Postwar Reconstruction in Lebanon." UNU-WIDER Research Paper No. 2005/44. Available at http://works.bepress.com/ghassan_dibeh/1. Retrieved November 18, 2008.

Doyle, Michael W., and Nicholas Sambanis. 2006. *Making War and Building Peace: United Nations Peace Operations*. Princeton, NJ: Princeton University Press.

Dwan, Renata, and Laura Bailey. 2006. "Liberia's Governance and Economic Management Assistance Programme (GEMAP)," May. A joint review by the Department of Peacekeeping Operations' Peacekeeping Best Practices Section and the World Bank's Fragile States Group. Available at www.gemapliberia.org/files/WB_Joint_review_of_GEMAP.pdf. Retrieved November 11, 2008.

"Evaluation of the Western Bosnia Rehabilitation Programme, 1996–1998." 1999. Interim report, May 1999, and final report, November 25, Centre for Defence Studies, King's College, London.

Gerson, Allan. 2001. "Peace Building: The Private Sector's Role." *American Journal of International Law* 95, 102: 102–119.

Glanz, James, and Richard A. Oppel Jr. 2008. "Panel Questions State Department Role in Iraq Oil Deal." *New York Times*, July 3, section A.

Goodhand, Jonathan. 2006. *Aiding Peace? The Role of NGOs in Armed Conflict*. Boulder, CO: Lynne Rienner.

Griffiths, Aaron, and Catherine Barnes. 2008. "Incentives and Sanctions in Peace Processes." *Accord* 19. Available at www.c-r.org/our-work/accord/incentives/contents.php. Retrieved November 18, 2008.

Hansen, Stig Jarle. 2007. "Civil War Economies, the Hunt for Profit, and the Incentives for Peace (The Case of Somalia)." AE Working Paper No. 1, Department of Economics and International Development, University of Bath, UK. Available at www.regjeringen.no/en/dep/ud/Whats-new/News/2007/somaliaseminar.html?id=464581. Retrieved November 18, 2008.

Höckel, Kathrin. 2007. "Beyond Beirut: Why Reconstruction in Lebanon Did Not Contribute to State-Making and Stability," July. Occasional Paper No. 4, Crisis States Research Centre, LSE Development Studies Institute. Available at www.crisisstates.com/download/op/OP4.%20Hoeckel.pdf. Retrieved November 18, 2008.

International Alert. 2006. *Local Business, Local Peace: The Peacebuilding Potential of the Domestic Private Sector*. Available at www.international-alert.org/peace_and_economy/peace_and_economy_projects.php. Retrieved November 18, 2008.

Kalyvas, Stathis. 2006. *The Logic of Violence in Civil War*. Cambridge: Cambridge University Press.

Keen, David. 2000. "War, Crime, and Access to Resources." In *War, Hunger, and Displacement: The Origins of Humanitarian Emergencies*, ed. E. Wayne Nafziger, Frances Stewart, and Raimo Vayrynen, 283–304. Cambridge: Oxford University Press.

Kinzer, Stephen. 2008. "Life under the Ortegas." *New York Review of Books*, June 12.

Kozul-Wright, Richard, and Paul Rayment. 2007. *The Resistible Rise of Market Fundamentalism: Rethinking Development Policy in an Unbalanced World*. London: Zed Books.

Mack, Andrew. 2005–8. "Human Security Report and Human Security Brief." Available at www.hsrgroup.org. Retrieved November 18, 2008.

———. 2008. "Conflicts." Copenhagen Consensus 2008 Perspective Paper. Copenhagen Consensus Paper. Available at www.copenhagenconsensus.com. Retrieved November 18, 2008.

Marchal, Roland. 2000. "The Somali Private Sector: Its Role in Governance." Paper commissioned by UN Development Programme for the Human Development Report on Somalia. In Woodward's collection.

———. 2003. "A Survey of Mogadishu's Economy." European Commission, Nairobi, September.

———. 2005. "The Somali Private Sector." World Bank Report, April.

Mwanasali, Musifiky. 2000. "The View from Below." In Berdal and Malone 2000, 137–153.

Norton-Taylor, Richard. 2008. "40% of Afghan Aid Returns to Donor Countries, Says Report." *Guardian* (London), March 25. Available at www.guardian.co.uk/world/2008/mar/25/afghanistan.internationalaidanddevelopment1. Retrieved November 18, 2008.

Oxfam. 2008. *Afghanistan: Development and Humanitarian Priorities*. January. Briefing paper, available at Oxfam America, www.oxfamamerica.org/publications/afghanistan-development-and-humanitarian-priorities.

Paris, Roland. 2004. *At War's End: Building Peace after Civil Conflict*. Cambridge: Cambridge University Press.

Peceny, Mark, and William Stanley. 2001. "Liberal Social Reconstruction and the Resolution of Civil Wars in Central America." *International Organization* 55, 1: 149–182.

Rubin, Alissa J., and Andrew E. Kramer. 2007. "Official Calls Kurd Oil Deal at Odds with Baghdad." *New York Times*, September 28, section A.

Ryan, Orla. 2004. "Can Mozambique Gain from Investment?" *BBC News*, December 9. Available at http://news.bbc.co.uk/go/pr/fr/-/2/hi/business/4002525.stm. Retrieved November 18, 2008.

Sogge, David. 2006. *Papering Over the Gaps: Dutch Policy and Post-Independence Fragility in Angola, Guinea-Bissau, and Mozambique*. Working Paper No. 262, December. Center for Social Studies, University of Coimbra, Portugal. Available at www.tni.org/docs/200702051110523676.pdf. Retrieved November 18, 2008.

Stanley, William D. 2007. "Multiple Transitions and Interim Governance in El Salvador and Guatemala." In *Interim Governments: Institutional Bridges to Peace and Democracy?*

ed. Karen Guttieri and Jessica Piombo, 123–146. Washington, DC: United States Institute of Peace Press.

Thale, Geoff. 1997. "Incentives and the Salvadoran Peace Process." In Cortright 1997, 181–203.

United Nations Department of Social and Economic Affairs. 2008. "Things Fall Apart: The Vicious Circle of Economic Insecurity and Civil Conflict." In *World Economic and Social Survey 2008: Overcoming Economic Insecurity*, chapter 4. New York: United Nations. Available at www.un.org/esa/policy/wess/wess2008files/wess08/wess2008.pdf. Retrieved November 11, 2008.

Watkins, Charlotte. 2003. "Provincial Reconstruction Teams (PRTs): An Analysis of their Contribution to Security in Afghanistan." Master's thesis, Oxford Brookes University.

Wood, Elisabeth Jean. 2000. *Forging Democracy from Below: Insurgent Transitions in South Africa and El Salvador*. Cambridge: Cambridge University Press.

———. 2003. *Insurgent Collective Action and Civil War in El Salvador*. Cambridge: Cambridge University Press.

———. 2008. "The Social Processes of Civil War: The Wartime Transformation of Social Networks." *Annual Review of Political Science* 11 (June): 539–561.

Woodward, Susan L. 2004. "Peace Operations: The Civilian Dimension: Accounting for UNDP and the UN Specialized Agencies." A discussion paper prepared for the Center on International Cooperation, New York University, and presented at the meeting "Strengthening the UN's Capacity on Civilian Crisis Management," Copenhagen, June 8–9. Available at www.um.dk/en/servicemenu/NEWS/ConclusionsCopenhagenSeminarOnCivilianCrisisManagement.htm.

World Summit Outcome Document. 2005. Available at http://daccess-ods.un.org/TMP/6305970.html. Retrieved November 18, 2008.

Notes

1. Andrew Mack (2005–8) has made this point in every Human Security Report and Brief since the first in 2005; see also Mack 2008.
2. Doyle and Sambanis (2006) are most associated with this argumentation, but it is also the core theme of all UN documents on peace-building, from Secretary-General Boutros-Ghali's *Agenda for Peace* (1992) and the Brahimi Panel Report on UN Peacekeeping (2000), to the creation of the Peacebuilding Commission and the Peacebuilding Fund by the 2005 World Summit Outcome Document, followed by resolutions of the General Assembly and the Security Council, in response to the recommendation of the 2004 High Level Panel on Threats, Challenges, and Change.
3. Although it is focused on conflict prevention, see the useful volume on incentives edited by Cortright (1997).
4. Most influential was the World Bank project on the Economics of Crime, Violence, and Civil War led by Paul Collier. See Collier and Hoeffler 1998 and Berdal and Malone 2000, but also Keen 2000; Ballentine and Nitzsche 2005; Collier 2007. For important exceptions to this dominant argument, see Wood 2003; Marchal 2003, 2005; Stanley 2007. Particularly useful critiques can be found in Hansen 2007 and in UN Department of Social and Economic Affairs 2008, 125–27.
5. This concept has blossomed in Iraq and Afghanistan into the practice of provincial

reconstruction teams, economic programs run by the military once a territory has been declared secure; see Watkins 2003.

6. See, for example, Oxfam 2008.
7. GEMAP places strict controls over revenue collection, public expenditure, and government procurement and concessions; and international experts with cosignature authority were assigned to many governmental ministries and state-owned enterprises (see Dwan and Bailey 2006).
8. Paris (2004) is most clearly identified with this characterization.
9. The risk-factor analysis by the Political Instability Task Force lays particular stress on the high correlation between a country's openness to foreign trade and a low risk of political instability, including civil war. Political Instability Task Force, "Internal Wars and Failures of Governance, 1955–2007," available at http://globalpolicy.gmu.edu/pitf/, retrieved November 18, 2008.
10. See the very useful analysis in Kozul-Wright and Rayment 2007, 283–294.
11. Blanca Antonini, personal interview by Woodward, April 3, 2008. Geoff Thale (1997) explains military support as a response, instead, to US military aid and the threat of its withdrawal.
12. See Call 2002, 395–396. Indeed, to the extent any land reform occurred at all, according to Thale (1997, 188–89), it was because USAID financed it (and it still faced "tremendous resistance from Salvadoran elites"). Call (2002, 391, 410–412) also emphasizes the vagueness of the other socioeconomic reforms and commitments in the peace settlement, its neoliberal model, and its failure to benefit the majority of the population over time.
13. Doyle and Sambanis 2006, 72–75. These authors code negative ("sovereign") peace as no resumption of the war after five years; undivided sovereignty; no residual, organized violence that challenges the state; and positive ("participatory") peace as a minimum level of political openness based on the Polity Index.
14. On the Somalia case, see Hansen 2007, 40.
15. As Kathrin Höckel describes his role, "reconstruction in the 1990s was mainly concentrated in Beirut's Central District (BD) and became almost synonymous with the name Rafik Hariri and his reconstruction company Solidere. This domination by a private actor, the Sunni Saudi-Lebanese billionaire Hariri, was possible because unlike the state institutions that had been marginalized by a protracted war he had the capability and means to completely take over this major task, influencing the political decision makers to achieve a transfer of power in favour of his planning proposal. His later position as prime minister allowed him to lift loyal supporters into influential positions in key institutions such as the Council for Reconstruction and Development or the local government of Beirut, thus managing to get official approval for his radical reconstruction programme against substantial opposition and criticism" (2007, 5).
16. But see Boyce on how little has been done—"accepted in principle" but almost nothing on "tools and capacities for implementation in practice" (2008, 24).
17. See "The Role of the Private Sector in Peacebuilding: Contribution of the PBC," summary of a strategy and policy discussion in the organizational committee of the UN Peacebuilding Commission, February 19, 2008; the conference concept note, "Private Sector Development and Peacebuilding—Exploring Local and International Perspectives," Berlin, Germany, September 14–15, 2006, organized by DFID, GTZ, International Alert, and the German Federal Ministry for Economic Cooperation and Development. See also International Alert 2006; Gerson 2001.

18. Xavier de Victor reports encountering this view harshly in Bosnia and Herzegovina, when he was World Bank desk officer for Bosnia immediately after the Dayton Accords.
19. Ismail Rashid, personal communication, July 2007.
20. Jonathan Goodhand (2006) distinguishes three types of economic spheres during civil war—the combat economy, the shadow economy, and the coping economy—but Mwanasali shows in detail in the case of eastern Zaire/DR Congo how interlocked these spheres are and how particularly difficult it becomes for those whose primary focus is survival.
21. This is a widespread pattern. One example is Bayardo Arce, one of the nine "commandants" who governed Nicaragua in the revolutionary directorate during the 1980s. Arce, who is currently special adviser to President Daniel Ortega on economic and financial matters, is "now a prosperous businessman." See Kinzer 2008, 62.
22. The economic activities of former South African president Thabo Mbeki are widely cited to explain his particular foreign-policy choices in Africa, for example. Afonso Dhlakama, an opposition leader in Mozambique, who is prominent in the literature on transforming militias into political parties (because of the trust fund that UN SRSG Aldo Ajello used as an incentive to gain his support for the peace agreement and run for elections), has recently become the main (90%) shareholder in Socadiv Holding Lda, which specializes in exporting wood and assorted material such as scrap metal. See "Afonso Dhlakama Goes into Business" 2007.
23. On the Somalia case, see Marchal 2000, 3.
24. Carnahan, Durch and Gilmore 2006. Quotations are taken from the Executive Summary, 1–6.
25. A study of aid to Afghanistan by Acbar (an alliance of international aid agencies working in Afghanistan, including Oxfam, Christian Aid, Islamic Relief, and Save the Children), written by Matt Waldman of Oxfam, for example, "estimated that 40 percent of all aid money spent in Afghanistan had returned to the rich donor countries, especially the US, through corporate profits, consultants' salaries and other costs," with the added effect of "significantly inflating the cost of projects." Quoted in Norton-Taylor 2008.
26. An exception to this argument, that PSD receives little or no attention in the short term, may be the US project in El Salvador described by Peceny and Stanley, for a private-sector think tank, FUSADES. Though it was also not specifically focused on entrepreneurs, its goal of transforming economic ideology through the design of government economic policies did, they write, provide "an organizational base for the more diversified and modernizing sectors of the elite" (2001, 165).
27. Although this point was made above in relation to Central America, and thus, the United States, it is not specific to the United States, as the example of DRC makes clear, or even the IFIs. See the very friendly but illuminating discussion in this regard on Lusophone Africa by David Sogge (2006).

TEN

Conclusions

CAROLINE A. HARTZELL AND MATTHEW HODDIE

Our goal of focusing on efforts by the international community to create stakeholders in peace helped to shape the structure of this book. From the outset, the contributors to this volume were agreed that we wanted to broaden our focus beyond the role peacekeeping forces play in the postwar peace process. Although peacekeeping troops address one of the central concerns that citizens have regarding the postwar environment, that of security, their charge generally has not extended to cultivating a variety of constituencies supportive of a durable peace. In addition, the limited number of instances of conflict in which peacekeeping forces have been deployed led us to concentrate on alternative means that third parties might employ in order to nurture stakeholders in peace.

Drawing on Donald Rothchild's expertise in the area of incentive strategies for conflict management, we decided to focus on the international community's use of incentives to persuade individuals and groups to support a fragile peace and disincentives to influence potential spoilers not to defect from an agreement. Based on this understanding of the relationship between third parties and postwar actors, we identified the two principal strategies the international community has relied on in its efforts to generate support for the peace in postconflict states: restructuring institutions and soft intervention. Accordingly, we organized the chapters to provide a detailed consideration of the international community's use of these two strategies.

How successful has the international community been in using these strategies to promote stakeholders, deter actors and groups hostile to stability, and secure the peace? As the chapters in this book suggest, the record is mixed. Although peace continues to hold in several of the countries in which third-party actors have intervened, in at least some instances the peace remains fragile and lacks legitimacy for some portions of the population. Based on the analyses offered here, the principal factors that explain this mixed record are a tendency on the part of third-party actors to impose their own visions of the peace on post–civil war states; problems involved in the coordination or sequencing of strategies; and a penchant on the part of the international community to focus on the interests of some members of society while neglecting others. Can the international community address these problems in a manner that would allow it to play a more constructive role in maintaining peace? Securing an affirmative answer to this question will depend in no small measure on the ability of third-party actors to take a critical look at the motives and consequences of their efforts to generate support for peace in post–civil war states.

Identifying Postwar Populations' Interests in the Peace

Not all postwar actors perceive themselves as having a vested interest in committing to a newly established peace. Potential defectors from an agreement include actors who have economic interests linked to their participation in plunder and other elements of the wartime economy. Equally problematic may be the leaders of groups who believe the politics of peace may lead to loss of the power they gained during the period of war. Contending with these types of spoilers may be so difficult that peace will not be secured until they pass from the scene. It was only with Jonas Savimbi's death and Charles Taylor's arrest, for example, that peace became a viable proposition for Angola and Liberia, respectively.

Although high-profile spoilers may command the bulk of the time, attention, and resources of the international community, peace may also founder if other actors, doubting that their interests will be served by peace, do not lend it their support. However, if significant portions of the postwar population come to believe that they have a stake in the peace, they should be more likely to acquiesce to the arrangement and may even act to defend it against the efforts of those who might seek to reinitiate hostilities. What are the interests citizens hope will be secured by the newly established peace? Three emerge as central from the analysis provided in this book. We focus on each in turn below.

Security and Order

Fear and the sense of insecurity that is prevalent in the immediate postconflict environment pose major challenges to efforts to stabilize peace. In an environment in which the state's claim to a monopoly on the instruments of violence only recently has been challenged by one or more armed factions, individuals and groups often worry about who will control the postwar state's coercive forces and about the ends to which they will be used. If citizens are to be persuaded to commit to peace, they must feel that they can safely leave their homes and pursue their livelihoods. Former fighters and armed groups must believe that they will not be targeted once they lay down their guns. In short, all must believe that they will not pay with their lives if they play by the rules that define the postwar order.

Some contributors to this volume emphasize the important role of establishing security and order in the postwar state in persuading actors to commit to peace. As David Lake underscores in chapter 2, the first order of business for those seeking to rebuild the state after civil war is to provide public safety and to guarantee that people and property will be protected from violence. It is only when individuals feel relatively secure, Lake argues, that they will consent to be governed by the state, thereby laying the groundwork for a stable peace. Establishing a secure environment is thus the first step in creating stakeholders with a vested interest in supporting a new social order.

Terrence Lyons, focusing in chapter 7 on the transformation of militias into political parties, observes that the legacy of fear can be powerful in the immediate post–civil war context. Those who seek to normalize politics must contend with the role "fear, polarization, and power derived from violence and predation" play in shaping the postwar political context (Lyons, this volume, 000). Unless politics is demilitarized, argues Lyons, peace is unlikely to endure. Demilitarizing politics does not mean ignoring security concerns. Lyons emphasizes that politicians are unlikely to prevail if they have no convincing answer to the issue of how to defend their followers from rival military forces or intimidators.

Shaheen Mozaffar echoes these insights regarding the central importance of addressing security concerns in chapter 4. Observing the role insecurity played in influencing voters in Liberia's 1997 postconflict elections, Mozaffar points out how fear induced citizens to elect Charles Taylor in response to his threat to reinitiate armed warfare if he lost the election. Liberian citizens had little stake in the postwar environment that followed Taylor's election, however, since during the campaign scant attention had actually been paid to substantive policy issues, including postconflict recovery and economic development.

Social Welfare

Beyond security concerns, individuals living in a postwar environment are also concerned about social welfare. They are thus more likely to believe that they have a stake in the peace if the postwar arrangement provides an opportunity to improve their sense of well-being. Access to services such as health care and education that may not have been available during the war can go a long way toward vesting citizens in the postwar order. As Lake points out, however, if some rudimentary social services were provided by warring factions to their followers during the course of the war, the postwar state will need to offer a larger or better set of welfare-improving services in order to generate meaningful support.

Donald Rothchild and Nikolas Emmanuel elaborate on this theme in chapter 6. They note that reconstruction of the economy following the end of the war and redistribution of the benefits of economic growth can provide the general public and its leaders with incentives to maintain a fragile peace. If third parties ensure that the end of conflict yields a recognizable peace dividend, Rothchild and Emmanuel contend, this can be used to persuade the wider national community that it has a stake in maintaining stability.

Economic Gain

Peace may be more likely to hold if it not only facilitates improvements in the general welfare of society but also provides economic elites or a local entrepreneurial class with economic incentives for supporting the peace. As Susan Woodward argues in chapter 9, in light of the fact that a number of analysts have identified the economic interests of local actors as a cause of civil war, it makes sense to examine how domestic entrepreneurs can help support a fragile peace.

Woodward observes that the business elite, sensitive to the costs of conflict and aware of the potential economic benefits of resolving a war, are often the ones who most actively press for peace. Citing Elisabeth Wood's work on El Salvador, Woodward notes that the war ended in that country when the changing economic interests of the landowning class led it to press the military to agree to negotiate an end to the war with the FMLN. Settlements designed in such a manner as to accord with the class interests of local economic actors, Woodward argues, ensure that these actors will play a role in implementing the agreement. She warns, though, that if the goal of peace for these actors is "a set of economic policies that have the consequence of increasing unemployment, both vertical and horizontal inequality in postwar society, and the antagonism of key political groups, then the peace process will remain fragile and at a stalemate" (Woodward, this volume, 000).

Strategies for Creating Stakeholders in the Peace

The contributors to this book analyze two strategies the international community has employed in its efforts to create popular support for the peace: restructuring institutions and soft intervention. In what follows we summarize the authors' key findings regarding the role that these strategies play in dealing with the disruptive influence of actors hostile to the peace and establishing conditions conducive to an enduring stability.

Restructuring Institutions

The outbreak of a civil war signifies the failure of the institutions of conflict management. If conflict is to be managed via rules rather than at the point of a gun, failed institutions must be replaced with new ones. As Timothy Sisk makes clear in chapter 5, civil wars ended during the past two decades have followed a common pattern of a "war-to-democracy" transition in which armed conflict is stopped through the introduction of a sequence of democratic institutions including elections and competition between political parties. Because democratic institutions as a means of managing conflict in postwar states appeal to members of the international community for both normative and practical reasons, third-party actors have played a significant role in brokering peace agreements that call for the use of these institutions and in providing support for the development of political parties and first-round elections in countries ranging from Angola to Nicaragua and Mozambique.

All four of the contributors who focus on the restructuring of institutions as a means of generating stakeholders in the peace are critical of the use of democratization processes in the immediate aftermath of war. Sisk observes that rather than promoting the interests individuals and groups have in security and order in the postwar environment, reliance on a "democratization formula" can actually exacerbate security concerns. The reason is that the potential loss of an election is seen as fraught with negative consequences by groups in postconflict states. For example, groups may fear that the winners in the election will use their control of security forces to punish the losers for their involvement in the war or that those who lose at the polls may be denied access to state resources vital to economic well-being.

Lake also sees the rush to establish democratic institutions as problematic. Observing that one of the defining elements of the state, a monopoly on the legitimate use of violence, is often either missing or contested in postwar states, Lake suggests that rather than immediately seeking to (re) construct political institutions in the aftermath of conflict, the international community should focus on establishing security and order as the basis for creating a legitimate state. Finding little evidence that democracy can produce legitimate governments in weak or fragile states, he warns that the process of democratization may even have a damaging effect by reifying divisions and distrust.

As Philip Roeder points out in chapter 3, different sets of institutional structures produce different incentives shaping actors' commitment to peace. Third-party actors must be cautious about the political institutions they support or undermine and the timing of their investments in civil society. Segmented states, most often created in the wake of negotiated settlements of civil wars, foster a polarized civil society that challenges the peace. Unitary states, typically associated with wars in which the central government emerges victorious, create conditions for a hegemonic civil society that is more likely to sustain the peace, but at the expense of disfranchising the secessionists.

Shaheen Mozaffar explains, in chapter 4, why democratic institutions adopted in the aftermath of civil wars sometimes fail to facilitate the transition to sustainable peace. Focusing on electoral systems, Mozaffar notes that although proportional representation (PR) electoral systems have been associated with several cases of successful postwar conflict management, including El Salvador, Nicaragua, and Mozambique, the use of such systems failed to prevent the resumption of civil war in Angola and Liberia. He accounts for these different outcomes by noting that electoral systems are embedded institutions and, as such, produce electoral outcomes contingently. The environment in which postconflict elections take place, Mozaffar warns, is one in which basic issues of survival, controlling violence, and securing law and order motivate the choice of rational voters. In this context, factors such as external mediators and the demilitarization of warring groups are likely to play a more significant role than electoral systems in persuading warring actors to play by the new rules of the game.

The analysis in these chapters suggests that the international community's emphasis on promoting democracy in postconflict states not only fails to contend with the security concerns individuals and groups have in the aftermath of war but may actually exacerbate their anxieties. Restructuring institutions along democratic lines has the potential to produce more challengers to peace than stakeholders. How, then, can the international community help to restructure institutions that will generate stakeholders committed to managing conflict in a nonviolent fashion? Four important points emerge from this study.

First, outside actors must be more cognizant of the implications stemming from the environment in which institutional replacement is taking place. The postconflict situation may range from a complete breakdown of order (e.g., in Somalia) to contention between centers of power, complete with institutions and rules that were developed by opposing groups during the course of the war (e.g., in Nagornyi Karabakh and Chechnya). In the first instance, order will need to be established before any type of institutional engineering can take place. Third-party actors likely will have to assume responsibility for protecting persons and property and adjudicating disputes before consideration can be given to institution-building.

If the environment is defined by competing centers of power, it may be necessary to develop political structures (e.g., power-sharing institutions) designed to bridge that divide. The most productive first step for the international community to take in these cases may be to understand why actors in a post–civil war setting feel driven to design institutions that are less than fully democratic. Either way, the international community must take into account the interests and concerns, foremost among them security, that actors will have in a postconflict setting. If actors are to develop vested interests in new institutions of conflict management, those institutions must be grounded in the realities of the environment in which efforts to manage conflict take place.

Second, more attention must be given to the sequencing of institutions. As several of our contributors take pains to emphasize, security concerns must be addressed if other institutions (e.g., electoral institutions) are to have a chance to secure the outcomes for which they were designed. Indeed, the degree of security felt by those actors—representatives of the government and rebel factions—charged with designing the postconflict constitutional order is likely to influence subsequent institutional choices. Only after rules regarding the cantonment of militias and government troops, the decommissioning of arms, and the future composition of state security forces have been agreed to should the international community turn its attention to the restructuring of other institutions. Many of these institutions may also have security-related implications (e.g., those focusing on the territorial distribution of power), thus making it all the more important to think about how the different pieces of the institutional order will fit together.

Third, although there is a tendency for the international community to focus on institutions at the political center as the principal tools of conflict management, these are not the only institutions that can help to develop stakeholders in the peace. Decision rights regarding control over school districts, water districts, and transportation districts can have a marked effect on the life of the average citizen. Not only can such institutions serve as tools for generating crosscutting cleavages, as Roeder points out, but if they are perceived as delivering social welfare goods, they can play an important role in generating support for the peace. This fact suggests that further attention should be devoted to the restructuring of local-level institutions with which citizens may have the most contact.

Fourth, as Sisk and Mozaffar emphasize, outside actors should recognize that institutions designed in a postconflict environment may need to be revised at some point in the future. Institutions, shaped by the context in which they are designed, themselves gradually alter the postconflict environment. The international community thus should not be surprised if national actors seek, at some point, to alter the institutions they once so carefully crafted. In fact, third-party actors may well want to encourage actors to build such a possibility into their thinking regarding institutional design. This process should be undertaken with great care, however, because actors are not likely to vest themselves in institutions they perceive as transitory. Institutional revision may also prove more difficult than expected because groups that benefit from the initial set of institutional choices may be reluctant to see those institutions changed. Nevertheless, making parties aware of the use of institutional revision as part of a larger strategy of restructuring institutions is another tool the international community may want to make use of in its efforts to create stakeholders in the peace.

In summary, a strategy of restructuring institutions seems to be of particular import if citizens' interests in security and order during the postwar period are to be met. This is not to say that the institutions created in the postconflict environment do not have an impact on individuals' and groups' interests in social welfare and economic gain. The extent to which institutions define property rights, for example, has a significant effect on the economic interests of different sets of actors. The most immediately felt impact of the institutions constructed in the aftermath of war, though, is likely to be on citizens' sense of safety. Helping to respond to individuals' and groups' other interests in the peace may thus require the international community to employ different sets of strategies. We turn now to one of these, the use of tactics of soft intervention.

Soft Intervention

As described by Donald Rothchild and Nikolas Emmanuel in chapter 6, tactics of soft intervention provide third-party actors with a variety of tools they can use to influence postwar peace. Some of these tactics take the form of incentives used to provide actors with a stake in the ongoing peace process or to reward behavior that is supportive of stability. Others consist of disincentives employed to punish would-be challengers of the peace who are intent on returning to conflict. From the international community's perspective, soft intervention strategies have the advantage of providing a straightforward means of shaping the interests and behavior of groups in a postconflict environment through a less cumbersome process than building new governing institutions. Soft intervention tactics are also flexible in nature, meaning tactics rewarding some groups can be used simultaneously with tactics penalizing others. Finally, this set of tactics for influencing behavior can be deployed at a relatively low cost, particularly when compared to the costs associated with peacekeeping.

How effectively has the international community used soft intervention strategies as a means of fostering a belief on the part of the postwar population that peace will serve the individual and/or group interests of citizens? Contributors to part 2 of this volume address this issue by focusing on the impact of soft intervention on three key sets of players in the postconflict environment: the political elite, civil society, and economic actors. As we see below, third parties have had varying degrees of success in their use of soft intervention strategies, persuading some of these actors to support the peace process while failing to get others to refrain from conflict.

The Political Elite

Like other contributors to this volume, Terrence Lyons emphasizes the role of organizational structures in supporting both war and peace. Postconflict stability, according to Lyons, requires demilitarizing politics, a process he characterizes as converting wartime institutions to new structures supportive of peace. However, he notes, institutional transformation by itself is not sufficient to secure peace. The political elite, powerful actors that developed and were sustained during a protracted civil war, must also be persuaded to play by the new rules of the game if the peace process is to have a successful conclusion. Based on his analysis of various post–civil war cases, Lyons finds that the use by third-party actors of soft intervention strategies, particularly purchase, legitimation, and sanctions, has been particularly useful in transforming the elite into stakeholders in peace.

Leaders of militarized organizations during the war, the elite who are part of a negotiated end to a civil war have an interest in retaining and exercising power during peacetime. Their ability to do so is based, in large measure, on the continued existence of the organizations they control. Whether or not these organizations manage to survive in a peacetime environment depends on how well they adapt to the new, postwar context in which they seek to compete. Particularly important in this respect is access to the resources needed to keep their organizations viable. With resources such as diamonds and looted goods sometimes more difficult for formerly armed groups to acquire after the end of conflict, leaders will need to seek out other sources of wealth that they can use for patronage and recruitment and to better prepare them for the challenges of using ballots rather than bullets.

The difficulties the political elite face in preparing themselves and their organizations to compete in the realm of demilitarized politics present the international community with an opportunity to build support for peace as well as to deter potential challengers. Third parties can seek to secure the commitment of political elites to peace through the use of *purchase*, by providing them with the resources necessary to ensure the survival and transformation of the organizations they lead. This tactic proved remarkably successful in helping Afonso Dhlakama, the leader of Mozambique's rebel group RENAMO, to transform that faction into a political organization, thereby ensuring that he and his supporters would follow through in implementing the country's peace agreement. *Legitimation*, the conferring by the international community of recognition and authority on leaders and the organizations they command, is also an important resource third parties can wield in their efforts to build stakeholders. Inclusion by the United Nations of the insurgent FMLN in El Salvador's peace process helped to ease the way for the organization to convert itself into a legal party, a move once resisted by the government. Finally, *sanctions*, the denial of resources to political elites and organizations that threaten to defect from the peace, have also been used with some success to punish actors whose behavior identifies them as potentially hostile to the peace.

Civil Society

Third parties face challenges in seeking to use soft intervention strategies to convince members of civil society that they should support an incipient peace. As Michael Foley points out in chapter 8, civil society is a diverse entity, so it is difficult to know which groups' and/or individuals' interests the international community should attempt to target. In addition, warns Foley, competing visions among members of civil society regarding what constitutes the "public good" means that this set of actors is not necessarily the virtuous, pro-peace entity that some analysts have conceived of it as being. Echoing a point made by Roeder in chapter 3, Foley further notes that civil society is a product of—or at least does not operate outside the constraints of—the political structures in which it finds itself. Based on this analysis, he concludes that there are limited opportunities for the international community to use soft intervention tactics to persuade civil society to support peace.

None of this is to suggest that civil society should be ignored by the international community. Civil society does have an important role to play, suggests Foley, via its capacity to get political elites to abide by their promises and to ensure a continued commitment to peace. If empowered through the use of soft intervention strategies of purchase and legitimation, the elements of civil society that are already committed to peace can perform this task more effectively. Civil-society organizations in El Salvador, for example, helped to secure the commitment of higher-level cadres of the FMLN to peace by providing employment for them. Resources provided to organizations associated with elite business interests in El Salvador also helped to nurture that important set of actors' commitment to peace.

Although the international community was successful in using soft intervention strategies to generate support for the peace by civil society in El Salvador, use of those strategies proved more problematic in both Bosnia and Northern Ireland. The institutional structure in Bosnia, Foley notes, limits the potential impact of civil society. In addition, third-party actors' nearly exclusive focus on funding NGOs in Bosnia has restricted the growth of other socially rooted civil-society organizations. In Northern Ireland, structural factors, including secure bases of support in the larger population, have meant that the political elite largely have been able to ignore civil society.

Members of the international community seeking to use soft intervention strategies to cultivate support for peace by civil society should be aware of the parameters within which they can effectively deploy these strategies. First, third-party actors must invest some effort in understanding the civil society that they seek to influence. How is civil society organized? Are there groups that are already committed to peace? As Foley asserts, resources are best directed at groups who are already working for peace, rather than those who might be sitting on the fence. Second, potential interveners must take into account the political structure within which civil society operates. If the political system is weak, or if it privileges ethnic divisions, citizens are unlikely to be able to wield much influence. Finally, Foley's analysis suggests that, in light of these parameters, it is soft intervention strategies such as purchase, insurance, and legitimation that *reward* citizens supportive of the peace process that are most likely to succeed in fostering stakeholders in stability.

Economic Actors

The international community has invested considerable resources during the past two decades in building economic bases for a stable peace in countries emerging from civil wars. As Woodward convincingly demonstrates, however, few of the economic tools employed by third-party actors have been directed at serving the interests of local economic actors. Since, as she argues, domestic entrepreneurs are essential to the creation and the sustainability of peace, the failure to target their interests through the use of soft intervention strategies should be considered a lost opportunity on the part of the international community to build stakeholders in the peace.

The current economic strategy of international peace-building, explains Woodward, consists of two elements, neither of which gives explicit attention to the role that local entrepreneurs might play in stabilizing peace. The first, a long-term agenda emphasized by major states and the international financial institutions, seeks to restructure postconflict economies, lowering barriers to trade and foreign investment so as to better integrate national economies with the global economy. The length of time this neoliberal strategy takes to show results, its tendency to benefit foreign investors and international nongovernmental organizations more than domestic actors, and the political consequences stemming from its use (i.e., defection from the political compromise that secured peace by actors whose interests are negatively affected by policies of tight credit and trade liberalization) render it ineffective as a means for making stakeholders out of domestic economic actors.

The second component of the economic strategy currently employed by the international community targets the general population, particularly citizens in zones most impacted by the war. In this instance, Woodward notes, economic incentives are not used as a selective reward or punishment but as a form of humanitarian aid and as a means of securing the population's vote in early postwar elections for leaders and parties deemed to be cooperative with the international community. This short-term strategy, warns Woodward, may actually be counterproductive for the peace process, since these projects typically fail to foster economic survival for the general public—a central priority for them. The types of microprojects initiated by the international community produce neither income nor jobs and do not serve to reconstitute the social networks upon which small-scale traders and farmers rely for survival. Further, citizens are resentful that members of the international community seek to buy their support through token efforts at economic reconstruction that they consider to be incommensurate with the nature of the sacrifices they made during the war.

Although current economic policies for gaining economic actors' support for peace must generally be viewed as failures, a strategy that provides economic support for local businesses and entrepreneurship can yield positive results, argues Woodward. In order for such a strategy to succeed, the international community must come to understand that economic and political interests are linked. Not only are domestic economic and political interests intertwined, but third parties' own interests, both economic and geostrategic, are endogenous to the design, implementation, and outcome of the peace process. Businesses will be willing to support a peace agreement only if they believe the new state will represent, or at least protect, their economic interests. If domestic economic actors and third parties have converging interests, the latter can provide the former with incentives that help to reinforce their commitment to peace. If their interests diverge, as has sometimes been the case concerning the implementation of neoliberal policies, there will be little the international community can do to make stakeholders for peace out of postwar entrepreneurs.

Policy Implications

Taken together, contributing authors to this book make an argument that the international community can employ strategies of institutional restructuring and soft intervention to generate support among a postwar population for the maintenance of peace. A close reading of the chapters further reveals that attention to the following three suggestions should help the international community to create stakeholders in stability.

Be Aware of the Destabilizing Effects of Democracy and Neoliberal Economic Policies

The international community would do well to think through how its vision of a legitimate peace may differ from that of communities just emerging from war. As several contributors to this book make clear, both third-party actors and many domestic actors share an interest in a stable peace, one that provides security and order for the postwar society. Beyond this important shared interest, however, the priorities of domestic and of international communities with respect to peace differ. The divergence of interests does not in itself pose a problem. Rather, what is problematic is that the international community's efforts to promote democracy and neoliberalism may make it more difficult to secure all three of the goals—security and order, social welfare, and economic gain—that domestic actors seek from the peace.

Although valued as a form of conflict management in the West, democracy, as some of the book's authors point out, may undermine efforts to stabilize the postwar environment. Democracy, because it institutionalizes uncertainty, is not likely to be very appealing for individuals and communities who associate uncertainty with insecurity. Holding early elections may exacerbate existing tensions and generate new ones (see Paris 2004; Mansfield and Snyder 2007). In the same vein, neoliberal policy, with its emphasis on scaling back state involvement in the economy, is likely to be viewed with skepticism by domestic actors who look to the state to guide the rebuilding of shattered economies and to provide much-needed social services. Furthermore, policies that mandate opening markets to foreign direct investment may well provoke resentment on the part of native entrepreneurs who fear the impact foreign competition will have on their businesses.

If third-party actors' support for a democratic and neoliberal version of the peace risks generating instability, what is to be done? In the absence of any evidence that democracy and neoliberalism produce a stable and legitimate peace, the international community would do well to show some flexibility regarding the promotion of these goals. Without denying the positive features of democracy as a form of conflict management and the efficiency-promoting elements of neoliberal policy, it may be prudent to delay the introduction of both of these sets of institutions until peace has been stabilized, some degree of state legitimacy and social trust has been established, and a national economy is functioning.[1] In the interim, both domestic and international communities can make plans for an institutional transition.

Seek to Improve the Coordination and Sequencing of Third-Party Interventions

Although we have referred repeatedly to the international community as a single entity, this group of actors is by no means cohesive in terms of its actions. Third parties with a potential interest in the post–civil war environment include nation-states, international organizations, nongovernmental organizations, foreign investors, diaspora communities, and so on. At least some of these groups are likely to have somewhat different goals regarding the type of peace they want to see take hold as well as how best to go about generating support for the peace. The United States and the international financial institutions (the International Monetary Fund and the World Bank), for example, argue that adoption of the neoliberal economic model by postconflict states best serves to promote economic growth, equity, and the economic interests of the majority of the populations of those countries. This position is contested, at least to some degree, in documents recently issued by the United Nations and the United Kingdom's Department for International Development (See "Investing in Development" 2005; DFID 2005). Lacking a common vision of the type of postconflict environment that will best promote the interests of a majority of the population, different members of the international community may at times act at cross-purposes, thereby diluting efforts to create effective incentives for individuals and groups to support the embryonic peace.[2]

Developing a shared understanding of the strategies the international community might best use to generate support for peace in post–civil war states is clearly a difficult task. It is not, however, an impossible one. As Suhrke and Buckmaster explain, the once ad hoc and programmatically incoherent multilateral aid regime that provided assistance to postconflict states became, with the end of the cold war, comprehensive and standardized, "with increasingly agreed-upon formulas for the nature and sequencing of aid, improved coordination and clearer division of labor among aid agencies" (Suhrke and Buckmaster 2006, 340). As the international community accumulates knowledge regarding the strategies that work best—and those that fail entirely—to stabilize peace, it should task some entity with the responsibility of sharing information and coordinating policy action. The centralized powers the international financial institutions (the IMF and the World Bank) hold with respect to neoliberal policy reform, for example, may be one factor that helps to explain the extent to which they have been able to implement policies for the liberalization of postconflict economies.[3]

Expand the Concept of Stakeholders in Peace

The structuring of peace agreements generally has been understood as an elite-driven process. Government leaders and the heads of rebel forces are the focus of attention as they meet to negotiate peace settlements and later as all wait to see whether they will follow through on their commitments.

Missing from this scenario has been an emphasis on the rest of the population, the individuals and groups who must live with the peace structured by elites. It is a central argument of this book that citizens in postwar societies also have a part in shaping the peace. They too should be considered to be stakeholders in the peace; their interests in the peace need to be analyzed and their commitment to the peace monitored in much the same fashion the international community has done for elites. Most important in this regard would be efforts by third parties to ensure that the actors associated with both civil society and the economy engage in actions supportive of the still-unfolding peace process.

Building a stable peace out of the wreckage of civil war is an inherently challenging process. The purpose of this book is to suggest that the international community has more tools at its disposal to address this challenge than typically has been recognized. Beyond the common emphasis on the deployment of peacekeepers in the aftermath of conflict, third parties may also help to facilitate an enduring peace through the tactics of restructuring institutions and soft intervention.

We have considered the strategies of restructuring institutions and soft intervention together, because they have complementary goals for post–civil war states. Both seek to encourage the citizens of countries emerging from conflict to identify the benefits of peace and become stakeholders in stability. By fostering an environment in which the majority of citizens recognize that stability is in their self-interest, these tactics increase the potential for a peace settlement to hold in the fragile months and years immediately following the end of hostilities.

While we identify these tactics as promising mechanisms for promoting peace, our analyses are not intended to be the final word on applying the tactics in post–civil war states. Our hope is that this book will serve to encourage more research and dialogue to identify the most effective third-party strategies for assisting states emerging from civil war. Further consideration of this subject will highlight the potential that exists for third parties to use a wide range of tactics as they try to facilitate peace in states emerging from civil war.

References

Boon, Kristen E. 2007. "'Open for Business': International Financial Institutions, Post-Conflict Economic Reform, and the Rule of Law." *Journal of International Law and Politics* 39, 3: 513–581.

Department for International Development (DFID). 2005. *Fighting Poverty to Build a Safer World: A Strategy for Security and Development*. London: DFID.

"Investing in Development: A Practical Plan to Achieve the Millennium Development Goals." 2005. Millennium Project, Report to the UN Secretary-General, New York.

Mansfield, Edward D., and Jack Snyder. 2007. *Electing to Fight: Why Emerging Democracies Go to War*. Cambridge, MA: MIT Press.

Paris, Roland. 2004. *At War's End: Building Peace after Civil Conflict*. Cambridge: Cambridge University Press.

Suhrke, Astri, and Julia Buckmaster. 2006. "Aid, Growth, and Peace: A Comparative Analysis." *Conflict, Security, and Development* 6, 3: 337–363.

Notes

1. This should not be interpreted as suggesting that the international community should condone any and all types of regimes that come to power in a postwar state as long as they stabilize the peace. Governments that abuse human rights or that engage in other acts of malfeasance that pose a threat to long-term stability should expect to see negative forms of soft intervention used by the international community.
2. For an overview of the sequencing issues involved in the disbursement of aid to postconflict countries, see Suhrke and Buckmaster 2006.
3. See Boon 2007 regarding the role of the international financial institutions in promoting a neoliberal model of economic reform in postconflict states.

CONTRIBUTORS

NIKOLAS EMMANUEL is Assistant Professor of Political Science at Oklahoma State University. His research, which focuses on developing countries, includes articles in the *Journal of Intervention and Statebuilding* and in *Africa Contemporary Record* and chapters in edited volumes.

MICHAEL W. FOLEY is an independent scholar, having retired from The Catholic University of America in 2007. His research emphases have been civil society and political change in Latin America and the United States, and postconflict settings around the world. He is the author, with Dean Hoge, of *Religion and the New Immigrants*; editor, with Bob Edwards and Mario Diani, of *Beyond Tocqueville: Civil Society and the Social Capital Debate in Comparative Perspective*; and coeditor, with Virginia Hodgkinson, of *The Civil Society Reader*.

CAROLINE A. HARTZELL is Professor of Political Science at Gettysburg College. Her research interests include the design of civil war settlements and postconflict quality of the peace issues. She is the coauthor of *Crafting Peace: Power-Sharing Institutions and the Negotiated Settlement of Civil Wars*.

MATTHEW HODDIE is Assistant Professor of Political Science at Towson University. He is the coauthor of *Crafting Peace: Power-Sharing Institutions and the Negotiated Settlement of Civil Wars* and the author of *Ethnic Realignments: A Comparative Study of Government Influences on Identity*.

DAVID A. LAKE is Distinguished Professor of Political Science at the University of California, San Diego. He has published widely in international relations theory and international political economy. Lake's most recent book is *Hierarchy in International Relations*. He is also the author of three additional books and coeditor of eight volumes. In addition, Lake has written more than seventy scholarly articles and chapters.

TERRENCE LYONS is Associate Professor at the Institute for Conflict Analysis and Resolution and codirector of the Center for Global Studies at George Mason University. Lyons's publications include *Avoiding Conflict in the Horn of Africa: U.S. Policy toward Ethiopia and Eritrea, Demilitarizing Politics: Elections on the Uncertain Road to Peace,* and numerous articles in a range of journals and policy-oriented publications.

SHAHEEN MOZAFFAR is Professor of Political Science at Bridgewater State College. His research focuses on institutional design, political parties, elections, ethnicity, and conflict management in emerging democracies, with particular focus on Africa. He is a coprincipal investigator of the African Legislatures Project, a comparative study of the role of legislatures in democratic development in twenty African countries. His published works have appeared as book chapters and in such journals as the *American Political Science Review, Comparative Political Studies, Electoral Studies, Nationalism and Ethnic Politics,* and *Party Politics.*

PHILIP G. ROEDER, Professor of Political Science at the University of California, San Diego, is a specialist on nationalism and the nation-state as well as on post-Soviet politics. His most recent book is *Where Nation-States Come From: Institutional Change in the Age of Nationalism.*

DONALD ROTHCHILD was Distinguished Professor of Political Science at the University of California, Davis. His research, which focused on Africa, centered on the resolution of ethnic conflict. At the time of his death, he was the author or editor of approximately two dozen books and had published more than 130 articles.

TIMOTHY D. SISK is Professor of International and Comparative Politics at the Josef Korbel School of International Studies, University of Denver; Director of the Center for Sustainable Development and International Peace, a research and policy institute at the School; and Director of the Korbel Program in Humanitarian Assistance. His publications include *International Mediation in Civil Wars: Bargaining with Bullets, From War to Democracy: Dilemmas of Peacebuilding* (with Anna Jarstad), and *The Dilemmas of Statebuilding: Confronting the Contradictions of Postwar Peace Operations* (with Roland Paris).

SUSAN L. WOODWARD is Professor of Political Science at The Graduate Center of the City University of New York. A specialist on the Balkans, her current research focuses on transitions from war to peace, international security and state failure, and postwar state-building. Her publications include *Balkan Tragedy: Chaos and Dissolution after the Cold War* and *Socialist Unemployment: The Political Economy of Yugoslavia, 1945–1990.*

INDEX